CREATING BUSINESS MAGIC

HOW THE POWER OF MAGIC CAN INSPIRE, INNOVATE, AND REVOLUTIONIZE YOUR BUSINESS

**David Morey, Eugene Burger
& John E. McLaughlin**

For permission requests, please contact the publisher at:

Mango Publishing Group

2850 Douglas Road, 3rd Floor

Coral Gables, FL 33134 USA

info@mango.bz

For special orders, quantity sales, course adoptions and corporate sales, please email the publisher at sales@mango.bz. For trade and wholesale sales, please contact Ingram Publisher Services at:

customer.service@ingramcontent.com or +1.800.509.4887.

Creating Business Magic: How the Power of Magic Can Inspire, Innovate, and Revolutionize Your Business

Library of Congress Cataloging

ISBN: (print) 978-1-63353-734-7 (ebook) 978-1-63353-735-4

Library of Congress Control Number: 2018930404

BISAC category code: BUS007000 BUSINESS & ECONOMICS / Business Communication / General, BUS063000 BUSINESS & ECONOMICS / Strategic Planning

Printed in the United States of America

This is one of Eugene Burger's very final projects and books on magic. We did not dream this would be the case when we together embarked on this project years ago, but he journeyed to what he himself called the "ultimate capital M Mystery of life" on August 8, 2017, while this work was nearing completion. For the sake of historical accuracy, references in this text to our magical mentor, our coauthor, and our friend are in the past tense. Of course, Eugene will always be with us and with everyone who loves magic. His tense is eternal. And we hereby dedicate our book—so much of which is also his book—to:

Eugene Burger, June 1, 1939–August 8, 2017

CONTENTS

ACKNOWLEDGMENTS

This book represents our journey to understand how magicians think and to apply this way of thinking to the challenges of business and life. Along this path, we are far from alone. We thank Alan Axelrod for his research and editorial legerdemain, Larry Hass for his inspirational contributions, Jeff McBride, Bob Fitch, Ross Johnson, Johnny Thompson, Tony Clark, and Max Maven for their unparalleled magical contributions, and Scott Miller for his one-of-a-kind strategic conjuring. We thank Jerry Wind, Kabir Khan, Bryce Kuhlman, Joe Michenfelder, Constance Warner, Ira Callier, Edgar House, Craig Helsing, Robert Charles, Michael Burke, Simone Marron, Stan Sieler, Jim Levine, and our marvelous Mango editor, Gary M. Krebs of GMK Writing and Editing, Inc., for their ongoing magical inputs.

Finally, John McLaughlin thanks his wife, Charlee, a woman of extraordinary patience and fortitude, and David Morey, too, thanks Xie Zheng for her own very special magic.

FOREWORD

The book you hold in your hand is unique. It demonstrates more powerfully than anything I've seen that there is a magician inside each of us. It explains how thinking like a magician can take you and your endeavors to new heights of success.

A political and corporate strategist who has advised winning global presidential campaigns and Fortune 100 CEOs, the former Acting Director of the CIA, and one of magic's true legends combine their perspectives to illuminate how the power of magic can ignite your own imagination, power you through barriers, and get way ahead of any competition. Fellow magicians David Morey, John McLaughlin, and Eugene Burger take everything they've learned from magic and other elements of their professional lives and pack it into a set of key strategies for meeting the special challenges in today's business world—and other realms as well. It is a magically powerful and important read.

Creating Business Magic takes the reader along a path of genuinely magical thinking. Beginning with imagination, the authors illuminate the power of perception, ways to innovate, to think out of the box, break down conceptual barriers and, finally, bring out the magician inside all of us. These are the essential ingredients of every powerful magic performance, and here the authors take you behind the scenes in magic to explain how thinking like a magician can move you into new realms of imagination, creativity, and accomplishment.

As I wrote in my own book, *Tales of the Impossible*, "The way I see it, there are common threads which bind together all those who aspire to being great artists, be they conjurors whose forum is the theater, or wordsmiths whose illusions are performed in the playhouse of the mind." This book shows us those common threads—binding together and synergizing the thinking of great magicians and transcendent leaders in business, the arts, education, and government. The authors powerfully make the case that the world today needs more magic; they demonstrate how exploration of the impossible—the essence of the magician's art—can energize, indeed revolutionize, endeavors in other fields.

I've long believed, have lived by, and tried to embody Albert Einstein's wonderful conviction that "imagination is more important than knowledge." Einstein, as always, was beyond prescient. Imagination is what has driven human progress from the invention of the wheel to the creation of the smartphone to humankind's ongoing exploration of space.

It's easy to think magic begins and ends on the stage, but the authors show the real secret—that the true magic occurs long before the performance begins—in the disruption of conventional thought, the experimentation, and the strategizing for success and against failure—steps that for any creative enterprise, whether in commerce or theater, ensure exceptional results.

Co-author Eugene Burger, one of magic's greatest teachers and philosophers, had a favorite pre-show mantra: "I have something wonderful to show you tonight." This book will help any reader bring out not only what is wonderful, but what is wondrous, too. It is a solid, sparkling argument that imagination empowers the real magician inside us all.

—David Copperfield

PREFACE

WHO SHOULD READ THIS BOOK?

Y ou may think you know what magic is. Abracadabra, hocus-pocus. Forget about it. Magic? Magic is what human beings do. It's just that some do it a lot better than others.

Take the wheel. Archaeologists tell us it's been around since about 4000 BC. Before then, if you had something heavy to move, you dragged it. Or at least tried to. That meant you probably couldn't move very much very far. Without even the idea of a wheel, you could either drag your things or imagine some magical force that could move them. The status quo—"the way things stand"—stood in your way.

What you needed was something to disrupt the status quo. The first step was to imagine the disruption—what it looked like, what it did, how people perceive the changes it makes. Imagine it thoroughly enough, and you could invent what you needed. Somewhere in our long history, some people began to realize that imagination was so powerful and useful, it should be made more available when and where it was needed. They were the people who systematized imagination and the disruptions it created. Today, we call such people designers, architects, engineers, scientists, artists, entrepreneurs, inventors, and innovators. In the past, they were more typically called magicians.

Once the wheel was imagined and invented—call it "conjured"—whenever you needed to move something, you no longer needed the disruption wrought by magic. All you needed were wheels. At least that's what you thought. The truth is that the wheels were the magic: the embodiment of imagination that made the impossible possible.

This is the course of history. Once the magic drove someone's imagination to disrupt the motionless status quo by inventing wheels, all anyone saw from then on were the wheels, and they forgot about the magic behind them. Wheels became the status quo. The disruption of reality became the new reality, which, after a while, wasn't new. That's the way all earth-shaking innovation works. First comes the magic, and then the magic becomes the reality.

Magic always was and always will be about creatively solving problems: satisfying a need, a want, a desire in some unheard-of way. The more creative and powerful the solution, the more disruptive of the status quo, the more magical it seems—at least until people cannot live without it. If, for instance, you were born in the age of the public phone booth, there is still magic in your smartphone—though even for members of the payphone generation, the smartphone magic fades a little day by day. That is what drives the journey from 5.0 to 6.0 to 7.0 and beyond.

Familiarity doesn't change the fact that our supply of magic is limitless. We just need somebody to help us tap into it. That's what *Creating Business Magic* is all about. This book uses the power and the metaphor of magic to help you unlock your imagination, creativity, and career, thereby disrupting your personal status quo.

Where did *we* get the magic?

We are practicing magicians who also happen to have other careers—in leadership, marketing, corporate strategy, political strategy, intelligence, education, diplomacy, global policy, philosophy, and the history of religion. We each make our living through what is often called thought leadership in our respective "day job" fields. Clients pay us to—in the words of Steve Jobs—"think different." Put another way, we sell disruption. We deliver magical ways to think differently.

For this reason, we put magic to work onstage as well as in everything else we do for a living. We learned a lot of our magic from the great magicians who have come before us, from stage magicians like Max Malini, Harry Houdini, Harry Blackstone, Tony Slydini, Doug Henning, and David Copperfield, but also from magicians known by other names: Isaac Newton, Albert Einstein, Kelly Johnson, Roberto Goizueta, Corazon Aquino, and Steve Jobs. In fact, we've drawn our magic from everyone we've worked with or known or just read about—from all the people who "think different," and in thinking differently, disrupt companies, industries, economies, cultures, and governments.

This book takes everything we've learned about magic and packs it into a unique framework that defines and captures the best of magic—from renowned magicians to performance art to empowering imagination—and relates it directly to key lessons learned in a variety of creative, governing, and commercial fields. Our "Strategies" conclude with a concise "payoff" that delivers specific, momentum-building action lists: *Creating Business Magic* strategies that will show you how to be the magician in your own life, career, and future.

INTRODUCTION

WHAT IS A MAGICIAN?

All three of us are magicians, and each of us is something else, too. One is a corporate and political consultant whose clients have included the likes of Apple, Coca-Cola, McDonald's, Corazon Aquino, and Barack Obama. Another is the former acting director of the CIA who now teaches at Johns Hopkins University, advises companies and governments on intelligence and foreign policy issues, and is a national security analyst with MSNBC. The third is regarded among his fellow magicians as something of a living legend and is the author of *The Experience of Magic*, *Gourmet Close-up Magic*, *Growing in the Art of Magic*, *Magic and Meaning* (coauthor), *Mastering the Art of Magic*, and *Strange Ceremonies*. He is also a highly-regarded philosopher and historian of religion with degrees in philosophy and divinity from Yale.

When we tell people what we do, the consulting, the CIA credentials, and the philosophy and divinity degrees stir interest, but it's the magic that unfailingly stops them in their tracks. Eyes go wide, and then they narrow to a squint. In some, this is a sign of bewilderment. In others, it's more like confusion.

Our typical audiences consist of political or community leaders, CEOs or teachers, symphony directors or software developers. And what ignites our own imagination is the experience of seeing audiences return in an instant to the magic of their childhood, to a place where dreams were bigger, where each moment was more present, and where magic was pure and real. What also excites us is when something we do fires the imagination of an audience to envision new possibilities in their own lives and work—to think different, to think magic, to disrupt from within themselves.

Understand, however, that most people have no idea what a magician is. Adults and older children do have an abiding faith in the visible, provable, and usually self-evident chains of cause and effect that create what we call business as usual. Ask a volunteer to pick a card from the deck, memorize it, return it to the deck, then shuffle the deck, and this abiding faith assures everyone watching that it will be very hard for the magician to retrieve the one and only correct card. If, contrary to ingrained expectation, the magician manages to produce it immediately, this faith is shaken—albeit delightfully. If the magician pulls the card not out of the deck, but out of the volunteer's shirt pocket, faith is not merely shaken, it is shattered. This creates, in some small way, the sensation of a whole new reality. In consequence, the delight is ratcheted up even higher.

But interestingly, when magicians try to capture the same effect before an audience of young children, they soon bump up against the challenge that, for children, this kind of magic is part of their everyday way of thinking. The effect, astounding to adults, challenges no innate assumptions of children. They have not yet had to struggle through the laws of physics or the elements of logic (they are developmentally incapable of doing so), so they assume that this is just "the way things are." In this sense, their thinking is quite naturally "magical thinking"—the belief that one's thoughts alone can bring about a tangible effect in the world.

In adults, magical thinking may find expression in religious faith or psychosis. In young children, by contrast, it is the normal way in which the mind creates reality from ages two to seven, as the great twentieth-century child developmentalist and self-described "genetic epistemologist" Jean Piaget demonstrated. A child holds a balloon on a string. In the yard next door, a dog barks. The balloon pops. Through her tears, the child understands that the dog's barking *made* her balloon pop—just as the chosen card appeared in the man's shirt pocket because the magician *made* it appear.

Magicians find it truly challenging to amaze little people who think magically. Only after we "grow out of" magical thinking does magic come to seem *magical* as opposed to *ordinary*—precisely because magic disrupts our expectations. The poet William Wordsworth keenly felt the heavy weight of nostalgia for childhood, which he saw as a wondrous age of magical thinking, a time in which simply to imagine reality was to create it. "Whither is fled the visionary gleam?" the thirty-eight-year-old poet asked in his celebrated "Intimations" ode; "Where is it now, the glory and the dream?"

***

What is a magician? The man or woman who can, in adult life, still summon the visionary gleam, the glory and the dream, and for whom magical thinking is the height of imaginative sanity.

Sanity, for most people, is first control: confidence in your competence to understand and productively impact reality. Second, it is normality: confidence that you have pretty much the same understanding of reality as others have.

But think deeper, and you will soon realize that we go through life *feeling* remarkably little control over reality: "Everyone *talks* about the weather, but nobody *does* anything about it," or "Accidents happen," or "Who knows what tomorrow will bring?" or "Bet on red, spin the wheel, hope for the best." And as for everyone thinking pretty much like everyone else, who among us admires the people who think just like everyone else? In fact, we celebrate the Shakespeares, the Beethovens, the Edisons, the Jobses. We revere the outliers, the people who think, who see, who imagine different. We honor the disrupters.

When the average member of the average audience watches a very good magician, everything in the show looks easy. Want to see a spectacular and inexplicable kink in the chain of cause and effect? Nothing to it. Yearning to witness a miracle? No problem. Very few are even dimly aware of the enormously complex and physically and intellectually elaborate undergirding beneath the surface of the show. Instead, what the audience believes it sees is an entertainingly adept performer spontaneously manipulating reality.

Spontaneity is the opposite of control. To bend the spontaneous moment to your will—that slice of time the content of which is impossible to foretell, a span of seconds utterly up for grabs—to bend this spontaneous moment to your will is to work a real miracle. Or to appear to do so.

A case in point is Max Katz Breit, born in 1873 in Ostrov, a hamlet straddling the Polish-Austrian border. It was a place of mud and misery, dull, oppressive, and hopeless. For a Jewish family like the Breits, it was decidedly a place to leave. They emigrated to America, hoping to find magic in New York. What Max found was the magic in himself by disrupting the status quo claustrophobia of mud, misery, and oppression that had shaped his first reality. His journey was, in every possible sense, a voyage from Old World to New.

Short, bald, and very round—five foot three and portly—Max Katz Breit performed as Max Malini. He astounded monarchs, presidents, senators, celebrities, regular folk, and fellow magicians with the utter audacity of his effects. A great man—an ambassador, a movie star—extends a handshake to him. Malini responds by seizing the proffered hand. Raising it, along with the great man's jacket cuff, to his mouth, Malini unceremoniously bites off a button.

Animal!

A moment later, amid the shock he has created, Malini magically restores button to cuff, stitches and all.

Bold and audacious, yes. But *spontaneous*? Hardly.

In the 1920s, Malini spent a year, perhaps two, systematically bribing a Washington, D.C. tailor who was patronized by the city's political upper crust to sew certain playing cards inside the suit and evening jackets of several of the most prominent United States senators. By now an entertainer who had delighted more than one American president and had delivered a command performance at Buckingham Palace, Max Malini, child of dull, dangerous Ostrov, now citizen of the New World, is at this time an avidly sought-after dinner guest. At a formal D.C. affair, he recognizes one of the senators he knows is a regular customer of the tailor he bribed months before. Malini greets the dignitary, and the man, unsurprisingly, begins cajoling him into doing a piece of magic.

"I'm not prepared!" the magician protests. "Please understand...out of the question..."

The more Malini demurs, the more the senator insists. With a sigh, at length the magician surrenders and asks if anyone—anyone at all—happens to have a deck of cards. Of course, no one brings playing cards to a formal Washington dinner. Indeed, had someone volunteered a deck, the audience rapidly gathering around Malini would have instantly smelled a rat. But no one thinks twice that the magician himself is carrying a deck. It's his stock in trade. He holds it out to the senator's wife, "forcing" a card on her—in other words, handling the deck so that she "chooses," apparently of her own free will (but only apparently), the very card he wants her to take.

With the "chosen" card securely in the lady's possession, Malini asks her to produce it.

"Of course," she giggles.

But she cannot. Flustered, she cannot find it. It has vanished.

"I *just* had it! Where did it go?"

Malini frowns.

"This is most unusual," he frets. Then, brightening, he asks, "Is anyone here carrying a knife?"

Of course not. Even in Washington, men and women in formal dress do not carry knives.

"Well," he says, "*I* have one."

Turning to the senator, Malini brandishes his blade. With the man wide eyed, the magician asks his kind indulgence to allow him to perform a minor operation. The senator, speechless for once, neither protests nor agrees as Malini begins to cut through the elegant evening coat, stopping just at the silken lining, where he finds—the missing card!

Spontaneity—the notion that a lot of things "just happen when they happen" and are beyond *anyone's* knowing or control—is an article of commonsense faith for just about everyone. It's part of the picture of "reality" all adults share. For this reason, the greatest magicians embrace spontaneity. They embrace it, but they never rely on it. They shape it. They bend it to their will. They anticipate it. They arrange for it.

The greater they are, the more they prepare. The props "casually" arrayed on their table? They *know*, by memory, precisely where every item is. All the magician needs to do is reach, never once looking away from the audience.

The stage is large. But magicians choreograph every move across it. They have thought through in theatrical terms every action and each event, no matter how small or apparently insignificant. Everything, they know, *everything* communicates, and the objective is to be several steps ahead of the audience at every step. The "miracle" the people are about to see has effectively already occurred—in the thought devoted to it, in the preparation for it.

Understanding how a magician *plans* spontaneity will help you plan the "spontaneity" of your next pitch, negotiation, criminal investigation, presentation, lesson, business consultation, marketing analysis, or design. We know it will, because all three of us use what we've learned from magic for purposes such as these all the time. By the same token, learning how great magicians stay steps ahead of their audience will help you to imagine how you can stay steps ahead of your competition, and even more important, ahead of the customers and clients you serve.

Great magicians are masters at analyzing their audience. They climb into their point of view. They create precisely the perception *they* want and that they understand the *audience* wants to perceive. And, having come into the performance steps ahead of the audience, they never let them catch up. They create empathy with their audience, and they adjust their approach by picking up the feedback continually sent to them via audience facial expressions, applause (or its absence), gasps, laughter, the collective intake and expulsion of breath, and (above all) silence. They work the audience as expertly as they manipulate the props they bring with them onstage, and they think ahead to how they might still achieve a successful outcome even if a trick goes badly wrong. The magic business is, in one respect, exactly like every other enterprise. It is a business of people—of understanding and anticipating wants, needs, desires, contingencies, and perceptions, and of using this understanding and anticipation to create delight and satisfaction.

A great magician once said that any good magic trick is performed three times. It is performed first when the magician "does" it. It is performed again when a member of the audience remembers it. And it is performed yet a third time when that audience member tells someone else about it. In this way, magic is like any truly valuable and valued product or service. It converts consumers into advocates, proselytizers, and champions. It creates followers.

***

The English word *magician* is derived from the Latin *magus,* usually translated as "magician," or more specifically, "learned magician"—hence the three *magi* in the Nativity story: "wise men." The Latin word is derived from the Greek *magos,* which the Greeks applied to any member of the ancient Persian learned and priestly caste.

Before it became *magician,* the Latin *magus* was anglicized as *mage.* It is difficult to ignore the fact that *mage* lacks but one vowel to become *image.* As a noun, *image* came into English from Old French early in the thirteenth century and referred at that time to any statue or painting or any other artificial visual representation of a person or a thing. As a verb, *image* debuted in our language later, toward the end of the fourteenth century, when it referred to the formation of a mental picture—that is, to "image" an *image* in the *imagination.* That last word, *imagination,* is also of fourteenth-century origin in English, derived from Old French *imaginación,* meaning a mental picture, a concept, even a hallucination, an "imagining."

Through all these etymological transformations, the core remains unchanged. From the beginning and always, *magic* and *imagination* share the same central syllable. And it is hardly an accident that they do.

In writing this book, our objective is not to create a new generation of magicians, but to publish in one place and for the first time the *CREATING BUSINESS MAGIC* strategies of the world's greatest magicians—to use the force and metaphor of magic to empower boundless imagination, drive leadership, and create success in your business, your career, and your future. At the core of this book is the belief that imagination can make magicians of us all.

PART ONE

IMAGINE

THE FIRST STRATEGY
FORGET REALITY

"Reality is merely an illusion, albeit a very persistent one."

—Albert Einstein

S cene: *This really happened[1] (https://www.youtube.com/ watch?v=xTxGC1OiWFs). It's the mid-1970s, and Doug Henning is re-energizing magic with his own form of magical wonder. He walks onto a Broadway stage, his pants one of those strange 1970s colors, and he's holding a newspaper, reading it, and turning to the audience: "The only thing a magician really does is to ask one question: 'What's real, and what's illusion?'"*

Henning pages through the newspaper and says: "Now, the illusion begins. I call this an illusion because I never actually tear the newspaper at all." He rips the paper in half, and again, and again, and again, five times in total. Each time you see and hear the newspaper tear. "In fact, some people even come back stage after the show." Henning admits. "And they say: I could have sworn you tore that newspaper.... But they've been deceived, because I haven't actually torn the paper at all.... You <u>can't</u> trust your senses. You don't believe me?" "Oh, look!" Henning instantly restores the entire newspaper! Or did he ever tear it at all? The audience gasps and claps, but still Henning's question runs in their mind: "What's real, and what's illusion?"[2]

This is the same question a now famous "scientific and experimental film about perception" inspires. You may have seen it: Three people in

white shirts and three in black pass a basketball back and forth. Viewers
are asked to count how many times the players wearing white pass
the ball. When the short film is over, audience members argue amicably
over the number. Fourteen? Thirteen? Fifteen? Not one of them,
however, comments on the man, dressed in an absurd gorilla costume,
who strolls back and forth through the frame, even pausing to pound
his fake gorilla chest. They are all "victims" of what psychologists call
"inattentional blindness." Asked to count basketball passes, basketball
passes are all they perceive. Asked whether Doug Henning is really
tearing the newspaper, seeing and tearing the newspaper is all they
perceive. As the saying goes, if all you have is a hammer, everything
looks like a nail.[3]

The hair of *Mad Men*'s Don Draper was reality from the late 1920s though at least half of the 1960s. If you watched cable television anytime between 2007 and 2015, you are intimately familiar with the thick, slick, shoe-polish black hair of actor Jon Hamm as the 1950s-1960s Madison Avenue ad man: unbearably handsome, impeccably stylish, and so thoroughly put together that not a single follicle or shaft was ever out of place. Never mind Don's tortured, alcohol-soaked psyche, that hair was the apotheosis of Euro-American manhood—and had been since the third decade of the twentieth century. For at least two or three overlapping generations, this tonsorial state was not only reality, but a very desirable form of the status quo.

In truth, human hair does not naturally assume such a sleek, shiny, and shellacked shape on the human skull. From the hairline up, the reality of the Don Draper look was real, but unnatural—and for good reason. It was manufactured at the County Chemicals Chemico Works, Bradford Street, Birmingham, England. The plant was owned and operated by Beecham, Ltd.—establishing its place in the world by turning out, beginning in 1842, Beecham's Pills, a concoction of aloe, ginger, and soap advertised to "Dislodge Bile, Stir up the Liver, Cure Sick-Headache, Female Ailments,

Remove Disease and Promote Good Health." It almost certainly did none of these, but the undeniable reality was that Beecham's Pills were one hell of a laxative, managing to keep British bowels in motion until 1998 when the successor to Beecham, SmithKline Beecham, shut down production after a run (as it were) of 156 years.

In all fairness to County Chemicals' hair product—introduced in 1928 and called Brylcreem—it did not issue from the same assembly line as the laxative. It was a pomade consisting mostly of water and mineral oil held together by beeswax and dispensed from a jar—or "tub," as the cosmetics industry calls such vessels—that fit comfortably in the palm of the adult male hand. (Today, as manufactured by Unilever, it comes in a tube.) If you are fortunate enough to be too young to recall the 1950s and 1960s television commercials for the product, several are available for your viewing pleasure on YouTube and Dailymotion.com. By the television era, Brylcreem was promoted with the jingle-borne injunction, "A little dab will do ya." At least one TV spot earnestly cautioned that "Brylcreem has a most extraordinary effect on women. (Young, pretty girls are especially susceptible.) So once again, as a public service, we'd like to caution all serious men to *use just a little dab*." This ad depicted a young fellow enduring the caresses of a mildly assaultive woman who just cannot keep her exploring hands out of his hair.

"This man dared to use two dabs. Now he's in trouble!"

The thing is, anyone who has seen Tyrone Power or Cary Grant in films of the 1940s—a time when dashing pilots flying for the Royal Air Force (RAF) were called the "Brylcreem Boys"—knows that old-school users could not confine themselves to a little dab or even two little dabs. Just look at photos of our last old-school president, Ronald Wilson Reagan, a lifelong user of the product.

Advance to 1962, the year Bristol-Myers gave Vitalis to the world. This product challenged the hegemony of the Brylcreem status quo and thereby changed reality. Vitalis was radically different from Brylcreem. It came neither in a tub nor tube, but in a bottle. It was not a "hair pomade" or even a "hair dressing," but a liquid "Hair Tonic," charged with an essence denominated V7, which the U.S. Patent and Trademark Office identified as "Polyglycol for use in a hair tonic."

We can reveal here that the current Vitalis formulation consists of SD Alcohol 40, PPG 40 Butyl Ether, water, benzyl benzoate, fragrance, dihydroabietyl alcohol, D&C Yellow 10 (CI 74005), and FD&C Yellow 6 Aluminum Lake. Whatever this formula does or does not do for human hair on the cellular or molecular level, what it did to Brylcreem is what Kryptonite does to Superman. In truth, we don't believe it's the SD Alcohol 40 or the FD&C Yellow 6 Aluminum Lake or any other chemical constituent of Vitalis that undermined the reign of the earlier reigning hair product. We are convinced the decline began as soon as Bristol-Myers decided to call out its incumbent rival neither by its brand name (Brylcreem) nor its generic name (pomade), but rather to redefine, revile, and dismantle it utterly by slurring it as "greasy kid stuff."

Here's how it worked. Both in print and on TV, the typical Vitalis ad was set in a locker room and depicted one pro athlete staring slack-jawed at the hair of a teammate. Barely suppressing a tone of contempt and nausea, athlete A demands of athlete B: "You still using that greasy kid stuff?"

Like Hamlet's "To be or not to be," the question struck a sustained chord with the public. In bars, at work, on the very streets of America, men asked one another, "You still using that greasy kid stuff?" Through the analog Web of predigital pop culture, Vitalis advanced against Brylcreem with the speed of Patton against Rundstedt. In 1962, honky-tonk song-writer

Cy Coben wrote a tune called "Greasy Kid Stuff," giving one-hit wonder Janie Grant her single Top 40 hit, with lyrics invoking Cleopatra and Mark Anthony, Stanley and Livingston, Sampson and Delilah, and Nikita Khrushchev and JFK—all of whom, the song complained, used "greasy kid stuff."

The following year, greasy kid stuff found its way into comedy stand-up routines and culture and became an even more embedded part of our popular consciousness.

FORGET REALITY, FOCUS ON PERCEPTION

It would be fair to say that reality changed in 1962 when Vitalis transformed Brylcreem into "greasy kid stuff." It would be fair to say, that is, if you look at the world from the magician's perspective—reflected here in a three-word sentence: *Perception is reality.*

This in and of itself is hardly a fresh insight. "Perception is reality" is at least as old as Plato's *Republic,* a product of the fourth century BC. In a dialogue between Plato's brother Glaucon and Plato's mentor Socrates, Plato (through Socrates) describes people who have lived lifelong as prisoners chained to the wall of a cave. They observe shadows projected on the wall from objects that pass in front of an unseen fire that burns behind the prisoners. The chained cave dwellers name each shadow, thereby identifying these mere shades as reality.

Now, Plato's Socrates is trying to sell Glaucon on the benefit of becoming a philosopher. His point in presenting the cave allegory is to demonstrate that prisoners in a cave *mistake* shadows for reality, whereas the philosopher understands the shadows for what they are because his mind has made him the freest of all men. This has enabled him to see the world of sun and substance outside the cave.

So now we arrive at the difference between the philosopher and the magician. The philosopher scorns and rejects the shadows and what the prisoners make of them, but the magician, while he is not deceived by them, doubles down on the shadows. Philosophers reject as false a "reality" that chains prisoners to impressions received via the senses. Magicians embrace and exploit these impressions because they regard them as something more than Plato believed them to be. They are not shadow impressions *passively* received, but shadow impressions *actively endowed* with reality by the human mind.

This brings us to the reason Gustav Kuhn, senior lecturer in psychology at the University of London, argues that "magic is so well-suited to explore human cognition and perception." It "comes down to one of the weirder facts of being human: Every experience we have in the world—everything we can see and hear and taste and feel, and everything we remember about it afterward—is in some ways virtual." That is, our picture of reality is created in our cognitive interpretation of reality—the way in which we sort through bristling fields of ambient data to understand what's happening *to us*. As Kuhn puts it, "magic happens to us all the time—our whole experience is a massive illusion, we're just not aware of it."[4]

Well, some of us—namely, we magicians—*are* aware. "Magicians," Kuhn says, "are trying to find loopholes in cognition, and they're trying to exploit those loopholes to create their illusions."[5] Vaulting from the fourth century BC to 1962 and the transformation of Brylcreem reality into greasy kid stuff reality, the magician says *perception is reality*, adding to that formulation the clause *or might as well be*. For the Platonic philosopher, nothing but reality will do. For the magician, perception is where the action is. Plato's Platonic version of reality may or may not exist. No one knows for sure, because the only way out of the cave is to *imagine* a realm outside of the cave. In other words, Plato's reality exists only in the mind when the mind is, by an act of will, isolated from the senses, those portals to the unreal (and therefore, for the philosopher, valueless) shadow realm. But the magician's reality is perception—or might as well be—because perception is all we really know.

Another "forget reality" example. In the drawing below, a simple question: not counting the arrows, which line is longer?

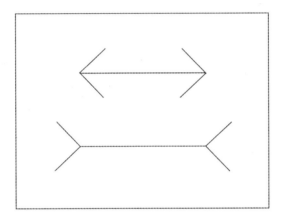

Answer: both are exactly the same. This is the famous Müller-Lyer illusion referenced in Daniel Kahneman's fascinating book, *Thinking Fast and Slow*. In his comprehensive work, Kahneman details dual parts of our mind, our system of perception, which he calls System I, the "faster" part of our brain that by necessity gathers information almost instantly, and System II, the "slower" and more powerful part of our mind that puts logic and reasoning to work. As we'll see below, great magicians operate inside both these systems, but at their best, they have an innate and almost Darwinian advantage in affecting and even temporarily controlling both.[6]

In a similar vein, John McLaughlin gives his graduate students an image from an illusion contest held at McGill University in 2007. It is the so-called Leaning Tower illusion.[7] Even though the two towers in the photographs are the same, the one seems to lean more than the other, and the eyes and brain are incapable of seeing the reality. The creators of the illusion explain that the brain insists on seeing the two sides as part of the same visual scene. The point for students in a course on intelligence and foreign policy is to always be skeptical of what they perceive as reality or truth. McLaughlin urges them to ask questions that challenge conventional wisdom.

PLACEBOS—CUPS AND BALLS

Placebo is a Latin verb form that requires a pronoun and two verbs to translate into English as "I shall please." That makes *placebo* more than a magic word. It is a magic spell. Doubtless, physicians in ancient times were familiar with the "placebo effect"—the way an inert pill or tincture or sham surgical operation or therapeutic procedure, or even a judiciously administered lie, can cause suffering patients to report amelioration of their condition or even experience clinically demonstrable improvement. The term *placebo* was not defined in any medical text, however, until it appeared in the 1811 edition of *Lexicon Medicum,* a medical dictionary published in 1717 by the English apothecary John Quincy, which was both plagiarized and expanded by Robert Hooper, a London physician. Hooper viewed placebos in much the same way as the Platonic philosopher viewed shadows—as a fraud to be scorned, calling the placebo a medicine "adapted more to please than to benefit the patient." It was not until December 4, 1920, in an article for the distinguished British medical journal *The Lancet,* that the physician T. C. Graves described the "placebo effect" in more positive terms, as producing "a real psychotherapeutic effect."

Modern research shows that not only do 30 to 50 percent of placebos have a positive effect, but that the placebo effect may account for half of the efficacy of "real"—physiologically active—drugs. That is, drugs tend to work about 50 percent more effectively when the prescribing physician tells a patient that she will feel better by taking the medication.[8] Rather more astoundingly, placebos appear to be becoming continually more effective, especially in the United States. The reason for this improvement is unclear, but some researchers believe it may be due to saturation advertising of prescription drugs, especially in the U.S., and perhaps also due to the demeanor of the personnel who administer the placebos. Friendly medical personnel tend to be associated with more positive placebo effects.[9] Eric Mead, a magician and theorist, cites studies suggesting that the better-looking the placebo is, the better it works. White pills work, but smaller white pills work better. Better still are smaller blue pills with a logo stamp on them. Capsules are generally more effective than pills, and colored capsules work better than plain capsules. The higher the indicated "dosage," the more effective the inert placebo is. But the biggest placebo effect of all is produced by injection.

The mere presence of a physician has a placebo effect, for good or ill. A white lab coat confers authority and authority confers confidence, but most people are also familiar with the "white coat syndrome," whereby the presence of the physician's lab coat measurably raises a patient's blood pressure. As the playwright George Bernard Shaw observed, "All professions are conspiracies against the laity."

The exterior of a capsule reveals nothing about the chemical composition of the powder or crystals inside it, let alone the physiological or therapeutic effect of the substance. Likewise, the shadows on the cave wall convey little or nothing of the substance of the objects that cast the shadows. Nevertheless, the senses and the mind work together to create a reality known as perception. They don't start from scratch each time we see a capsule or a shadow. For better or worse, we come to every encounter prepared.

Penn & Teller, the renowned magic/comedy team, started performing together in 1975 as magical buskers on Philadelphia street corners and at Renaissance festivals. After one gig, they stopped to eat at a New Jersey diner. Raymond Joseph Teller—that is his full original name—sat at the table practicing Cups and Balls, a close-up magic trick at least as old as the conjurers of ancient Rome and a routine that is performed all over the world. It is a series of vanishes and transpositions. In one common version of the illusion, three balls are placed on top of three inverted cups. The magician picks up one ball, vanishing it "into thin air," only to see it reappear beneath the cup. Experienced magicians will work numerous variations on the pattern, with multiple balls appearing under one cup or with small balls turning into one or more big balls or—as Penn & Teller sometimes do it—the balls becoming several potatoes or objects or pieces of fruit. That evening in the Jersey diner, Teller had no props, so he used what was at hand, wadded-up napkins and clear water glasses. In a traditional performance, opaque cups are used. With clear glasses, anyone watching could follow the wadded napkins as Teller palmed them and moved then from cup to cup. Common sense dictates this would make the illusion impossible. But no. The illusion persisted. As Teller explained later, "The eye could see the moves, but the mind could not comprehend them. Giving the trick away gave nothing away, because you still couldn't grasp it." Today, Penn & Teller perform the illusion on stage, using clear glasses. It never gets old because the reality—the source of the illusion—is not in the props, but in the structure and physiology of the human brain.

We create the reality our brains prepare us for. Most of the time and in most situations, this preparation is useful. There are three opaque cups on a table. You have placed your house keys under the middle cup. You leave the room. You return an hour later. You need your keys—fast. Your memory, together with your life experience (reminding you that inanimate objects don't move by themselves), prompts you to lift the middle cup instead of wasting time by looking under all three. You lift that cup, retrieve your keys, and are on your way. But if those keys had been placed by a skilled magician well practiced in so-called sleight of hand, your brain might well fail you. The keys you *saw* the magician put under the middle cup are now under *none* of the cups. Your brain, prepared to see the keys go under the middle cup, failed to see them disappear into the magician's hand and thence into his pocket.

SPOTLIGHT ATTENTION AND CHANGE BLINDNESS

Natural selection is a brutally straightforward evolutionary concept. Variation exists within all populations of organisms. Some variations produce characteristics in individuals that promote survival in an environment. Others fail to promote survival. Call the former variations "favorable adaptations" and the latter "unfavorable adaptations." Over time, more individuals with favorable adaptations survive to reproduce, whereas fewer with unfavorable adaptations survive to reproductive age. Eventually, the result in such a species is a population exhibiting only the favorable adaptations.

We human beings are equipped with brains that have acquired, through natural selection, certain characteristics that contribute to our survival—at least under most conditions. Among these characteristics is something we might call spotlight attention. The world bombards us with stimuli, potentially and quickly overwhelming us, leaving us vulnerable to harm from a plethora of sources—were it not for our unconscious ability to focus exclusively on (or "attend to," as psychologists put it) those inputs that are most likely to affect us for good or bad. Without this narrow-beam spotlight focus, we are doomed. When we cross a busy street, we are attuned to traffic—not to the sound of a random bird or the hum of an errant bumblebee. For this reason, we stand a good chance of getting across the road unscathed. Spotlight attention works very well in "normal" situations, but when the status quo is disrupted—as it is when a magician performs— spotlight attention can create what psychologists call change blindness.

A classic example was videotaped in 2007 by the British psychologist Richard Wiseman. It shows the psychologist performing what he describes as the "amazing color-changing card trick." Seated at a table, he introduces himself and Sarah, the woman sitting beside him. He spreads the cards out in front of Sarah, face down. The backs of the cards are blue. He instructs her to pick any card and push it toward the camera. Wiseman gathers up the remaining cards, narrating the action all the while. He announces that he is going to ask Sarah to show us the card she selected. She picks it up, turns it toward the camera, and announces that it is the three of diamonds. The magician puts the card back into the deck, which he now holds fanned out in his hand, cards facing toward the camera. He spreads the cards face up on the table and pulls out Sarah's card, the three of diamonds. He turns it over and shows that it has a blue back.

"Not particularly surprising," he says, "but what is more surprising is that all of the other cards have changed to red backs!" He flips them over to reveal this. "And *that* is the amazing color-changing card trick," he concludes.

What Wiseman does not draw our attention to is the fact that his shirt, Sarah's shirt, the tablecloth, and the backdrop behind them have all changed color, too, because Wiseman and his assistant changed them and the decks—without any camera breaks—when the angles allowed. We never noticed these far more dramatic color changes because we were focused—

narrowly, like a spotlight—on the cards and the magician's ongoing patter. "Change blindness" is a side effect of a favorable evolutionary adaptation, spotlight attention, and it can cause us to miss a huge transformation in the reality that, although right before our eyes, remains beyond our perception.

THE TRUTH? PIGS FLY!

Focusing, as we normally do, on the status quo—the expected and the anticipated—we miss some truly amazing thing, like pigs flying. Throughout most of 2015 and 2016, the answer pundits and other experts reflexively gave to the question, "Will Donald Trump be elected president?" was "When pigs fly!"

As it turned out, the pundits, who focused exclusively on the expected and anticipated, were afflicted by change blindness. They did not see what many voters saw in Donald Trump, a candidate capable of bringing the change they deeply craved. Therefore, the pundits did not—because they *could not*—believe what many voters believed, that Trump should and would be president. If voters (assuming you are in the punditry business), consumers (if you are in the making, advertising, or selling business), or audience members (if you are in the magic business) believe pigs fly, it's time to get out your pig-proof umbrella.

What's the point of all this? Pundits, business strategists, and magicians must start from a simple and ineluctable understanding: The voter, the consumer, the audience is boss. We play by *their* rules at *their* party on *their* terms. As the brilliant magician Tommy Wonder once challenged, "Imagine what the audience thinks." Like great magicians, great marketers know how to put themselves inside the simple, daily reality of their customer's world to understand what is missing, to understand the opportunities, to understand what this customer may *"need"*: *You get up, go to the bathroom, shake off whatever sleep you found, ponder, sit, shift this morning's stupid urgencies away from the strategically important, hear your email beeping, jump onto your computer, check Facebook, hear about another scandal in Washington, D.C., and you realize you "need"....*

This is what the great marketers understand—these perceptions, what consumers *need* but don't have, and how to get ahead by fulfilling those needs.

The first corporate client David Morey's company served, Steve Jobs, had this in mind when he answered a hostile question from the audience at a 1997 Q&A. In the fullness of time, the question has ceased to be important, but the answer remains valuable—and always will. In developing a product, Jobs explained, "you've got to start with the customer experience and work backwards to the technology. You can't start with the technology and try to figure out where you're going to try to sell it. I've made this mistake probably more than anybody else in this room. And I've got the scar tissue to prove it." Jobs went on to explain that in trying to come up with a vision for Apple, he and his team asked, "What incredible benefits can we give to the customer? Where can we take the customer? Not starting with 'let's sit down with the engineers and figure out what awesome technology we have and then how are we gonna market that?'"[10]

This is even more "right" in what today is often called our "reset environment," in which disruption is the norm, and where change is not only accelerating, but accelerating exponentially and unpredictably. It is an environment in which outsiders are the new insiders, winning power, and governing nations, and where companies such as Uber, Lyft, Facebook, Airbnb, Alibaba, and Bitcoin are creating industries unimagined just a few years ago. Beginning and anchoring business strategies—not to mention life strategies—with perceptions is today's new reality.

Fortunately, magicians give us secret tools to do this. They challenge our sense of what is "real," of how we define *real*. By challenging our assumptions, they prompt us to do as they do: figure out how their audience thinks, feels, and acts—and how this relates to what we *want* them to think, feel, and do. Somewhere in the dialectic between these two *hows* is our reality. The late eighteenth-century philosopher Immanuel Kant divided reality into what he called the *Ding an sich* (the thing in itself) and the *Ding für uns* (the thing for us, or the thing as it appears). These days, magicians, marketers, and political strategists have pretty much given up on finding the *Ding an sich* and have instead settled for the *Ding für uns*—because perceptions rule, and it is the magician's, marketer's, and strategist's job to begin with, understand, and shape these perceptions.

Brylcreem was the key to the kingdom of civilized virility until it became greasy kid stuff. Bounty was just another paper towel—a dull commodity—until some ad man or ad woman pronounced it "The Quicker Picker-Upper." Now it is the nation's leading paper towel product. The phrase is a magic word, an incantation, a spell, endowed with its magical power through a combination of language and the context of "information" created by incessant advertising. The lilting "Quicker Picker-Upper" pricks our memory of TV sequences showing Bounty *absorbing* several times as much water as any competing towel soaks up. This perception, reinforced by the incantation, is our reality—as solid as the image of a Volvo calling to mind the magic word *safety* or the vivid blue, red, and orange of a Southwest Airlines jet evoking the incantatory utterance—*value*.

THE MARKETING-MAGIC NEXUS

We marketers and magicians may not always like what the audience thinks and believes. As the late Arizona congressman and presidential candidate Mo Udall proclaimed the day after losing an especially close election, "The people have spoken.... The bastards!" David Morey particularly recalls how a client, a famous (but nameless here forevermore) high-tech CEO, banged on the soundproof two-way mirror of a focus group session, impotently yelling at the truth-telling consumers inside: "These... people...just...don't...*understand*!"

Well, they don't. But their misunderstanding was my famous client's problem and responsibility, not theirs. We report to *them*—consumers, constituents, audience, voters. They are the boss.

So how do we discharge *our* responsibility and solve *our* problem? Let's break it down.

The very first thing in both magic and marketing is to provide a context for and a summary of the perceptions you want your audience or your customers to have. This is crucial because—remember—perceptions are reality, or might as well be. To provide both context and summary, both magicians and marketers exploit the concept of *brand*. Bestselling author, entrepreneur, and marketing guru Seth Godin defines "brand" as a set of "expectations, memories, stories, and relationships that in combination drive the decision to choose a particular company, product, or service."[11] David Morey describes "brand" as a bucket into which we pour our expectations and our sense of relevance, difference, and credibility, along with the thousands of images we gather about any leader, country, company, product, or service. Either way, a great brand sums up and reveals to the world how you or your product are different, special, and better.

Next, having contextualized and summed up your merchandise (product, idea, whatever you are selling) in a brand, apply the rules magicians follow every time they perform. David Morey and his business partner, political and marketing consultant Scott Miller, have developed a framework around consumer and voter perceptions that has added exponential business value and won global elections. They call it the *6 Cs*.

These days, with more choice on every shelf and in every brick-and-mortar and online store, it is harder than ever to know what consumers will decide. But it is relatively easy to know *how* they will decide. Six factors drive the decisions of consumers, audiences, and voters. Luckily for us, all six happen to begin with the letter *C*: Control, Choice, Change, Customization, Convenience, and Connection. Behold:

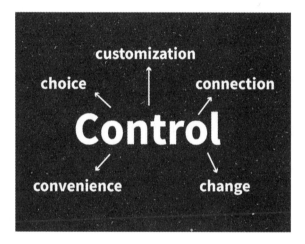

- **Control** is at the center. Consumers make decisions that will give them a greater sense of control—over their personal safety, their economic security, their health and wellness, and in opposition to the influence of powerful institutions. A soda pop, piece of software, or athletic shoe can give a consumer the feeling of control. It's a matter of product development and positioning. Orbiting *Control are the five following satellite factors.*

- **Choice** provides more consumer control. It does not limit or force the hand of today's increasingly knowledgeable consumer, but instead provides cost, quality, and value comparisons. Technology is an enabler here. The Internet has trained us all to expect Choice. If we aren't confronted by what we have been taught to expect, we quickly find Choice on our own.

- **Change** usually leads to more and newer choices. Change used to induce anxiety in many people, but ever since Steve Jobs revolutionized personal electronics, consumers have anticipated change positively. These days, the negative dynamics of political leadership have been making change especially attractive to voters. "Anybody *but*" has become a viable—and often winning—candidate everywhere.

- With more Choice and more Change, **Customization** is now more attainable than was ever before anticipated. During the bygone era of mass marketing, consumers accepted the tube sock dictum of "one size fits all." With the technology-driven penetration of the controllable search concept, consumers now accept, embrace, and demand the idea that "*I can find that* one *size that fits just* me.*"

- **Convenience** is a known decision driver. It is taken for granted in a world of increasing Choice. Although early adopters will seek out a new idea, once they adopt it, they expect to find it distributed ubiquitously. What is more, in contrast to the early days of the personal computer, they expect the initial usage experience not to give them too many headaches. Nor do they want the burden of thick instruction manuals in seventeen different languages, none of which ever quite come across as native to anyone.

- **Connection** is not a new driver, but it is now empowered by new tactics and new media. The urge to associate with "people like me, people I like, and people I'd like to be like" still pulls consumers toward brands and voters toward candidates.

These six factors are essential today to great marketing and are at the core of how great magicians manage audiences and their perceptions. In fact, the greatest magicians take command of these 6 Cs. Take, for example, the legendary Spanish card magician Juan Tamariz. His virtuoso performance allows the audience to feel in *control*, even as he fools them badly and beyond any logic. He offers anyone and everyone just the card *they* want, he constantly changes the tempo and jolts the audience with ongoing surprises, he acknowledges every helper by name, creating almost intimate connection and making it all seem completely and utterly simple; and finally, he brings the audience to a sense of connection, earning a standing ovation every time. For Tamariz, all 6 Cs are on magical performance overdrive.

Or consider the late, great Harry Blackstone Jr. When he asked for children to join him on stage, he ceded *control* to the audience—any kid who could make it to the stage was welcome. Every parent within reach of the stage could *choose* whether to let their child join. Then Blackstone, stepping out from the wings carrying a small bird cage and canary, invited the children to place their hands on the cage, on the top, bottom, back, front—on all the sides. By the time every kid stretched out a hand, the cage and even most of the magician were covered. Then, in a flash, the cage and bird would vanish from Blackstone's hands and the children, who were invited to look under the magician's coat—still more ceding of *control*—could find nothing. Imagine the *connection* Blackstone made with a vast swath of his audience literally touching him. At that point in the show, his audience was prepared to suspend disbelief and come along for the ride. They were *sold.*

In business, the 6 Cs are the instruments essential to performing an autopsy on a dead brand or business:

1. Did the deceased take away that sense of Control (as the major airlines so often do)?

2. Did the cadaver before me narrow choice (in the whole category or in its own portfolio)?

3. Did the victim stop changing and refreshing?

4. Did the stiff insist on positioning itself as "one size fits all?"

5. Was this floater inconvenient even for its most loyal users?

6. Did the dear departed discourage the connection of one user to another?

The 6 Cs will help you engage and hold today's most difficult audiences, consumers, and voters. And in our hyper-challenging environment, we need all the help we can get.

Finally, we need to delve more deeply into magic by asking how we can learn from the stage instincts of today's great magicians so that we can better understand how each member of our audience—our consumer— thinks, feels, and acts. Magician, marketer, political candidate, we each sell something to somebody. So how can we "think ahead" (as magicians put it)—think one step ahead—to understand and thereby influence the purchasing process through which audiences/consumers/voters are led by their perceptions?

How? Get the answers to the ten questions that follow. (Magicians get the answers through long experience and close observation. Marketers— well, marketers simply *ask* consumers.)

1. **What surrounds your customers' world?** In what context do they live? Overall, what are the most critical dynamics, forces, changes, products, services, and brands that touch them every day? How do they perceive that world? Every magician asks: Who is my audience? It's one thing to perform for a group of children on Saturday afternoon, but quite another—as John McLaughlin has done recently—to work corporate events for audiences of electrical engineers, information scientists, or mainline journalists and government officials.

2. **How do they see the future?** Is it headed in the right or the wrong direction? Remember to ask your customers the classic question Ronald Reagan planted in the minds of voters to win

the 1980 election: "Are you better off than you were four years ago?" What do they expect from your company or brand in the future? What do they expect from your competitors? A great magician will always try to understand how his or her audience experienced magic in the past—in order to aim his or her show toward the future. Has this audience seen an excellent magician before, or a magician that in some way disappointed? And how has this conditioned their expectations?

3. **What do they dream about?** What is their ideal product, service, or offering in your category? Since 1984, David Morey has worked with partner Scott Miller and political pollster Pat Caddell as they developed the groundbreaking "Candidate Smith" research, which asked voters not to react to existing candidates, but to construct their own perfect, ideal candidate for president. Once you understand your customers' ideal product and service brands and brand relationships, you can probe ways to fill in the gaps. For a magician, the relevant question is: what will your audience perceive if they believe you *really* can do magic?

4. **What's in their hearts?** What emotional drivers are most important to your customers? Because more and more decisions are being made impulsively, more and more of marketing is driven by emotion. For example, in politics, one of the most telling measurements of any campaign is the degree to which people believe that a candidate "cares about people like me." Behind this question is a combination of curiosity and cynicism. "Can this person understand my life? And can I understand this person and the way she or he makes decisions?" They want to know the same thing from the companies and brands that they decide to deal with in the marketplace. In magic, the best magicians, such as David Copperfield, don't have to deal with quite the same factors, but they do work hard to show they *care* about and treat their audiences well; and, too, they seek to establish an *emotional* context for their illusions—to touch the audience's hearts as well as their minds and embed illusion in a meaningful framework.

5. **Where is their pain?** What are your customers missing that they most need? What do they worry about at night? For example, in the Internet gold rush of the late 1990s and the recession of the late 2000s, far too many companies received funding—without being able to articulate what specific marketplace "pain" their offerings uniquely addressed. Chances are those companies' stock certificates are about as coveted today as two-day-old sushi. Similarly, the magician's job is often to take his or her audience away from any pain they feel in their lives, even if temporarily, and at their best, to inspire and help these audiences to rise above pain, and to help relieve it by the wonder of magic, all the time working to entertain and astonish.

6. **What's relevant and different?** Value is created by relevant differentiation—by the benefits *you* provide to targeted customers and the way *you* provide them uniquely among all market choices. To achieve relevance, you've got to know what matters most to your customers. Most importantly, you must know what attributes communicate and prove differentiation *for them.* Consider using a "laddering" technique that asks customers to rate a product's or service's most important attributes in order of importance *to them.* If you learn only one thing from market research, that one thing should be how your target consumers define *relevance* and *differentiation* in your market segment. For magicians, this is a variation of "know your customer"—what is it that this audience will find especially relatable, different, and astonishing?

7. **Are they movable?** What are your customers' attitudes toward your product, service, or company? Are they experiencing hard opposition? Soft opposition? Undecided? Soft support? Or are they hard supporters—that is, loyalists? In other words, ask your customers to tell you if *they* should be a prioritized marketing target. Get your customers to help you order your targeting priorities. Don't waste time and resources trying to move the unmovable. On this score, the magician asks: am I facing a group of skeptics…are there people in this audience who don't like magic, find it challenging, or want to think only like engineers and understand how it works? If so, how can I bring them around?

8. **How can you over-deliver on their expectations?** What are your customers' current expectations based on today's market choices? What would constitute an over-delivery on these expectations? And when and how should you claim this success? How can you clearly define expectations in line with their perceptions, over-deliver on them, and then remind customers of your success at delighting them? These are the most constant questions magicians ask themselves—how can I exceed my audience's expectations? How can I give them an experience of wonder that goes beyond what they know?

9. **How can you best define yourself?** In the end, how must your customers see you? What must you stand for? And how can you define your competition most advantageously? (Ideally, positioning yourself to advantage will result in positioning the competition to disadvantage.) With a consumer company/ brand, as with a political candidate, people are interested not only in *what* they decide to do, but in *how* they decide to do it. Self-definition tells consumers what they can expect from the candidate or the company/brand in the future. Great magicians think constantly, "Who is my character? Who am I portraying on stage? (Recalling the words of the famous nineteenth century French conjuror, Robert-Houdin, that 'a magician is an actor playing the part of a magician.') How do I want my audience to remember me?"

10. **How can you control the dialogue in your favor?** You must understand and objectively evaluate the effect of your competitors' claims in the marketplace. If the competition consists of the incumbent market leaders, chances are that they have control of the market dialogue. The question is, how can you take it away from them? What perceptual opportunities must be seized to turn consumers' attention to you? What core message and themes will help up the ante in the marketplace? The magician is competing not so much with other magicians as with the audience's version of reality—and the magician constantly asks how they can control all the elements of their

45

performance and bring an entire audience to a state of wonder, delight, and surprise.

Before a performance, John McLaughlin always looks at his favorite magic poster—one from the early 1900s depicting the greatest British magician of that era, David Devant. He does this to remind himself of why magicians perform and what they can give to their audiences. The poster is titled "All Done by Kindness," and the audience it depicts shows every emotion of delight, skepticism, and expectation that we've just discussed. Overwhelmingly, what we behold is a happy and satisfied audience, and although Devant may not have consciously asked himself the foregoing ten questions, we are sure he answered them successfully.[12]

PRACTICE, PRACTICE, PRACTICE

The moment you embrace the equivalence of reality and perception, you feel a rush. But then you start thinking, and then the rush yields to doubt, self-consciousness, and even a tinge of guilt. David Morey had been an avid magician in childhood since the age of five; to his surprise, he returned to the study of magic as an adult, after a twenty-five-year hiatus. What struck him was the "fragility" of the initial embrace. When you try to learn, or relearn, magic, you become self-conscious about the reality-perception equivalence, so that you tend to see it not as an equivalence, but as a dual reality. You yourself know how you are doing a sleight-of-hand effect, and that self-consciousness will kill the magic, if you let it. So, if you are serious about continuing with magic, you adapt by shifting 180 degrees until your natural inclination is to think from the perspective of the audience's reality.

This takes practice. You know where the card is hiding, so the challenge becomes erasing all guilt about this, trimming away any blinks or tics or other tells that are signs of something else at work, anything that signals to the audience that, no, perception is *not* reality. You need to practice until all your tells are purged. The thing is, the audience, like Agent Mulder in TV's *The X-Files, wants* to believe. Operating inside their own reality, they *want* to believe it *is* reality, period. It is the job of the magician—and the marketer—to oblige them by fulfilling, not fighting, their desire to believe. This is *not* deception, because perception is reality—or might as well be.

As an aspiring magician, how do you know when you have practiced enough? Our sense of the "fragility" of the perception-reality equivalence often lands in the very mirror before which we magicians begin to practice. We start fooling even ourselves, because our minds simply cannot follow our own tools of deception and sleight of hand, and, in this, we fully assume the role of the audience member or the consumer. We become the audience. At this point, practice has nearly made perfect. The next step is to stop using a mirror altogether and instead perform in front of a video recorder. Watch yourself onscreen in recorded time—unreal time, rather than mirrored time, real time—and you will see the magic happen. Never mind that you are the magician, you will begin to wonder how you did *that*. When you cannot honestly answer how the magic happened, you have practiced enough.

In magic, the great effects go far beyond "fooling" people. They rise high above simple deception. Here is the secret of the world's greatest magicians: *their* magic does not *trick* the mind, it *transforms* perceptions— disrupting our preconditions, assumptions, and prejudices. The magic of the great magicians is like the physics of the great physicists. When Einstein showed us that space and time were equivalent, he felt no guilt— though he was obliged to remind us that "Reality is merely an illusion, albeit a very persistent one" and that "Common sense is the collection of prejudices acquired by age eighteen." When the marketers of Vitalis transformed Brylcreem into greasy kid stuff, they did not repent but rejoiced. Great marketers, like great physicists and great magicians, do not deceive. They transform perceptions—of their marketplace, their product, their service, their brand, and the very future of their industry, sometimes even of their culture and their world.

THE SECOND STRATEGY
REBOOT ASPIRATION

"A computer on every desk and in every home."

—Bill Gates

Scene: *This really happened. It's the early 1920s, and Harry Houdini is the world's most celebrated magician. Right now, he's sitting behind a closed curtain, having just escaped from one of his signature magical props, the Chinese Water Torture Cell. Moments ago, onstage before a live audience, his feet were locked into stocks fixed into a restraint brace, and he was hoisted upside down, suspended in midair by his ankles. The brace fits on top of the Torture Cell proper, which is a sinister-looking device, a phone booth size glass box reinforced with a steel framework and filled with water.*

Head-first, ankles locked, Houdini is lowered into the water, which sloshes over the top of the Cell as his body enters. Once the brace that holds his ankles is fitted securely atop the Cell, assistants lock it into place. The audience glimpses the writhing struggles of the fully immersed magician just before a curtain is drawn across the Cell.

The audience knows it's a show. They know Houdini has escaped from the Torture Cell before. Yet they somehow feel certain that this time he will drown and die.

Unseen, Houdini quickly escapes. He kills time behind the curtain, swimsuit-clad, dripping, passing the minutes, waiting, his ears attuned to the buzz, groan, gasp, and suppressed screams of the unseen audience. When their collective crescendo of suspenseful anxiety just begins to fade, Houdini knows the audience has just begun to lose hope. That is when he bursts out from behind the curtain, smiling, dripping, taking his bow before a theater full of witnesses giddy with the combination of awe, relief, and joy that comes from an aspiration realized.

"The American Academy of Achievement"—there actually is such a thing[13]—was founded in 1961 by a photographic journalist named Brian Blaine Reynolds "to bring aspiring young people together with real-life heroes—the kind of achievers [photographer Reynolds] met every week on assignment." On March 17, 2010, the Academy published an interview with Bill Gates, a 1992 inductee into the Academy and a former client of David Morey. As anyone who has followed Gates and Microsoft knows, he issued in 1980 a most memorable statement of the Microsoft mission. It was an aspiration of boundless ambition: *A computer on every desk and in every home.*

"When did you first have the vision of a computer on every desk at work and in every home?" the Academy interviewer asked Gates.

"Paul Allen and I had used that phrase even before we wrote the BASIC (programming language) for Microsoft." This would have been 1975, when Gates, Allen, and Monte Davidoff were hired by the makers of the now-legendary Altair computer to create the first high-level programming language for their machine. Released before Micro-Soft shed its hyphen, Altair BASIC was Microsoft's very first product. "We actually talked about it in an article in—I think 1977 was the first time it appears in print—where we say, 'a computer on every desk and in every home...'" [14]

Talk about an *aspiration!*

Consider... The famous phrase became a formal mission statement in 1980, at a time when Microsoft, a software maker, did not even make computers. Three years earlier, in 1977, it was just beginning to make software. Two years before that, in 1975, three guys who were among a small group of "hobbyists" tinkering with the Altair 8800 were paid to write a version of BASIC that could squeeze some degree of practical functionality out of 256 bytes to 64 kilobytes of RAM with a processor chugging along at 2.0 MHz in a computer programmed via toggle switches and lights rather than with a keyboard and monitor. Altair BASIC, Microsoft's foundational piece of software, was itself an aspiration.

"It's very hard to recall how crazy and wild that was, you know," Gates told the Academy interviewer, "'on every desk and in every home.' At the time, you [had] people who are very smart saying, 'Why would somebody need a computer?' Even Ken Olsen, who had run this company Digital Equipment, who made the computer I grew up with, and that we admired both him and his company immensely, was saying that this seemed kind of a silly idea that people would want to have a computer."[15]

DREAM BIGGER DREAMS

In 1975, 1977, and 1980, when typewriter repair was a job you could count on, Bill Gates was writing, thinking, imagining, and dreaming the way Harry Houdini had done some fifty years before. Magic, you see, is at its very best all about dreaming bigger dreams. *Dream bigger dreams* could have been the mission statement of Harry Houdini, the very archetype of a modern magician. It was he who redefined magic for modern audiences by making it relevant to their innermost and yet most universal dreams. Houdini's *astounding* escapes were also great escapes, because they were intensely relevant to an audience who dreamed of magically freeing themselves from the myriad chains of everyday life.

Arguably, Harry Houdini's appeal would only have increased had he lived beyond the Roaring Twenties and continued to perform during the 1930s. The twenties were an era of relative prosperity—or at least of its glittering promise. The decade both embodied and encouraged aspiration. In bleak contrast, the thirties, marked by a global economic Great Depression of unprecedented severity, amputated dreams, locking people into the financial and emotional equivalent of the boxes, cells, and vaults from which Houdini had routinely escaped. A fascinating article published in the August 1932 edition of *Popular Aviation* asked the age-old question, "Can Man Propel Himself Through the Air by His Own Power?" The article's author, W. I. Oliver, "[n]oted student of aviation history and ornithopter flight," cited the Greek myth of Icarus, who flew on magical waxen wings his father Daedalus had fashioned for him as well as for himself to escape from the impenetrable labyrinth of the monstrous Minotaur. Young Icarus, exhilarated by the freedom of flight, sheered away from his father to fly higher and higher until, having approached too near the sun, the wax began to melt, and he fell back to earth and his death. This end notwithstanding, Icarus had realized—for a time, at least—the dream of human-powered flight.

Turning from mythology and the heat of the sun, Oliver went on to explore a more practical limitation of animal-powered flight. He invited his readers to "picture a sparrow and an eagle in a pen," forty feet square, with no top, and with walls four feet in height. "The small sparrow rises vertically at the rate of nine to ten feet per second and could easily clear the walls. The eagle, on the other hand, could not escape, because the eagle requires a wing flapping run of sixty feet to clear the four-foot fence....the same rule applies to the condor, buzzards, seagull and other large heavy birds..." [16]

In the 1930s, *Popular Aviation* advertised itself as having the "Largest Sale of Any Aviation Magazine." That was really saying something, since the early thirties were a golden age of aviation. As the Great Depression threatened to drag everyone down, the wonders of flight promised to lift everyone up. The dream of escape and transcendence that Houdini had offered in the 1920s, flying machines offered in the 1930s. Too bad Houdini had succumbed in 1926 to peritonitis following a ruptured appendix, which may or may not have been aggravated by multiple gut punches delivered (all in good fun) by a fan. If anything, the 1930s offered an even bigger market than the 1920s for the kind of magical aspirations to which Houdini catered. As for W. I. Oliver's practical mathematical calculations concerning the aerodynamics of birds and the human beings who sought to emulate them, perhaps the more important point is nature's instinctive belief that we all need lots of room to take off, to aspire to bigger dreams, to escape from our version of the forty-foot-square pen. Houdini, it turns out, was not all about mere entertainment any more than the myth of Icarus and Daedalus was just a good story or Oliver's fascination with bird flight was no more than an aerodynamic calculation. All these things were and are about the magic of aspiration.

"THE MAGIC IS OUT THERE"

In 1999, Michael Eisner handpicked Bob Iger to succeed him as CEO of The Walt Disney Company. During this time, Iger happened to be a client of David Morey's company, and David's business partner, Scott Miller, asked him a critical question. *Do you really want the job?*

The thing is, Iger was doing very nicely, thank you, as president and CEO of ABC, Inc., which Disney had purchased in 1996. Disney itself? Not so much. In fact, the company was in sharp decline. It was no longer delivering on the aspirational promise founder Walt Disney had invented way back in 1923. No, the parks, movie business, broadcast and cable television, and retail operations were all sliding. As for the Disney digital and gaming business, it never even got off the ground. To add proverbial insult to proverbial injury, the company seemed to be doing its damnedest to destroy its aspirational relationship with young parents by over-licensing the Disney brands, putting its beloved characters on everything from pasta to toilet paper, and generally abusing moms and dads with an ill-conceived Disney Store concept guaranteed to turn even the sweetest little kid into a spoiled rotten undersized tyrant.

As for tweens and teens, core Disney mainstays since the mid-1950s, the company was neglecting if not undoing these all-important consumer relationships. Half-hearted efforts to revive the classic 1950s *Mickey Mouse Club* TV show in 1977 *(The New Mickey Mouse Club)* and 1989-1994 *(The All-New Mickey Mouse Club)* were about as imaginative as the "New" and the "All-New" prefixes tacked onto the original name. True, Michael Eisner had performed like the bona fide business genius he was when Roy E. Disney and others brought him on board as CEO and Chairman in 1984. But by the 1990s, by many accounts he had become a manager who had challenges delegating, and he was attracting significant criticism. The trouble was his sincere conviction that he and only he possessed the secret of the "Disney magic." This prompted him to commandeer every decision, soon sending the company's frightened shareholders into revolt. So by the time Bob Iger asked our advice about the job, things had gotten relatively ugly.

"Do you really want the job?" Scott asked him.

"Yes," Iger replied. "I want the job."

"Well, okay, you've been *selected*," Scott replied. "But now you must be *elected*."

Morey and Miller understood Disney's plight. In kid's entertainment, Disney was the long-established "incumbent" player and had been for seventy-five years of the soon-to-end twentieth century. Like all too many incumbents, however, Disney had forgotten its original dreams. To recover its magic, the company needed done for it precisely what magicians do for their audiences. Disney needed its aspirations rebooted. The metaphor is appropriate. When any digital device runs too long, it tends to slow down and even seize up. The only thing you can do to fix it is to reboot. Often, this means pulling the power plug, plugging it back in, and starting all over. Similarly, when a company is an incumbent for too long, it slows down or seizes up and finds itself in need of radical intervention in the form of an aspirational reboot. "I hold it that a little rebellion now and then is a good thing," Thomas Jefferson wrote to James Madison on January 30, 1787, "and as necessary in the political world as storms in the physical."[17] Rather more savagely, Jefferson wrote to William Stephens Smith on November 13, 1787, "[T]he tree of liberty must be refreshed from time to time with the blood of patriots and tyrants, it is its natural manure."[18] Incumbency requires an assault from insurgency. And *that* is precisely what Bob Iger delivered.

He conducted nothing less than an insurgent political campaign, beginning what would be one of the most successful runs of any American CEO, a trajectory that continues to this day. He aimed to reboot and satisfy the aspirations of the company's stakeholders. He set out to recapture the aspirations of customers whose loyalty had made Disney legendary for over eighty years. With a keen understanding of perceptions, he took control of his stage and focused his performance to win over the dissident Disney factions he faced coming into the leadership role: dissatisfied shareholders, disaffected young parents, and alienated teens and tweens, as well as demoralized division heads, employees, and partners in the global creative community. His objective was to define himself in such a way that *all* stakeholders would come to feel that his leadership selection had been *their* idea all along. He wanted to be perceived as *their* choice for CEO, *fulfilling their* aspirations.

A tall order? Absolutely. And we told him that he had to pull it off within the space of no more than a year.

We worked with Bob to put into action a strategic approach that we have found rarely fails. It consists of defining three things:

1. Yourself

2. The aspirations of your leadership

3. The future

Using this approach, Bob quickly differentiated himself from his predecessor. Whereas Eisner had firmly believed that only he understood the "Disney magic," Bob met with his top managers in his corner suite at Team Disney Burbank, a Michael Graves building adorned on its façade with the Seven Dwarves. Facing his management team, he spread his fingers and placed his palm flat against his chest.

"The magic is not in here," he said. After taking a beat, he continued: "It's not in this building. It's not in Burbank."

Now he met the eyes of each executive. "The magic," he said, is out there. Our job is to find it."

Successful magicians possess the knowledge and skills of their craft, but they know that the "magic" is not theirs at all. It belongs to their audience. Some call it a capacity for wonder and astonishment. We call it aspiration. Without aspiration, there is no magic because there is no motive for magic. "Nothing great was ever achieved without enthusiasm," the American essayist and philosopher Ralph Waldo Emerson wrote. Doubtless, he was inspired in this thought by the German philosopher Georg Wilhelm Friedrich Hegel, of whom he was a great admirer. "Nothing great in the world was accomplished without passion," Hegel wrote. We believe this declaration can support at least two more variations: "Nothing great was ever achieved without aspiration" and "Nothing great was ever achieved without magic."

At Disney, Bob Iger has consistently defined himself as an executive who leads people to discover and act upon their aspirations, which if they are thinking like magicians, are parallel to and even coincide with the aspirations of their customers. Through this approach, Iger did a brilliant job of restoring the company's relationship with young families and moms and resetting its relationship with teens and tweens. The aspiration he expressed for Disney was as iconic as Mickey's ears: "We will define family fun everywhere in the world."

THE NON-MIRACLE OF *NET-A-PORTER*

Magic looks miraculous. It isn't. And Bob Iger worked no miracles at Disney. Yes, the company was in trouble when he took it over, but let us acknowledge that when Iger took the helm, the Disney organization already had a formidable brand. The good news is that any company—anyone in business—can learn to create brands that not only imagine consumer aspirations, but imagine those aspirations achieved.

Consider the story of Net-a-Porter, a London-based high-fashion retailer founded in 2000 by Natalie Massenet. She pioneered the Web as a platform on which consumers could achieve their most fashionable aspirations. Born Natalie Rooney in Los Angeles to an American journalist/ film publicist father and a British model for Chanel mother, Massenet spent her early childhood in Paris. She grew up in close contact with the fashion industry and became a fashion journalist for *Women's Wear Daily* and *Tatler*. This experience not only gave her a unique perspective on the fashion industry, it also inspired her to develop the concept of a magazine-format website capable of converting readers into consumers with a mouse click on clothing items they encountered while browsing. In 2000, this concept was met with a great deal of skepticism, but Massenet was convinced of the power of the concept: a magazine platform that created interest *and* functioned as a retail store, providing the means of instantly acting on interest. Massenet was among the early generation of e-retailers who recognized the magic of the digital platform, which could variously anticipate, create, and shape consumer aspiration while enabling the effortless transformation of aspiration into reality.

The naysayers notwithstanding, Massenet launched her company from a flat in Chelsea, London. Remember, this was 2000, a year in which "dot-coms" were being lavishly overvalued and recklessly overfunded. Often, what they promised far exceeded the state of Internet technology at the time, and many dot-coms turned into dot-bombs. Massenet walked straight into this situation with Net-a-Porter. Not only were overly hyped dot-coms imploding all around her, the concept of selling exclusively online was almost unimaginable. Most computer users were still literally *dialing into* this thing called the World Wide Web. Designers as well as investors were justifiably wary of putting merchandise, money, and reputation into an enterprise that lacked the brick-and-mortar presence of a Saks Fifth Avenue or Barneys. Whenever Massenet tried to pitch her business ideas, there was always the same question: "But where is the actual store located?"

Her persistence, however, paid off. In 2001, she persuaded up-and-coming new designer Roland Mouret to sell his first collection on her site. That was sufficient to overcome inertia, and by 2004, Net-a-Porter was turning a profit. A fashion discount site, *The Outnet*, followed in 2009, and Massenet sold Net-a-Porter to the Swiss-based luxury goods holding company Richemont in 2010, remaining as the company's executive chairman as well as a prime investor. Today, Net-a-Porter grabs the attention of over five million women a month, who read, browse, and shop the latest runway looks from the season's most sought-after collections.

Not only does Net-a-Porter act as an online retailer, it also presents the latest fashion news, trend reports, and style advice to women around the world. Endorsements from celebrities like Victoria Beckham (in WWD, April 18, 2012) further strengthen its appeal: "I do like using style apps on my iPad and I also like to shop online. I love Net-a-Porter in particular. Being a working mum with four children, having the ability to shop online is wonderful."

The average Net-a-Porter customer is a thirty-three-year old female who is affluent and accomplished. Typical customers hold such positions as CEO, senior executive, attorney, fashion director, or media director. They have plenty of household income to spend on luxury and fashion, and the members of this target audience are not bashful about their own aspirations. They want the best, and they want to get it the way they want to get it—conveniently, at the mere click of a mouse. Net-a-Porter's website was created with a clear layout resembling any hardcopy fashion magazine. When browsing and scrolling across any of the magazine's editorial pages, a pop-up window near the user's mouse curser conveniently enables purchase. Net-a-Porter gives buyers literally no excuses for failing to buy. Fulfillment of aspiration is just a click away.

Over the years, Massenet focused on aspirational consumers like herself, who value time over cash. Her goal was to provide effortless shopping to people who are so busy earning money that they crave the convenience of getting luxury goods with minimal digital effort. Massenet then included the final touch on the packaging itself. An elegantly mysterious black box is delivered to your home—or office—tied up in a bow. Such attention to detail from order to delivery is a signature of the brand. Today, Net-a-Porter's deliveries make the receiver feel more than anything else valued as a customer. Consumer aspirations are delivered with each purchase.

Net-a-Porter blazed a new path within the retail industry. Massenet created it as the Web's first one hundred percent shop-able publication. In serving her customers' aspirations, her goal was to redefine the magazine industry. In the process, however, she ended up redefining the retail industry. Supremely well-executed digital enterprises share with magic the ability to render the universe seamless and frictionless. Physical effort, distance, and time itself are made, in the wave of a wand or the click of a mouse, to disappear.

INDULGENCE IS NOT THE ONLY ASPIRATION

The aspirational principles of magic readily lend themselves to the entertainment and luxury sectors, but their application is by no means limited to these. Antivirus software is neither entertaining nor luxurious, but in 2010, when David Morey's client, digital security firm AVG Technologies, sought to create a successful IPO, David drew on his experience as a magician to create a strategy. Common sense tells us that digital security is a consumer need, not a luxury. Magic, however, has more to do with uncommon than common sense, and David therefore decided to focus AVG Technologies not on customer need but on customer *aspiration*. Consumers aspire to peace of mind in their digital lives. Trapped by Internet threats and the increasingly complicated burden of managing their online worlds, the consumer of 2010 shared the position of those who in the 1920s gaped and cheered as Harry Houdini escaped from handcuffs, strait jackets, and "torture cells." Modern consumers want the freedom that comes with mastery of life online, so David helped to build a marketing approach that empowered and liberated AVG Technologies to deliver a message not of grim necessity, but of aspiration—more precisely, of aspiration achieved. In the jam-packed digital security sector, AVG Technologies' 2012 IPO was a homerun.

THE ASPIRATIONALS

Like magicians, today's most innovative business leaders are at their best when they transcend and seek to fulfill their customers' higher aspirations. For example, a first-quarter 2016 study of 21,000 consumers from twenty-one countries showed the power of "Aspirational Consumers" is steadily rising—even if half of this defined segment cannot name a "purposeful" brand they themselves feel good about. This study defined these "Aspirationals" based on their "love of shopping, desire for responsible consumption, and their trust in brands to act in the best interest of society." The research concluded that 40 percent of today's global consumers are "Aspirationals," a big and powerful target market for the business leaders who are thinking like magicians.[19]

Because the data in this study is both new and novel, Aspirationals are as yet very much insufficiently studied as well as underserved, and even their marketplace potential is still largely untapped. We know that they are hungry for brands with a strong ethic, or what could be termed a strong "conviction." Put another way, the Aspirational Consumers seek brands with a higher purpose, brands that know and appreciate what their founders and creators believe, and companies that know how their brands fit into their customers' lives. The Aspirational Consumers are young, mostly millennial and Gen X populations (think Burning Man). Most live outside the United States, in emerging markets.[20]

Some of David Morey's favorite clients, such as Apple, Nike, and The Coca-Cola Company, exemplify "aspirational" brands. Grey Goose Vodka is another example—and perhaps among the most revelatory. We challenge readers to a blind taste test of the three leading vodkas. Good luck distinguishing one from the other. But, of course, chemical substance is not the issue here. It is the look, feel, packaging, imagery, and aspirational fulfillment of Grey Goose that allows it to charge more and lead its marketplace. Arguably, in fact, the higher price contributes to the aspiration. After all, nothing is less worthy of desire than a "bargain brand."

Like religion, magic often imbues ordinary things, people, events, and environments with magnified significance. The entity in question becomes, under the force of religion, sacred. Under the influence of magic, it becomes magical. Likewise, "aspirational" brands stand for more than what they actually are or do. They execute against a product perception that extends well beyond devices, sneakers, sugar water and brown food coloring, or distilled clear spirits. Among the most potent aspects of managing consumers' perception of aspirational brands is something we call "image associations." The world's greatest magicians, like the world's best marketers, understand these instinctively. The most effective image associations are distilled through something called the "One Emotion" test. It goes like this: If you had to choose to evoke only a single emotion from your audience—or your customers—what would it be? Here's what two former David Morey clients chose:

- ◆ Focusing on male consumers, BMW chose an emotion and aspirational fulfillment associated with an automobile—e.g., "Pride"… "The *Ultimate* Driving Machine."

- ◆ Focusing on female consumers, LVMH (LVMH Moët Hennessy Louis Vuitton SE), the French-based luxury goods conglomerate, chose pocketbook brand imagery that allows the company to charge what it charges, namely prices that are exponentially higher than the cost of manufacture—e.g., "Richness"… "Exceptional *Luxury*."

The greatest magicians align every single detail of their own personal brands by instinct and purpose to connect with the higher aspirations of their audience. For example, our friend David Copperfield, with the obsessiveness of a brilliant marketer, controls every element of his own show, celebrity, and image. Just try taking a selfie with the world's most famous magician. It won't happen. Copperfield won't deny you a photo with him. It just won't be *your* selfie. One of his staff or Copperfield himself will take the picture for you and send it along. You will have your souvenir, and Copperfield will have exercised his control over it. Nothing he does happens by accident or passive acquiescence. Like David Copperfield, rising and steadily powerful brands always play offense and never settle for defense. This is a hallmark of what we call "insurgent brands," and today they are in every marketplace, insurgent hordes that swarm like ants—we do admire ants—around the pedestals on which traditional incumbent brands perch. The insurgent brands keep scrambling, climbing, and fanning out as they climb, until they cover whole product categories—or create entirely new ones. Like magicians, insurgent brands play by a different set of rules than the incumbent market leaders. Today, it is insurgent rules that rule markets.

GETTING AHEAD

By definition, aspiration focuses on the future. The Rolling Stones owe their creative and commercial success to the fact that Mick Jagger couldn't get no satisfaction. The German Romantic poets of the early nineteenth century understood that all creative energy was in aspiration, not fulfillment. *Sehnsucht*, they called it—longing, yearning, craving: in other words, aspiring. Johann Wolfgang von Goethe ends his epic poem Faust with the line, *Das Ewig Weibliche zieht uns hinan*—"The Eternal Feminine leads us upward." Thus, the greatest poem by Germany's greatest poet ends not with a period but with an aspiration—the promise of a future so great as to be eternal precisely because Faust, the archetypal human being, can't get no satisfaction.

Think now of the great companies and their CEOs and the way that they, at their best, focus on delivering something beyond a product or service to their customers. Apple, Red Bull, Netflix, Spotify, Zappos, Sam Adams, Starbucks, Instagram, Under Armour, Twitter, 5 Hour Energy, Big Ass Fans, and Uber, to name a few, make or sell a variety of products, but all cater to aspiration. The last thing these companies want to do is finally satisfy their customers. Mick can't get no satisfaction. Faust follows the Eternal Feminine. The Black Eyed Peas on YouTube or iTunes just can't get enough. CEOs like Iger and Massenet are so good at what they do that they lead their companies *ahead* of their consumers' aspirations, violating outworn conventions and models to deliver more and better than their competitors. They think out of the box, like magicians, and are unafraid to imagine how to give people the solutions they want—even if their companies must ultimately plant the *Sehnsucht* inside their consumers by giving them a hunger they never knew they had. The furthest thing from their minds is satisfying the hunger they create. Why doesn't the magician reveal the secret of the trick? Because to do so would end the hunger for a solution to the mystery.

Who finally gets satisfaction? Who finally stops yearning? Who finally gets enough? Answer: The incumbent brands and those who lead them. They, the incumbents, are the antithesis of the start-ups and upstarts of David Morey's first book with Scott Miller, *The Underdog Advantage*.[21] For everything that is stacked against them, the insurgents have all the advantages of underdogs—first and foremost, a lot less to lose and, conversely, a lot more to gain. Insurgents know how their customers think. They understand aspiration far better than the state of indolent satiety known as incumbency. And it is no coincidence that all great magicians are underdogs. They are the ones trapped in the Chinese Water Torture Cell, who are therefore super-powered by the desire to escape, transcend, and save their necks.

We Americans live in a country born of revolution, conceived by underdogs. Insurgency is in our bloodline, and it's why we all love an underdog—because few of us need to go too far back into our own lineage to find one, whether you are descended from a Pilgrim, an immigrant from a Russian *shtetl*, or a refugee from the violent instability of—well, of so many places in the world that are not the United States.

Give it some thought, and chances are you will conclude that you've been at your best when you've thought and fought like an insurgent, an underdog, coming up from behind, a stranger to complacency, acutely on offense, pulling, hauling, yanking your way up; following your dreams, empowering your aspirations—and, in the process, fulfilling the aspirations around you.

HARSH REALITY

The great operatic and symphonic conductor Arturo Toscanini recalled in an interview, "When I was a young boy in my native Parma, I heard people from the audience say, 'Tonight, it's *Rigoletto*. Let's go boo the tenor!' They went to the performance with this intention already in mind..."[22]

Face it: A great performer can never afford to phone it in. The most dedicated opera fans, at least at one level, attend to the performance with the expectation that it will merit an attack. The diehard NASCAR fan watches hour upon repetitive hour of cars racing around a noisy track in the expectation that a fiery, bloody catastrophe is just around the next bend. Harry Houdini drew crowd after crowd because the exhilarating pleasure of vicarious escape and transcendence was always counterbalanced by the possibility that this time—*this* time—Houdini would fail, fall to his death while escaping from the bonds that suspended him from the skyscraper or drown when he just couldn't hold his breath long enough to get out of a locked trunk submerged in the murky, icy river. Or maybe Fred Astaire and Ginger Rogers will finally trip and fall and break their necks tap dancing on some fantastically polished floor. Or the man on the flying trapeze— maybe he'll fly off and end up in a broken and bloody heap. Or Blockbuster, or Tower Records, or Radio Shack, or the Ringling Brothers and Barnum & Bailey Circus, maybe these venerable institutions will take their eyes off the prize just long enough to be mowed down by new technology, new markets, new interests, or even animal rights activists. The brilliant singer-songwriter and satirist Tom Lehrer—"Don't write naughty words on walls if you can't spell"—walked away from a successful career at the height of his popularity at the end of the 1960s. When asked why, he reportedly replied: "What good are laurels if you can't rest on them?"

Tom Lehrer, who is a spectacular eighty-nine in 2017, may be quite happy today, and he may have been perfectly pleased for the last forty-seven or so years in which he was out of the public eye. As he put it on the liner notes of a retrospective album released in 1997, "If, after hearing my songs, just one human being is inspired to say something nasty to a friend, or perhaps to strike a loved one, it will all have been worth the while."[23] But most people, most business owners, CEOs, and shareholders cannot content themselves with such rewards. The harsh reality is that in business or magic or any reasonably high-stakes endeavor, you are either on the attack as an insurgent, or on the defensive as an incumbent—you are either rebooting your aspirations, or you are not. The truth is incumbents who rest on their laurels typically end in obscurity. (When is the last time you even *thought about the once-ubiquitous Circuit City?)*

It's no accident that history's greatest magicians—Jean Eugène Robert-Houdin, Howard Thurston, Harry Houdini, Max Malini, Harry Blackstone, Doug Henning, David Copperfield, Lance Burton, Jeff McBride, David Blaine, Criss Angel—never stopped acting like underdogs, and never stopped rebooting their own aspirations. They performed as insurgents, even after they were universally acclaimed as "forever" among the greats. They continued or continue to cut new paradigms by carving out their own territory, often playing by their own rules, and by doing so, continually fulfilling their audiences' highest aspirations.

As for brands and businesses, God help you if you are playing by incumbent rules without the incumbent's balance sheet. For the harshest of harsh reality is that for every Netflix or Uber, there are eight start-up flameouts. While there is magic in insurgency, there are no miracles. That 8-to-1 failure rate has held true for many years. Eight out of ten start-ups fail. Period. Council on Foreign Relations military historian Max Boot, in his incredible book *Invisible Armies*, delivers a scorecard for global political and military insurgencies since 1775. The stats? Sixty-three percent failed. As with escaping from a Water Torture Cell for a living, revolution is risky business.

Failure, by the way, need not be abject, let alone final. Even in failure, insurgent brands can change markets and fulfill aspirations. They often lead or empower others to more successful developments. For example, David Morey's and Scott Miller's company was advising board members and top executives of Deja.com, a promising newsgroup and product review service in 2000—the year that saw the tech bubble burst. Time ran out for the terrific CEO Tom Phillips, who the Internet Capital Group had sent in to rescue the company—unfortunately, a few months too late. We found ourselves helping Tom with the mundane but morose details of renting out the company's office space and selling off its used furniture and supplies. One day, Tom called with a final, brighter note: "I was able to sell the software," he told us.

"That's terrific. Who bought it?"

"A little company called Google."

Silly name! Hard as it is to believe, Google was pretty much a start-up in 2000. In his classic 1782 eyewitness commentary on America at the close of the American Revolution, *Letters from an American Farmer*, Michel Guillaume Jean de Crèvecoeur describes the first frontier settlers, the backwoods pioneers, as "a kind of forlorn hope, preceding by ten or twelve years the most respectable army of veterans which came after them."[24] "Forlorn hope" is eighteenth-century military jargon for the advance guard or shock troops, who are calculatedly sacrificed to secure a position for the main body of soldiers in a major attack or invasion. Crèvecoeur uses the term to define the semi-barbaric state of the first pioneers, who chose to live far from established civilization and were therefore lost to civilization in the very process of securing the frontier for the *expansion* of civilization. The sacrifice of such pioneers is real and maybe even tragic, yet it makes possible the spread of civilization into the unknown. It makes possible the growth of a revolutionary nation. Think of the Internet flameouts like Deja.com, Napster, or Netscape, all of which faded or failed entirely, as the "forlorn hope" whose sacrifice enables the transformation of a revolutionary wilderness into a viable marketplace for even more revolutionary and insurgent businesses. Those flameouts light the fires of change.

It used to be that the big market leaders competed only with other big market leaders. It was incumbents versus incumbents; superpowers versus superpowers. And they played by clearly understood rules. Sure, there was competition, and there were the occasional Pepsi Challenges or guerilla campaigns, but even those were played according to the well-understood rules of incumbent engagement. The campaigns may have been insurgent, but the war itself was strictly conventional. Today, to believe that insurgent brands will play by traditional market rules is to believe that ISIS will adhere to international law and the Marquess of Queensberry Rules to boot. Insurgent brands hold the cards today, and they shuffle the deck.

MAGIC LESSONS FROM THE "FOUNDER/PERFORMER" CEOS

Magic legends such as Robert-Houdin, Thurston, Houdini, Malini, Blackstone, Henning, Copperfield, Burton, McBride, Blaine, and Angel call to mind the recent and current crop of Founder CEOs, such as Uber's Travis Kalanick, Facebook's Mark Zuckerberg, Alibaba's Jack Ma, and Airbnb's Brian Chesky, all of whom have literally invented new industries. The success of these magicians as well as the Founder CEOs is based on five strategic drivers:

1. **Discovery:** Allowing early fans—early adopters—to find your brand themselves, on their own aspirational terms, and then to harness the most powerful marketing force on earth: word of mouth.

2. **Craft:** Today, millennials are leading U.S. business trends, both in the B2C and the B2B marketplace. Millennial consumers expect products to be as simple and as natural as possible. They demand what you might call "Honest Farmer" quality, just as they expect their favorite performers to be totally real, honest, and genuine.

3. **Authenticity:** Truth is the best propaganda. Brands must be transparent and aligned in terms of message throughout their development, packaging, distribution, placement, promotion, and pricing. Similarly, great performers show their true colors in every small detail on stage. Any deviation dilutes the brand's power and meaning, and any differentiation must be relatable, credible, and simple.

4. **Founder/Visionary Narrative:** Consumers these days associate new products with individual entrepreneurs and passionate visionaries. They want to know their "story," especially the parts that explain *why* they developed their product, for whom they developed their product, and what marketplace "pain" it is designed to relieve. Today's audiences are looking for the story that explains who the performer or the product is, what it (she/he) does, and how it (she/he) is different, special, and better than others.

5. **Quirky/Un-Marketing:** Mass marketing is over. The collapse of the effect of advertising in the U.S. is epic. Today, your target audience of early adopters seeks "un-marketing"—ideas that possess—or appear to possess—the purity of passion and conviction. From businesses to performers, today's audiences want to follow their own bread crumbs to the apotheosis of their own aspirations.

CONVICTION

You cannot be a world-class magician unless you know—and deeply understand—why you are performing magic. This has always been true of magic, but has only become true of business and brand leadership in the new era of "un-marketing." Like the best magicians, today's business leaders cannot mount an effective campaign without a clear definition of how they see the world and how they intend to commit to achieving their goals in that world. This means defining the moral imperative driving what you do. Companies such as Nike, The Coca-Cola Company, and Disney have successfully defined their conviction and applied it as a powerful competitive advantage in their marketplaces.

Another example is Starbucks. From the beginning, the company put neither its faith nor its resources into advertising or other aspects of traditional marketing. Its communications have been singularly focused on the meaning of coffee as a total experience—not just a jolt of caffeine, the twenty-five-cent "Cup of Joe" defined by traditional market leaders like Maxwell House. In fact, faced with diminishing consumption of coffee by the rising generation, coffee marketers began diluting the beverage's meaning in a desperate attempt to reposition it closer and closer to soft drinks, for which the young had a seemingly unquenchable thirst.

Starbucks took a different path, the path of conviction. It made coffee magic by elevating it beyond a bitter hot brown fluid that delivers a jolt of caffeine. Coffee became a source that instead delivered a magical—that is, quasi-sacred—experience. This redefinition of the coffee experience revitalized the product by bringing back to the fore its core meaning: not the bright, quick, effervescent, youthful refreshment of soda pop, but the slow, flavorful, contemplative experience at the heart of coffee's tradition. It is not a refreshment but an elixir that depending on the aspiration of the consumer, engenders social conviviality or quiet contemplation. Either way, it conjures up an experience of an oasis of unhurried pleasure in a world moving faster and faster around it.

Competent magicians appeal to the mind. Great magicians move the heart. Move the heart of the audience, and their minds will follow. Psychologists believe there is no such thing as a rational decision. Unfortunately, most CEOs can't quite bring themselves to believe this. They do not readily accept the necessity of understanding and embracing the power of aspiration and emotion in decision making. This is remarkable because, presumably, most business leaders accept that great performers—actors, musicians, magicians, and, for that matter, political leaders—appeal first and foremost to the heart. The truth is that aspiration and the emotions associated with it are just as critical in business as they are in performance or politics.

David Morey's business partner, Scott Miller, tells a great story about how back in the 1990s, he was asked to help with the strategy for Billy Graham's then-forthcoming autobiography. He was summoned to meet with the Billy Graham Evangelical Association in Minneapolis. There, the association's CEO, John Corts, was trying to be polite by demurring and deferring to marketing guru Miller.

"We're sure glad to have you here, Mr. Miller. We don't know anything about marketing."

"Oh, bullshit!" Scott replied.

He knew—and, what is more, they knew—that American evangelicals virtually invented the most powerful form of aspirational marketing, what today is called viral marketing. In the process, they gave the lie to the clichéd admonition, "Don't *just* preach to the choir." Evangelicals revel in preaching to the choir—and then in turning the choir into missionaries. Early on, before anybody, they perfected inside-out communicating—and always with high emotional and aspirational content.

A competent CEO is a good manager, much as a competent magician is a good stage manager. Both make themselves fully responsible for everything the audience sees. But a great CEO, like a great magician, must also be a leader—one who addresses more than the senses and the brain, and who also uses aspiration and emotion to lead the aspiration and emotion of the consumer or the audience. In the First Coming of Steve Jobs at Apple, he was a maestro of corporate aspiration and emotion. Under his leadership, Apple put millions of dollars into the production of corporate meetings to rally the troops and feed the aspirational emotions of the company's Dolphin vs. Shark battle against IBM. And Jobs' Apple not only developed the Macintosh, but also Windham Hill Records to provide appropriately emotional theme music for its meetings.

Or think historically—back to the desperately dark early days of World War II. Winston Churchill did not rally his small island nation to victory in the fight for its very life by inflating the chances of achieving that victory. Instead, with unparalleled eloquence, he painted a chilling and realistic picture of the fight ahead, pledging on behalf of his people:

> We shall go on to the end. We shall fight in France, we shall fight on the seas and oceans, we shall fight with growing confidence and growing strength in the air, we shall defend our island, whatever the cost may be. We shall fight on the beaches, we shall fight on the landing grounds, we shall fight in the fields and in the streets, we shall fight in the hills; we shall never surrender...

The reality was that, as of June 4, 1940, when Churchill delivered his "We Shall Fight on the Beaches" speech, Adolf Hitler was winning. France was falling (it would surrender twenty-one days later) and, as Churchill had written on May 15 to President Franklin Delano Roosevelt, whose America had yet to join the fight, Poland, Norway, and the Netherlands had been smashed "like matchwood." That was reality at that point, and Churchill compelled his audience—his customers, his fellow countrymen—to see it, feel it, and believe it. But then he turned their focus toward a far more powerful reality, the reality of aspiration, of the future. Winston Churchill worked magic by making that reality appear more real and more significant than the reality Hitler had actually wrought as of June 4, 1940.

Know that the leader of a beleaguered underdog business, like the prime minister of a beleaguered underdog nation, must be a great magician in the way he communicates the goals, character traits, and values that drive his very aspirations. In government, business, or magic, you must above all define yourself so that others will not define you. It is critical to define *how* a leader decides as much as *what* he decides. It is critical to define the values and character traits involved.

Having defined yourself—now define aspirations. Your audience, your people, your customers, your employees want to know and understand the key benefits *to them* of *what you propose to do*. Give them a compelling reason to join you in fighting on the beaches.

Aspirations naturally open onto the future. Now, finally, you need to define that future. All people want to know where the leader—the ultimate performer—proposes to take them. It is up to you to define the destination, the route, the milestones, the obstacles, and how they will be overcome. Your audience, your people, your customers, your employees need to know where you are taking them, why you are taking them there, and how the rewards of arrival will outweigh the costs and the risks of the journey.

THE THIRD STRATEGY
IMAGINE FIRST

"The true sign of intelligence is not knowledge, but imagination."

—Albert Einstein

Scene: *This really happened[25] (https://www.youtube.com/watch?v=CBLcinheVWg). It's 1983, and the world's most famous illusionist, David Copperfield, is performing in a worldwide television special—his ninth. This time, he's in China. Think* China, *and you cannot help but think* Great Wall. *Now, with the cameras feeding video across the planet, and with a live audience arrayed on both sides of the timeless landmark, David Copperfield makes his appearance.*

Begun in the seventh century BC, the Great Wall of China extends over three thousand miles and was built to prevent the passage of the most powerful invading armies in history. Copperfield proposes not to storm it or climb over it or travel three thousand miles around it, but rather to walk through *it.*

Among the many cameras deployed to cover the event is one mounted on a crane and boom, remote-controlled to follow him from one side of the Great Wall to the other without ever cutting away. A platform on which an open-framework cubical rises has been erected against the Wall. White sheets are now affixed to the frame, creating a curtained cube through which only silhouette shadows are visible. Copperfield enters the cube. In the background, we hear the electronic beeping of a heart monitor. It is the sound of his heart.

We clearly see Copperfield's silhouette, one hand extended to caress the stones. It looks as if he is feeling for a way through the incontestably solid wall, when, suddenly, the hand, then the arm, the shoulder, leg, torso, and profile dissolve into the Great Wall of China. We see his other arm, the trailing arm, stretch backward, and we watch as it, too, slips into the Wall, outstretched fingers the last part of his body to disappear. Assistants scurry to remove the sheets, revealing a totally empty cubical.

Now the crane-mounted camera dollies in, up, and over the Wall, passing in one continuous shot to the other side. The picture settles on another framework cube, identical to the one Copperfield had entered. It is open, not draped in sheets. Assistants mount the stairs to the cube platform and raise a single white sheet against the stonework of the Great Wall itself. As they hold the sheet in place, we see first one hand, then two, and then a face push against it—from beneath the sheet and, presumably, from inside the Wall. It is as if we are witnessing some otherworldly being struggling to be born into our dimension...

Suddenly, the sound of the heart monitor, persistent and steady throughout, increases urgently in tempo—beep, beep-beep-beep. Just as suddenly, it becomes a single continuous tone. Flatline!

The assistants instantly let the sheet drop from the Great Wall. No one—nothing—is there! One of the assistants hurriedly presses his ear to the stones. Again, however, there is nothing and no one.

As the assistant slowly backs off and draws down a sheet to cover one side of the cube frame, the heartbeat sound slowly returns. Another assistant draws a sheet to cover the side of the cube that faces the camera, and a third sheet is secured to completely enclose the cube. The assistants then step away.

One of Copperfield's outstretched hands appears in silhouette, then the other, followed by the shadow profile of his face and upper torso. The magician seems to be dragging himself—willing himself—to the *other side, when suddenly, he tears off the sheet facing the camera and appears before us, all smiles. He has just walked through the Great Wall of China.*

They say that, in accordance with an unwritten but universally accepted code, magicians never reveal their secrets. This is only partly true. Magicians don't reveal the mechanics of a given illusion or effect, but some of the greatest magicians speak very freely about the creative process behind their magic. Among the greatest—and most successful—of living magicians is David Copperfield. As with most performing arts, evaluating magic generally calls for a good deal of subjective judgment. But we can quantify Copperfield's success objectively. He has been performing for more than four decades, during which time he has sold more tickets than Michael Jackson or Elvis, grossing over $4 billion. He has won twenty-one Emmys for his TV specials, lays claim to eleven Guinness World Records, averages fifteen performances a week, 640 shows a year, and has a dedicated venue, the David Copperfield Theater, at the MGM Grand in Las Vegas.

In an early 2017 interview with filmmaker Judd Apatow published in *Interview,* Copperfield spills the beans, explaining (in the magazine's paraphrase) that he "has always tethered illusions (flying, walking through the Great Wall of China) to universal stories of longing and overcoming fears." How does he come up with these illusions? Well, he reveals that as well:

Thirty years ago, when I was doing specials, it was all about getting the story right and getting the combination of magic and theater to work. Some of it was great, some of it not so good. For one of my specials, I said, "I'm going to make an airplane disappear." Okay! And the next day, everything went crazy—it was like breaking the Internet before the Internet. Everyone was talking about having airplanes disappear. And I said, "Wait, wait, wait. *That's* what you like? I'd tell you a story about something like my girlfriend leaving me, and the magic was really hard. The airplane thing was comparatively easy, and people liked *that* thing?" I realized at that moment, the power of the simple idea. A simple concept, from a brand-new standpoint, really resonates. So then I said, "Now the Statue of Liberty is going to disappear, but I've got to make this have more meaning."[26]

Copperfield combines magic with theater and a story. He understands that making magic requires these three elements, just as a baker who proposes to make a Tres Leches Cake understands he needs to buy evaporated milk, condensed milk, and heavy cream. How does he know that he needs these three things? Because, like David Copperfield, the successful baker of a Tres Leches Cake begins with the desired end in mind. In fact, whether you are a magician, a baker, or business leader, the prime directive is the same: *Begin with the end in mind.* Put another way, *Imagine first.*

Like a great CEO, Copperfield breaks existing magical paradigms by first imagining and then working backward from this visualization to arrive at creative solutions. As magicians, we begin by asking: *What is the effect?* Then, like Copperfield, we backtrack to how we can create the effect. Put simply:

- ◆ Effect *before* method
- ◆ Objective *before* process
- ◆ Dream *before* mechanism

We imagine "What" *before* we struggle with "How." This is the working method almost all successful performing magicians employ—and it reminds us of the way the greatest CEOs and business leaders think. The effective application of imagination is also one of the two critical faculties—the other is marketing—that the late management guru Peter Drucker said all businesses need to succeed: "a level of imagination capable of intensive innovation." No wonder the revolutionary psychologist Carl Jung called imagination "the mother of all possibilities," and Einstein judged it "more important than knowledge."

Some requisites of imagining first are more nitty-gritty than others. A Three Milks Cake requires three milks. A David Copperfield illusion requires magic, theater, and a story. Other aspects both invite and require greater breadth of imagination—what we might call inspiration. A mediocre magician may imagine pulling a rabbit out of a silk top hat. Copperfield says, "I'm going to make an airplane disappear."[27]

Now, if Copperfield were merely a successful magician, having discovered that making an airplane disappear pleases an audience, he would simply find more planes to vanish—and he would repeat this as long as he was selling tickets. But Copperfield is a great magician, for whom vanishing an airplane is a powerful "simple idea"; however, developing that simple idea "from a brand-new standpoint" is necessary, he believes, to create an effect that resonates magically. Having disappeared an airplane, he then says, "Now the Statue of Liberty is going to disappear..." For one thing, the Statue of Liberty is bigger than a plane. For another—and far more important—it is familiar to everyone and sacred to some. Making it disappear creates a genuine fear: the loss of liberty itself.

Recall the final scene in the original 1968 version of *Planet of the Apes,* when astronaut George Taylor (Charlton Heston) stumbles upon the ruins of the Statue of Liberty and realizes that his nightmare experience on the "planet of the apes" is really the nightmare of earth destroyed by thermonuclear war in the distant future. Falling to his knees, all the astronaut can utter is "Damn them, damn them all to hell!" The iconic statue represents everything good and valuable, not only about the United States, but about civilization itself. The filmmakers knew this in 1968, and

David Copperfield knew this when he made the statue disappear on April 8, 1983. He explained to his interviewer, the comedy film director Judd Apatow, that making people anxious is necessary for the magic to work, but it is not sufficient. He had to find some way to "make this have more meaning."[28]

Imagining first can be done alone, but few truly important innovations are created without help. Copperfield told Apatow that he called on "Frank Capra, one of my idols," for help developing the story to go along with the Statue of Liberty illusion. He explained to the director of such classics as *Mr. Smith Goes to Washington* and *It's a Wonderful Life* that he wanted to do the disappearance "as a lesson in freedom, how valuable freedom is and what the world would be like without liberty." To Copperfield's chagrin, Capra pushed back, telling the magician that he loved the idea but that what Copperfield had to do is to *try* to make Liberty disappear, but fail. The magician understood the film director's point, but told him that failure was not an option. In response, Capra "lambasted me. 'You cannot do this. You will fail.'"[29]

Imagining via collaboration is not all about agreement. As the great American general of World War II George S. Patton Jr. said, "If everybody is thinking the same way, nobody is thinking." Instead of capitulating to his idol, Copperfield spoke with Capra, and "after another hour of conversation, I convinced him to help me write the speech."[30]

In the end, Copperfield did make the Statue of Liberty disappear,[31] and that meant that he had to imagine even bigger for the next televised illusion. He explained to Apatow that he started working on an escape from a volcano. "I was going to float out of a volcano.... So as I'm thinking about that, I go home and I'm taken by the technology, how I was going to do it. I'm walking around, and something inside me said, 'You know something?

It's not an escape from a volcano; it's going to be flying. I'm going to fly....
Okay, now I'm on the right track.'"[32]

***

The right track. For Copperfield, the right track led from one triumph of
imagination to another—the one innovation both requiring and enabling
the next greater innovation. As imaginative innovation is at the heart
of the magic, as mentioned above, so it is the driver of what the late
management guru Peter Drucker called "intensive innovation." A "level of
imagination capable of intensive innovation," he wrote, was one of the two
critical faculties all businesses need to succeed. (The other is marketing.)
Of course, the value of imagination goes far beyond magic or business.

But habit can get in the way of imagination, "intensive innovation," and
thinking anew. Take the cliché "the right track." Consider why the noun
in this phrase is *track*, not *station* or *destination*. Once on the right track,
you still must get somewhere. Innovation is not about arrival. It is about
departure and movement and getting somewhere other than where you are.

"You Press the Button, We Do the Rest" was the slogan of a revolution
when George Eastman first used it to sell his new system of photography
in 1888. Before the appearance of the innovation behind this slogan,
photography was a complicated, cumbersome business best left to
professionals. Eastman, however, imagined photography as the technology
of everyman—and every woman and every family. As Bill Gates imagined
the end he wanted to achieve— "a computer on every desk and in every
home"—so George Eastman imagined a technology that enabled the
sequence "You Press the Button, We Do the Rest." He invented the
"Kodak"—the very brand name a nonsense word that nevertheless
conveyed the sound a shutter makes when "you press the button." It was a
camera purchased preloaded with a roll of film for one hundred exposures.

Operating it required exactly two user actions: point and click. After performing these one hundred times, the customer sent the camera to the factory, which developed and printed the film, returning to the customer prints and negatives, together with the camera reloaded for another hundred exposures.

Before Eastman's leadership by imagination, studio professionals monopolized photography. He knocked them off the mountain top, and his company, Kodak, quickly became the leader in the field of photography, making George Eastman and generations of Kodak stockholders very rich through sales of cameras and film and processing. The company was on the right track, a track that proved to be a very long one—eighty-seven years, from 1888 to 1975, the year Kodak switched tracks by pioneering the core technology of an invention even more momentous than Eastman's celluloid roll film: digital photography.

Bravo, Kodak!

Unfortunately, the new track proved very short. In 1976, one year after the company embarked on a digital program, Kodak's market share of U.S. film sales hit a staggering 86 percent. Management could not resist the appeal of so cushy a number. A number whose supreme comfort defined a marketplace incumbent, it prompted management to kill the brand-new digital camera program for fear of losing dominance in the film market.

As Kodak recoiled from innovation, others—many others, as it turned out—laid the new track Kodak had abandoned. As digital photography caught on, film sales inevitably flagged. Kodak was still the film market leader. It's just that the film market was evaporating. Late in the 1990s, Kodak frantically administered CPR to its digital division, but it was way too little and way too late. Chapter 11 filings came in January 2012, and the company emerged from bankruptcy on September 3, 2013, but not before selling its most valuable patents to its competitors—the new leaders-by-imagination who were busy making a new market and defining the future of their industry.

If you're Kodak—or Woolworth's or Blockbuster or Borders or the Union of Soviet Socialist Republics—you may have wished you had empowered your imagination more, asking better questions, inverting these questions, thinking differently along the right track, just like a magician, and just like a magician, imagined your way out of the proverbial box. But if you're Apple, or Disney, or Google, you simply refused to stop imagining in the first place.

***

So, here's another movie you might recall. Released in 2002, *The Emperor's Club* is about a dedicated prep school classics instructor, a rather more put-together version of Mr. Chips named William Hundert (Kevin Kline). On the first day of his class "Western Civilization: The Greeks and the Romans," he asks a student to read an inscription on a plaque above the door:

> *I am Shutruk-Nahhunte, King of Ansham and Susa, sovereign of the land of Elam.*
>
> *I destroyed Sippar and took the stele of Naram-Sin and brought it back to Elam, where I erected it as an offering to my god.*
>
> —Shutruk-Nahhunte, 1158 BC

Mr. Hundert then asks the students in his class if any of them are familiar with Shutruk-Nahhunte. Silence. Mr. Hundert tells them they can look in their textbooks. But after a beat, he adds that in no textbook will they find a discussion of Shutruk-Nahhunte.

Why not?

"Because great ambition and conquest...without contribution...is without significance," he answers.[33]

In business, commerce, and technology—and in magic—continuous innovation is all that counts as "contribution." Rest on the laurels of incumbency, and you fade into irrelevance. In magic, there are many great performers, and they are justly admired; but within the profession, some of the highest honors go to the creators and the innovators, who feed the insatiable requirements of performers for new material—so that *they* don't fade. Because the pace of innovation is extraordinarily fast these days, the "fade" is more rapid than a complacent incumbent may hope for. Get off at the station instead of staying on the track, and you get nowhere—fast. You don't fade. You implode.

Consider: Jerry Wind, Lauder Professor of Marketing at the Wharton School, points out that 88 percent of Fortune 500 companies from the 1950s are not just missing from today's list, they're gone! Bankrupt! Out of business! They are as over and done with and gone as Shutruk-Nahhunte. In contrast, companies such as Uber, Facebook, Alibaba, and Airbnb have created markets that did not even exist ten or fifteen years ago. Real estate mogul, super-investor, and billionaire Sam Zell writes in his recent book *Am I Being Too Subtle?*: "Take the Forbes 400 list, except for inherited wealth, and the great majority went 'left' when others went 'right.' "

***

Imagination, our ability to think and invent beyond what we can see, hear, feel, experience, and know, elevates us above all the other species on the planet. We have seen this happen again and again: how the empowering crossover between a feat of magic or a stroke of business success begins in the imagination. We have seen again and again how successful entrepreneurs, like great magicians, imagine beforehand what the win is going to look like and sound like and taste like. There are those who will tell you that such "imagining" is just so much wishful thinking, or counting your chickens before they're hatched, or living on airy hope rather than solid reality.

Well, they're right. Imagining the win *is* all of this. So what?

Much of what we think of as reality exists to be changed. Change begins in the imagination. The reality of the future therefore begins in the imagination. And that means that reality itself begins in the imagination. Imagination then helps drive innovation day after day. Read any story, see any film, watch any television show created before the mid-1980s or treating that era. Now, think about how many fictional plots involve the reality of pay telephones. These are essential props in story after story. The hero is out on the street. He has an urgent message to convey. He searches wildly for a pay phone—and that puts the audience on the edge of their seats. The imperative need to find a working pay phone is key to the plot of countless stories and films and TV shows. Pay phones were once reality, and perhaps the only people today who yearn for the good old pre-cell phone days are novelists and screenwriters, who have lost a valuable plot device. They can no longer create urgency and suspense by means of a desperate search for a pay phone. Pay phones are so rare today as to be nearly *unreal*. Why? Because imagination innovated the cellular telephone and created a new reality. Without imagination, we would all still be putting quarters in slots.

In 1950, the idea of placing calls with "Touchtone" push-buttons was tantalizing to a global population of finger-sore rotary dialers. Tantalizing—but it did not require a heroic stretch of the imagination to imagine a push-button alternative. While rotary dials were reality, push-button "dials" certainly seemed a plausible possibility. But the wireless cellular telephone? In 1950, it did not exist in anyone's imagination—at least as far as we know. The idea of being able to place a call to anyone at any time using a small hand-held device was, in 1950, magical.

In this vein, John McLaughlin underscores that there is a constant requirement for intelligence services to imagine in ways that alter reality. In the 1970s, for example, long before the concept of a cell phone, the CIA developed the Short Range Agent Communication (SRAC) device. This was a small hand-held instrument that allowed a CIA officer to wirelessly send a burst of encrypted communication to a secret agent across the street, who received the message on a similar device from which it could be decrypted and read. Pretty magical for its time.

In Europe, until the seventeenth century and the rise of the scientific method and preeminence of rationality and common sense, magic reigned supreme. With the triumph of the Enlightenment, however, magic started having to compete with common sense, rationality, and the scientific method. Magic might be scorned as trickery, but it invited the imagination to soar. Science and rationality, while elevated as the only truth, brought imagination back down to earth. Even as late as 1950, the notion of a portable wireless telephone capable of communicating with just about anyone was magic or perhaps that species of magic known as science fiction. In either case, it could not withstand the competition from the "reality" of common sense, rationality, and the scientific method.

Today, science and technology are still cited as rivals of magic—not because magic is fantastic and technology is mundane, but, on the contrary, because recent technology has produced such wonders—including not just the cellular telephone, but the smartphone—that mere magic has a hard time keeping up, let alone overtaking it. In many spheres of activity, imagination has transformed reality faster than magic ever could. Slow motion video playback, Googling information, digitally printing solid objects in three dimensions, using the Hubble Space Telescope and its successor device, the James Webb Space Telescope, to look back in time to the creation of the universe—how can magic hope to compete with these examples of present-day technological reality? The great British science fiction writer Arthur C. Clarke formulated three "laws" concerning the prediction of the possible versus the impossible. The first two are thought-provoking:

> Clarke's First Law: When a distinguished but elderly scientist states that something is possible, he is almost certainly right. When he states that something is impossible, he is very probably wrong.

> Clarke's Second Law: The only way of discovering the limits of the possible is to venture a little way past them into the impossible.

But it is the third that is most often quoted:

> Clarke's Third Law: Any sufficiently advanced technology is indistinguishable from magic.[34]

For magicians, the fun and the challenge is to imagine how to make magic exceed our present-day technological reality. We never said that either magic or innovation was easy or obvious. But consider this example, another story about former David Morey client Bill Gates. Picture him at age thirty. He looks fifteen, and he's leading a young company he has recently founded. The phone rings—the phone is on his desk, which is tethered to a wire, by the way. He picks it up and is talking to a company based in Albuquerque. The voice on the other end of the line tells him they are working on something called a "personal computer," or PC. They've got the hardware going just fine—it's almost ready—but to run it, they now need the "basic software," which they call an *operating system*. They need it precisely because no such thing exists at the time of this phone call. In fact, nobody, including Bill Gates, has ever really thought about an "operating system," for the very good reason that there has never been a need for one.

No matter. Bill Gates is the most desperate person on the face of the planet: a start-up entrepreneur. So, he speaks to the voice on the phone with perfect confidence and authority.

"Yes," he says to it. "Yes, of course we can create your operating system." He pauses, and then continues: "And we can deliver it in a matter of weeks."

That is what he says. That is what Bill Gates says. Fortunately, it is also what he *imagines*. And so he and his little company—soon to be called Microsoft—work backward from imagination to build what they decide to call Disk Operating System, or DOS.

The rest, as they say, is history—except that Gates, of course, did not stop with DOS. Microsoft became wildly successful, not because of the efficiency and effectiveness of the OS it built. Arguably, even at Microsoft's corporate zenith, there were better operating systems to be had. The point is that Gates did deliver DOS, which drove the success of the PC. Propelled by that success, Gates went on to make Microsoft even more wildly successful by imagining an even larger mission. In Las Vegas, David Morey once heard Gates, who was at the time leading Microsoft at its zenith, deliver a speech without even once mentioning the name of his own company. Instead, he talked about the future and invited his audience to imagine with him what that future could bring. Ultimately, he expressed what was in his imagination with the deceptively simple motto we discussed earlier: "A computer on every desk and in every home."

***

Indispensable to magic and business, imagination is, in fact, critical to innovation in any field. Innovation, after all, is creating something that *is not*. It is the act of looking out at reality—*what is* at any moment in time—and seeing *what can be* or *might be* or *should be*.

Track and field is a set of athletic endeavors—as much a part of the physical realm as muscle and flesh can make it. Arguably, no single track and field event is more spectacularly physical than the high jump, in which competitors jump unaided over a horizontal bar, landing on a landing pit or crash mat. In the early 1900s, Olympic champions used a so-called scissor technique, in which the jumper clears the bar in something like a sitting position, torso essentially perpendicular to the bar as one leg clears the bar in preparation for the other to follow it. The advantage of this technique is that it allows jumpers to land on their feet. This was an important advantage in an era of landing pits that consisted of a thin layer of sawdust or other marginally effective cushioning material.

Through the early twentieth century, jumpers innovated with new techniques, always looking for added altitude. The traditional scissors jump evolved into something called the "Eastern cut-off," which then evolved into the more efficient "Western roll." No radical innovation, the Western roll was propelled by the jumper's take-off leg closest to the bar—and it ushered in officiating changes such as a rescinding of the "no dive" rule.

Evolving from the Western roll, the "straddle" technique gradually developed during the 1950s and 1960s. The innovation was enabled in large measure by the development of friendlier landing pits. In the straddle, the high jumper's arms and lead leg power their way up as the body rolls around the bar. Finally, the jumper lifts the trailing leg just in time to clear. Led by master coach Vladimir Dyachkov, the Soviet school fully developed this technique with Yuri Stepanov, who used the straddle to break the world record in 1957. Soviet jumpers Robert Chavlakadze and Valery Brumel went on to win Olympic gold medals in 1960 and 1964 respectively, with the legendary Brumel upsetting the U.S. favorite, John Thompson, in the climax of a classic rivalry captured in grainy black-and-white *Wide World of Sports footage*. Brumel, the master of the straddle, with superior speed and raw strength, raised the world record to 2.28 meters, just short of 7´6˝. The technique required jumpers to land on both hands and side—a landing made possible (that is, without injury) by softer pits padded either with better sawdust or thick foam rubber.

There is a clear, gradual, evolutionary sequence from the original scissor high jump techniques to the straddle. But then something new was imagined. Seemingly out of nowhere, a young man named Dick Fosbury introduced a pure and sudden innovation. In other words, it looked just like magic.

A Portland, Oregon, high schooler whom teammates remembered as "independent and imaginative," Fosbury was willing to try something different—very different. As a sophomore, he began going back and forth between the scissor technique and something no one had seen before.

The scene is a track meet in May 1963. As the bar is raised to increasingly challenging heights, Fosbury does something totally instinctive. While taking off in the old eastern cut-off style, he starts to arch backward and then lifts his hips up, helping to drop his shoulders over the bar. The bar goes higher. Fosbury reclines even more as he sails over it, as if lounging on a sofa. Eventually, at that meet, he clears a new personal best of 1.78 meters or 5´10˝.

The young man works to transform instinct into technique. During his junior and senior years, he adds a curved "C" approach, and rather than lying back from the scissor position, he plants his take-off foot at a 45-degree angle to the bar with his lead leg parallel to it, driving up—hard—and setting up a rotation of his body that completely turns his back to the bar. Leading with his shoulders, his center of gravity is now *below* the bar, increasing the physics of efficiency and clearing head-first as his body rolls around the axis of the bar. The result? Fosbury is national junior champion, with a 2.01 meter or 6'7" jump. He advances to Oregon State University, where as a freshman, he works with an initially skeptical coach, Berny Wagner. At first, Wagner tries to change Fosbury back into a conventional straddle jumper, imploring him to abandon this crazy "flop" and instead focus on the tried-and-true straddle technique, which has served all the incumbent competitors so well. It worked for the Olympic champion and world record holder, Valery Brumel, the coach argues, and it can certainly work for Fosbury.

Fosbury yields to his coach—and immediately goes from jumping 6'7" to 5'6" his freshman college year. But slowly, yet inevitably, the reality of gravity and innovation begin to take hold. Before they do, let's leave Fosbury as he is about to enter a sophomore college competition in Oregon. Let's travel a century and a half back and thousands of miles east to Potsdam, Prussia, in 1804. There and then Carl Gustav Jacob Jacobi is born. He will die a few miles away in Berlin in 1850, but before his forty-six years on earth are done, he will make foundational contributions to advanced mathematics in the areas of elliptic functions, differential equations, dynamics, and number theory. But Jacobi will be best remembered for his maxim "*Man muss immer umkehren*"—usually translated as "invert, always invert." This is how he describes his breakthrough approach to the most difficult of problems. Jacobi believes that seemingly intractable problems can be solved most efficiently in the inverse, by working backward. It is a variation on the magician's approach: Imagine the effect, and work back from that to discover the process.

We don't know whether Dick Fosbury studied Jacobi at Oregon State, but we do know that when he jumped as a sophomore he confronted the bar quite literally in the same way Jacobi confronted a mathematical problem. He inverted—inverted to an Oregon State record of 2.08 meters or 6′10″. The following year, safer and more welcoming landing pits along with a mesmerized press all welcomed his innovation of inversion, which was now called the "Fosbury Flop." As an Oregon State junior, Fosbury became the most consistent 2.13 meter or 7-foot jumper in America. That year, 1968, he flopped his way to a jump of 2.21 meters or 7′3″, winning an NCAA Championship and a berth on the U.S. Olympic team.

As an Olympian, Fosbury faces a showdown against the straddling Russians in Mexico City. With defending Olympic champion Valery Brumel recovering from a motorcycle crash, Fosbury is in the competition of his life against two Russians and two other Americans. All of them use the straddle. Time, then, to *invert.*

Fosbury clears every height in the thin air of Mexico City on his first attempt—until the bar rests at 2.22 meters. This setting defeats both the Russians. Only fellow American Ed Caruthers stands in his way. Fosbury faces the bar, raised now to 2.24 meters, misses once, misses twice, and, on his third and final try, floats backward over the unforgiving bar and into history as Olympic champion. The legend of the "Fosbury Flop" is born.

Four years later, in the 1972 Olympics, twenty-eight of forty high jumpers used the Fosbury Flop. By 1980, thirteen of the sixteen Olympic finalists were Fosbury Floppers. Of thirty-six Olympic medalists in this event from 1972 to 2000, thirty-four used the "Flop." Today, the once-ubiquitous straddle is as hard to find in an Olympic final as a cinder track.

TAKEAWAYS

"Man muss immer umkehren"— "Invert, always invert": This simple paradigm-crushing maxim solved mathematical puzzles in the eighteenth century, and in the mid-twentieth century, proved indispensable to the success of the Allied air forces' bombing missions over World War II Germany. Years later, Charley Munger, cofounder and vice chairman of Warren Buffett's Berkshire Hathaway, used the Jacobi admonition to invert to create the firm's extraordinarily successful investment strategies.

Look around. You'll find the idea of imagining the end and working backward everywhere. It is, for example, at the heart of detective stories from Edgar Allan Poe to Sir Arthur Conan Doyle. Poe's fictional detective, C. Auguste Dupin, like Conan Doyle's Sherlock Holmes, found clues—and sometimes the absence of clues ("the dog not barking" in Conan Doyle's "The Silver Blaze," for example)—from which they worked backward to solve the most mysterious crimes. As for bombing Germany in World War II, the Germans on the receiving end of the Allied bombs were not the only people who had big problems. The lumbering aircraft sent on these raids— most often United States Army Air Forces B-17s—were being lost to enemy antiaircraft fire at a devastating rate, threatening the very prospects for an Allied victory. One option was to provide more plate armor for the "Flying Fortresses." But the sheer weight of any extra armor meant that it had to be used very sparingly, covering only the most vulnerable areas of the aircraft.

But how to identify the most vulnerable areas? The data hardly existed. Planes that were hit in vulnerable areas crashed and burned—behind enemy lines. Aeronautical engineers could not study the aircraft. The problem of where to add armor was seemingly intractable since the dataset was so incomplete. In 1943, the British Air Ministry proposed simply examining the damaged planes that had been able to return and then adding armor to the areas that showed the greatest damage. In the absence of anything better, that solution was common sense. But as Albert Einstein famously remarked, "Common sense is the collection of prejudices acquired by age eighteen." Enter another great mathematician, Abraham Wald. He drew directly on Jacobi to propose something magically different. Like most magical solutions, it blatantly defied common sense—inverted it, in fact.

Relying more on intuition than statistical or computing power, Wald inverted the problem. Rather than examining bombers that returned, Wald shifted backward to imagining the perspective of the planes that did *not* return. Examining the damage on the planes that *did* return, he asked what it would have taken to make these aircraft crash. By way of answer, Wald concluded that the areas of the returned B-17s that showed little or no damage from enemy fire—around the main cockpit and fuel tanks—were the truly vulnerable areas. The reason these planes had survived to limp home, even though they were damaged elsewhere, was that it had been their good fortune not to have been hit near the cockpit or fuel tanks. This insight, later confirmed by rigorous computer-driven mathematical analyses not available during the war itself, shifted the momentum toward the Allies in the air war. Confronted with damaged survivors, Wald inverted the problem based on what he did *not* see.

Again, this is strikingly similar to the inversion concept Warren Buffett's partner Charley Munger uses in analyzing investments. Munger understands as a fundamental principle that often, more can be learned from looking at reverse-success examples—at people and portfolios that failed—and asking: "Why?" Fundamentally, Munger argues that successful investment is often less about being clever than it is about avoiding mistakes. As Buffett himself says: "Protect the downside, the upside will take care of itself." By not just avoiding failure, but *debriefing* failure, we often find the most powerful lessons for success.

For a classic magical example of *"invert, always invert,"* see the unique performance of Penn & Teller on *Saturday Night Live*, seemingly defying all forms of gravity and logic until, well, visit the link below to see what they do, which required weeks of training, and how it is done: https://www.youtube.com/watch?v=D87DSLe4Eqw. The universal principle behind *imagining first* is Jacobi's admonition to invert. Beyond this, we suggest the following.

ASK BETTER QUESTIONS

As former acting director of the CIA, coauthor John McLaughlin explains that intelligence work frequently requires imagining the future. This means asking: *What is it, if we could do it, that would "revolutionize" our world?*

For example, back in the late 1950s, at the height of the Cold War, the Agency was frustrated that it did not know all it needed to know about the Soviet Union, especially its military capabilities. CIA innovators began to imagine something that today is an accomplished fact, but which seemed impossible back then. The imagining started with a question: *What if we could take photographs from space?*

Working with the U.S. Air force and U.S. industry specialists, CIA technical officers addressed the question and tackled the problem. Remember, this was in the infancy of space rocketry. The Soviet Union had just stunned the world by putting the first space satellite, Sputnik, into orbit in 1957. U.S. efforts had repeatedly failed. Nevertheless, it was possible to imagine doing all sorts of things with satellites. More difficult to contemplate was the power of digital technology. In the end, therefore, the

Agency's collective imagination fell back—albeit ingeniously—on pieces of familiar analog technology. The proposal was to mount a conventional camera carrying the chemical film of the day on a rocket, get it into space, take photographs, bring the exposed film back to earth, and recover, develop, and analyze the photographs. The rocket was to carry the camera and orbit the earth while it snapped photos. It would then eject a capsule carrying the camera, which would plummet through 600,000 feet of space, enter the earth's atmosphere at about 65,000 feet above ground level, deploy a parachute, and float down, to be caught in a basket trailing a slow-flying C-119 USAF "Flying Boxcar" cargo plane.

Rube Goldberg could not have imagined a more complex or accident-prone process. Predictably, in try after try, something went wrong somewhere in the sequence between launch and recovery. It was only on lucky try number thirteen that it all came together. Although supremely finicky, the concept was shown to be workable! The fact that it worked meant that imagination had pushed beyond the edge of the technological envelope of the day. This in turn enabled engineers to imagine far better methods as technology progressed to digital photography and the ability to transmit images from sophisticated satellites in real time. This development was a race between imagination and technology, but it was an act of imagination that served as the starter's gun to begin the race. The process is remarkably like that of the magician who imagines an effect, experiments with many methods to achieve the effect, comes up dry time and time again, but persists until an illusion is perfected—whether it's flying on a stage or making a lady vanish before your very eyes. Audiences who see the finished "miracle" have no idea of the stops, starts, visions, and revisions that enabled the magician to make it look easy.

How can we get the technological edge on intelligence? is another question the CIA asked on the threshold of the twenty-first century. Intelligence gathering was becoming increasingly technology-dependent. And the challenge this posed to the CIA was how to ensure it would always have technology well ahead of the rest of the world. Everyone, after all, adversaries included, will always have whatever is commonly available. CIA leaders looked at cutting-edge tech companies in the private sector. It was quickly clear that Silicon Valley innovated through small, highly inventive, insurgent start-ups. The traditional notion was fading fast that you could give a large sum of money to a big defense contractor and tell them to go invent something. So much invention was occurring at the periphery of big industry, in garages and basements and small labs operating on a shoestring, that the question became: How can intelligence take advantage of this? And the answer was another question: *What if the U.S. government could act like a venture capitalist?*

The answer to this question was the birth of In-Q-Tel, the CIA's answer to a challenge similar to the one magicians face when technology is always stealing the show. In-Q-Tel was chartered from the CIA's budget in 1999 as an independent investment firm charged with searching for technology solutions to problems the Agency articulates. Through In-Q-Tel, the CIA puts out a problem it is trying to solve and solicits bids from companies large and small willing to tackle the challenge. The winner presses ahead on the problem, and if successful in solving it, gets to keep a commercial spin-off of whatever they create. Over the years, In-Q-Tel has invested millions of dollars and delivered countless technology solutions to the CIA. A good example is the development of Keyhole, a CIA-funded satellite-mapping software program: It was eventually acquired by Google and became that company's version of what we know today as Google Earth.

Asking the right questions is a highly effective method for seeing what is coming and preparing for it. John McLaughlin recalls the challenge presented in the mid-1980s as it became increasingly apparent that the Soviet Union and the economic system it had created was in deep trouble. When Mikhail Gorbachev came to power in 1985, he set out to reform a system he recognized as moribund by introducing *glasnost* and *perestroika*—a freer media and a somewhat liberalized economy. Alas, it was too little and too late, and as the 1980s approached their end, it was apparent to CIA analysts that the pillars of command economics were weakening in both the Soviet Union and its Eastern European satellites.

In 1989, McLaughlin briefed President George H.W. Bush in the Oval Office two days before the Berlin Wall came down. When the President asked McLaughlin if the Wall would crumble, he replied that for all practical purposes it had been gone for weeks. The pressures for German unification were irresistible, he said. Indeed, at this point thousands of Germans were in the streets on both sides of the Cold War divide demanding change. But what enabled McLaughlin's confidence was that the CIA, in its own internal organizational structure, had in a sense united Germany months earlier.

Traditionally, the CIA divided its work between two administrative units in two separate divisions, one focused on west Germany and the other on east Germany. From these perspectives, analysts were so convinced that pressures were building, making unification inevitable—a conclusion CIA analysts reached long before most Germans could even imagine this outcome—that the Agency ended years of tradition by putting its east and west units together under a single leader in what was called the German Working Group. The idea of this internal reorganization was to enhance analysts' ability to see across this divide, get ahead of the event horizon, and begin thinking about the effects of what they were convinced was inexorable change—*before* it was upon them and our foreign policy decision makers.

Creating conditions conducive to imagining trends before they begin allows individuals and organizations to be prepared to ride the coming trend, to master it, or even to leap ahead of it. This is the magician's approach as well. We who perform magic call it the "one-ahead" principle. A good magic effect is usually over, as far as its internal elements, long before the audience realizes it. If a magician is very good, he approaches the "reveal" at about the time the audience just begins looking for the method.

THINK EXPONENTIALLY

The world's greatest magicians emulate the world's greatest scientists in finding ways to break the linear logic trail in what they do. Linear thought—*a* to *b* to c and so on—is comfortable. Innovation, however, is uncomfortable. It requires strenuous effort. Call it exponential effort.

Great magicians understand that magic begins with audiences thinking in a linear way, setting up a causal chain where everything makes sense and flows logically out of that which comes before it. This is what allows the magician to explode the causal chain so the audience exclaims, *"No Way!"* As Eugene Burger argues in an essay called "On The Structure of Magic Effects," for magic to work, the audience must think: "That was fair, that was fair, that was fair, that was fair...NO FREAKING WAY!" In other words, magic can be broken into discrete moments that separately must not arouse suspicion, and may then all lead to a final moment of magic—so the general structure of magical effects is: Fair/Fair/Fair/Fair/Wow!

For the magician, this is precisely how the causal chain is broken and the linear logic demolished—taking the audience to a place of exponential thinking. Magicians, in fact, are the creators of and operate every day inside this world of exponential thinking—it is their job. They must put exponential thinking into action because there is no magic if the magician does not explode and transcend linear thinking, and by so doing, ignite an audience's imagination.[35]

In the world of science, imagination provides the lever that raises linear thought to exponential thought. As Archimedes famously proclaimed: "Give me a lever and a place to stand and I will move the earth." His proposition is a metaphor—that is, an imagining—of how a lever multiplies force exponentially. It is also a straightforward explanation of what a lever does. Finally, Archimedes' proposal is both a metaphor of the power of imagination and itself the product of that very power.

In science, imagination powers the exponential thinking necessary for breakthroughs of insight. In his works on Einstein, including *Einstein's Cosmos: How Einstein's Vision Transformed Our Understanding of Space and Time*, physicist Michio Kaku enumerates five reasons the great genius could think so exponentially:

1. He was a theoretical physicist, not an experimental one. He lived in thought and imagination, constantly conducting what he himself called "thought experiments."

2. He spent up to ten years on a single thought experiment. From age sixteen to twenty-six, for example, Einstein focused almost exclusively on the problem of light, which behaved both like a particle and like a wave.

3. He had an off-center personality. Einstein was a rebel, a bohemian, an insurgent who constantly used his own formidable imagination to think outside of any box.

4. The old physical world of Isaac Newton was beginning to crumble at just the time Einstein was coming into his prime. He had the good fortune to live in a time ripe for imagination and innovation.

5. Finally, as Kaku puts it, he *was* Einstein...

Great scientists, magicians, and business leaders partake of the same inverted imagination. Back in the 1940s, for example, Walt Disney was planning Disneyland. His associates were deeply worried that he was seemingly quite unconcerned with the ideas basic to any traditional amusement park: How many rides to build? How many parking spaces to set aside? What food should be sold? And so on. Disney did not begin with these building blocks. Instead, he imagined the end—the effect—he wanted to achieve with Disneyland. And so he asked just one question, which was much larger than any of those smaller building-block inquiries. It was, in fact, a question big enough to accommodate his imagination: "How can Disneyland make its visitors feel as though they are having a more magical customer experience?"

Ask the right question, get the right answers.

Walt Disney did not begin with facts. He began with imagination. Bosses with common sense are very critical of those who fail to begin with facts. "Face facts!" they command. Failure to face facts, the acolytes of common sense are quick to tell you, is why fantasy is not reality and why science fiction writers are not scientists. Except that Jules Verne's *Twenty Thousand Leagues Under the Sea* (1870) and *The Clipper of the Clouds* (1886) inspired, respectively, the invention of the submarine (the first truly successful one was the USS *Holland,* not commissioned until 1900) and the helicopter (not a mass-produced "fact" until Igor Sikorsky's R-4 of 1944).

And then there's Martin Cooper, who led the Motorola team that developed the world's first hand-held mobile phone. An electrical engineer by profession, Cooper was a fan of TV's *Star Trek* by avocation. Deeply troubled that Motorola's mammoth rival AT&T was almost certain to beat his much smaller company to the release of new "car phone" technology, Cooper sought soothing distraction in an episode of *Star Trek.* Suddenly,

the spectacle of Captain Kirk using his hand-held "communicator"
triggered his imagination. Turning from the TV screen, he realized he had
an extraordinary idea. Motorola would make an exponential leapfrog bound
over the "car phone" and instead create a *hand-held* mobile phone. In 1973,
the company released its 800 MHz cellular telephone prototype. AT&T had
nothing like it.

The lesson? Exploit any available source to hypercharge your imagination.
It is one of the most underutilized advantages in business today.

Magicians use imagination to disrupt business as usual, to confront
resistance to change, to transform resistance into embrace, embrace into
use, and use into change. This sequence, we argue, is the very engine
of innovation, what *In Search of Excellence* coauthor Tom Peters calls
"re-imagination." Tactics for re-imagination include *reverse mentoring,*
differentiation, brainstorming, and *destination planning,* all of which help
you to move away from conventional thinking and toward creative problem
solving and strategic imagination—the approaches necessary to win in what
is arguably the most difficult and complex business environment in history.
For example:

- ◆ *Reverse mentoring.* This is a technique the Wharton School's Jerry
  Wind endorses. Recruit a Millennial who can tutor *you* on the
  latest fads, social media dynamics, and anything else they see as
  powerful age-group consumer terms of reference.

- ◆ *Differentiation.* In business, the best category to be in is a
  category of one. Carve out a space in your market that disrupts
  the status quo. That's what Apple did and continues to do
  brilliantly. Find a strategic vacuum, a place where there is
  unaddressed consumer pain. Ultimately, this is the place
  where the *differentiation* of your brand can truly make a
  difference. Being sharply differentiated from your competitive
  set is key to success in magic for the simple reason that too
  many magicians look alike. In business, the most popular brand

positioning in the marketplace is, *"Me, too!"* In fact, most brands take comfort in following the leader. But more imaginative competitors take comfort in deviating from the leader's path. As our former client, Coca-Cola CEO Roberto Goizueta, advised: "Be different or be damned."

♦ *Brainstorming.* Bill Gates believed in getting away for at least three to five days in his own retreat—he favored a cabin in the woods—where he would spend a few hours a day solo *brainstorming* ideas to deliberately stretch and expand his thinking. Done right, brainstorming is all about asking bigger and better questions, thinking more exponentially, and then beginning to categorize the resulting ideas into clusters—round about day three. A hundred ideas can be bundled into three mega-shifts with the potential to create your own powerful advantage in your marketplace.

♦ *Destination planning.* Work with your most trusted group to conduct "destination planning," by which we mean imagining what your business success *will* look like, what the "win" *will* and *must* be. Many people make the mistake of thinking of the imagination as a gauzy sort of place that spins out ideas like cotton candy. In fact, business goals are seldom as crisply defined as they should be. So apply clarity to your imaginings. In your small group, for instance, work to imagine success in the most granular and meaningful terms. Start by asking the right questions: "If we achieve all our goals over the next twenty-four to thirty-six months, what will our success look and feel like...for us and all our key constituents?"

Great magicians are role models for empowering more creativity, innovation, and imagination in business—something we need so much more of today. Turning the way we think upside down, asking bigger and better questions of ourselves, finding exponential ways to problem solve, and putting to work the magical concepts of *reverse mentoring, differentiation, brainstorming, and destination planning set the stage not only for imagining first, but imagining better.*

PART TWO

PLOT

THE FOURTH STRATEGY
DISORGANIZE INNOVATION

"There's something about the center of any bureaucracy—
it's as if the water tastes different there...."

—Robert Shapiro

S cene: *This really happened[36] (https://www.youtube.com/*
watch?v=f9PL-uhjG5U). We are in the suburban Las Vegas home
of Jeff McBride, one of the best magicians in the world today. Gathered
here are some of the other top American magicians, taking a five-day
master class sponsored by the world's most famous magic school. In
the desert heat, this select group comes together to hear lectures, try
out new material, and endure more or less polite critiques. Most of all,
they create new ideas in a professional magicians' equivalent of the
experimental "Skunk Works" that legendary aircraft designer Kelly
Johnson led for Lockheed—where he and his crew developed the likes
of WWII's war-winning P-38 Lightning fighter, the Cold War's U-2 spy
plane, and the SR-71 Blackbird, still the fastest aircraft ever built. Or
think of it as akin to Steve Jobs' famed "Mac Group," set up in a strip
mall in Cupertino, California, physically separate from official Apple
HQ and topped by a Jolly Roger pirate flag. It was the perfect place to
imagine and build a computer that shifted the PC paradigm.

Today, imaginations are fired up inside an unassuming desert home,
the very environment in which McBride synthesized the shamanistic
roots of magic to make new again a very old effect: The Water Bowl
Illusion. (Ultimately, on September 7, 2017, this is the effect that will fool
Penn & Teller on their Fool Us television show.)

Take your mind outside the suburban house and into a great Vegas showroom. There onstage, eerily lit from above, dressed as a shaman from an earlier age, McBride displays two metal bowls, obviously empty. Suddenly, in response to an ancient musical call, he looks up, appealing to the gods of water for their bounty. After all, he and his audience are in the middle of a desert.

He asks, he prays. And the water comes, filling both bowls. He drinks, drinks it all, and then shows the bowls, now dry.

McBride asks for more. Again, the bowls fill. He drinks. They fill again...again...and yet again. It seems too much. Yet the bowls fill again. And again. A thankful McBride accepts at long last the final drops. He says nothing, but the audience understands. The magic of life is good.

(The lights go out: Cut to black.)

William Thomson, 1st Baron Kelvin, president of the Royal Society and the first British scientist to be elevated to the House of Lords, formulated the first and second laws of thermodynamics. The first is a version of the law of conservation of energy adapted to thermodynamic systems. Essentially, it applies conservation of energy—energy can be transformed from one form to another, but can neither be created nor destroyed—to thermodynamic systems. The second law is about the irreversibility of natural processes and the tendency natural processes usually have toward entropy. In short, Lord Kelvin was among the founders of modern physics, creating a mathematically certain vision of how energy can and cannot behave and how, ultimately, the universe slouches toward the changelessness of absolute zero, the value of which (-459.67 degrees Fahrenheit) he calculated.

In 1884, this colossus of modern science visited Johns Hopkins University in Baltimore, Maryland, where he led a course on molecular dynamics and the theory of light, anchored by twenty lectures and delivered to an elite group of students filling a small lecture hall. Catalyzed by the informal yet high-powered atmosphere of this talented group of outsiders and renegades, some of the students gathered here will go on to make a plethora of scientific breakthroughs. The university called this a "master class," borrowing from the tradition of the famed musical conservatory at Strasbourg, France, where elite teachers and learners came together outside of their daily routines for the sole purpose of elevating their collective knowledge by lecturing or performing "works in progress." The master class was a safe, honest, and constructive venue aimed at creating the kind of synergies that advance civilization itself.

It is 2016, and welcome to Paradise. A town outside of Las Vegas, it is home of the legendary McBride Magic & Mystery School, founded by magician Jeff McBride, winner of many magic awards, including the International Grand Prix of Magic, "Magician of the Year." The Founding Dean of the school was Eugene Burger, one of the authors of this book. Paradise and the Magic & Mystery School were as far outside the mainstream in 2016 as an obscure Johns Hopkins lecture hall was in 1884. And *that*—location on the periphery—is part of the master class magic. The Conservatoire de Strasbourg is, after all, in Strasbourg, not Paris.

What the flame is to the moth or the fluorescent bug zapper is to the mosquito, the bright lights and big city are to most seekers of success. Pulled to this light, we want these little town blues to melt away right in the very heart of it, New York, New York, as the song goes. F. Scott Fitzgerald can break your heart with "Absolution," a short story in which a sad priest hears his parishioners' confessions in one of northern Minnesota's "lost Swede towns" while secretly dreaming of "the best places" where "a lot of people get together" and "things go glimmering."

Speaking to a young, lonely boy who seeks his sacred counsel, the priest asks, "Do you hear the hammer and the clock ticking and the bees?" Without waiting for an answer, he warns him: "Well, that's no good. The thing is to have a lot of people in the center of the world, wherever that happens to be. Then...things go glimmering." That, of course, is the way Fitzgerald, child of Minnesota, lived his life—Paris, New York, bright lights, big cities, where things go glimmering. In the end, he died young in what many believed was the *true* center of the world, Hollywood—or as close to it as he could get to it at the point of a fading career, Encino, in the San Fernando Valley.

Like the sad priest of his story, Scott Fitzgerald failed to understand that the very worst place to be is in the center of the world—at least if you want to create innovation, what we call "decentralized or peripheral innovation." The truth is that the center of the world, or the center of any organization, bureaucracy, or marketplace, views innovation as insurgency and is so threatened by it that it attacks and attempts to destroy it, as antibodies attack and destroy an infection. That is why bold innovation happens outside and along the periphery—in places like Lockheed's fabled Skunk Works, Apple's legendary Mac Group, Lord Kelvin's master class, the Conservatoire de Strasbourg, or the McBride Magic & Mystery School.

INNOVATION DEMANDS DISORGANIZATION

Paradise. In the front row of the McBride Magic & Mystery School, David Morey and John McLaughlin listen to Eugene Burger and Ross Johnson, one of the world's top mentalists—non-magicians call them mind readers— teach. Right now, Johnson, a former teacher as well as a mentalist revered by other mentalists for his groundbreaking works and performances over several decades, commands the stage, fooling even us professional magicians with his effects.

Paradise. "Die Gedanken sind frei" is the title of a famous old German song, rooted in the Middle Ages: Thoughts Are Free. Everyone knows that. And everyone also knows that they are free precisely because they are our own, secret, until we choose to give them expression in words or pictures or music or gestures. "Die Gedanken sind frei, wer kann sie erraten?" is the first line of the song: "Thoughts are free, who can guess them?" The privacy of thought is one of those truths we call self-evident. It is an aspect of reality, the way the world, or even the universe, is. And therein lies the power of any great mentalism act. We watch and listen as the magician reads the mind of someone he has never met before. Die Gedanken sind frei? Our thoughts—suddenly—are his!

What could be more amazing, eye-opening, and disorganizing? Which is another way of saying: What could be more innovative?

For the nature—the heart—of innovation is disorganization. The truly new disorganizes the old, the familiar, what we already know and have known for a long time and assume everybody knows and has known for a long time. The essence of innovation is destructive. Thank goodness.

So, David, John, and Eugene are sitting in Paradise, listening to Ross Johnson deliver the secret codes of how he staggers and disorganizes reality to create something new from within his own imagination. As we listen, Johnson takes us ahead years, if not decades, in terms of our own performing abilities—jump-starting our ability to "read minds," allowing us to stand on his shoulders even as he stands on the shoulders of *his* teachers. In Paradise—*out here* in Paradise—we're all thinking, imagining, scribbling notes. Out here, in this slice of the creative periphery, the magic of innovation is alive and kicking. Really kicking.

Out here in Paradise, for example, the school highlights what are called "works in progress." In this way, students take the stage with their best and most rehearsed effects and then absorb creative and affirmational feedback from their teachers—often creating moments wherein "light bulbs" illuminate not just within the performers of the works in progress, but also inside the imaginations of all who watch. Importantly, this process does not destroy participants' status quo, but rather disrupts and disorganizes it.

Paradise can be in Nevada or Baltimore or Strasbourg. So let's look at some business examples of extraordinarily disorganized innovation before we return to magic.

Back in 1943, Paradise was in Burbank, California, at the Lockheed Aircraft Corporation. In World War II, the contest in the skies of Europe was at a tipping point. U.S. Army Air Forces brass were sending representatives of the Air Tactical Service Command (ATSC) to the Burbank headquarters of Lockheed. They had a problem. While the Allied air forces were beginning to gain air superiority over the vaunted Luftwaffe, German engineers were making big strides with jet fighter aircraft. The technology was in its infancy. But wars make babies grow up fast, and if the Germans could deploy significant numbers of jets, the piston-and-propeller air forces of the United States and Britain would be instantly outclassed. The jet could be a war-winning weapon—for the enemy, if they had it and you did not.

Lockheed had access to the new British breakthrough, a jet engine called the Goblin. Convinced that this project was a hot rush, Lockheed management gave the job to a young engineer named Clarence L. Johnson, but better known as "Kelly." Kelly for sure could think outside of the box, like a magician, well out into and along the creative periphery. He and his team delivered the proposal for an experimental jet fighter, the XP-80, one month after the ATSC came calling. And two days after receiving the proposal, Lockheed was given the green light to start development. With that, the "Skunk Works" came into being—headed by Kelly Johnson.

The Skunk Works is a registered trademark with the company today known as Lockheed-Martin, but the exploits of Kelly Johnson and the Skunk Works became universally famous, so much so that to this day, the phrase "skunk works" is used to describe any gathering of innovators—disruptors—outside the center of their own bureaucracy. This freedom from conventional thinking and time-wasting red tape empowers disorganized and disorganizing innovation. True to the Skunk Works concept, Lockheed did not receive a formal government contract for the XP-80 until October 16, 1943, by which time Johnson and his team were four months into the project. This established a precedent. When a customer came to the Skunk Works with a project, work began—then and there—on a handshake.

The XP-80 prototype was designed and built in 143 days, seven days less than the contract had stipulated. The aircraft made its first flight on January 8, 1944, but did not go into full production during World War II. It did, however, become the first successful turbojet-powered combat aircraft in the fleets of the U.S. Air Force and U.S. Navy as the P-80 Shooting Star and was used in the Korean War. As it turned out, the World War II U.S. Army Air Forces had a propeller-driven fighter aircraft, the remarkable Lockheed P-38 twin-engine Lightning, which was capable of long range, high altitude, and high-speed flight—432 miles per hour—a combination that made it more versatile than the early Luftwaffe jet aircraft. German pilots feared the P-38, which they called *der Gabelschwanz-Teufel*, the Fork-Tailed Devil, because of its innovative twin-boom fuselage design. Japanese adversaries called it *Ni hikoko, ippairotto*: "Two Planes, One Pilot." The P-38 had been designed by Kelly Johnson in 1939, before the official founding of the Skunk Works.

"Disorganized and disorganizing innovation" does not mean random improvisation or waiting for genius to strike. Johnson's record of innovation at Lockheed lasted nearly forty-five years, and it was driven by fourteen "rules and practices"—yes, rules:

1. The Skunk Works manager must be delegated practically complete control of his program in all aspects. He should report to a division president or higher.

2. Strong but small project offices must be provided both by the military and industry.

3. The number of people having any connection with the project must be restricted in an almost vicious manner. Use a small number of good people (10 percent to 25 percent compared to practice in the so-called normal systems).

4. A very simple drawing and drawing release system with great flexibility for making changes must be provided.

5. There must be a minimum number of reports required, but important work must be recorded thoroughly.

6. There must be a monthly cost review covering not only what has been spent and committed but also projected costs to the conclusion of the program.

7. The contractor must be delegated and must assume more than normal responsibility to get good vendor bids for subcontract on the project. Commercial bid procedures are very often better than military ones.

8. The inspection system as currently used by the Skunk Works, which has been approved by both the Air Force and Navy, meets the intent of existing military requirements and should be used on new projects. Push more basic inspection responsibility back to subcontractors and vendors. Don't duplicate so much inspection.

9. The contractor must be delegated the authority to test his final product in flight. He can and must test it in the initial stages. If he doesn't, he rapidly loses his competency to design other vehicles.

10. The specifications applying to the hardware must be agreed to well in advance of contracting. The Skunk Works' practice of having a specification section stating clearly which important military specification items will not knowingly be complied with and reasons therefore is highly recommended.

11. Funding a program must be timely so that the contractor doesn't have to keep running to the bank to support government projects.

12. There must be mutual trust between the military project organization and the contractor, with very close cooperation and liaison on a day-to-day basis. This cuts down both misunderstanding and correspondence to an absolute minimum.

13. Access by outsiders to the project and its personnel must be strictly controlled by appropriate security measures.[37]

14. Because only a few people will be used in engineering and most other areas, ways must be provided to reward good performance with pay not based on the number of personnel supervised.

Notice that these rules are "granular"—that is, practical, nitty-gritty, even nerdy. But notice as well that they codify creative informality: one manager is given complete control; project offices are to be "strong but small"; the "number of people having any connection with the project must be restricted in an almost vicious manner"; the drawing system must be "very simple" and "flexible"; reports are to be kept to a minimum, but everything must be recorded (so that no ideas are lost); costs are to be reviewed monthly—with an eye toward the outcome; avoid unnecessary duplication of inspection; the *contractor* must test fly—it's the best way to learn; all specs must be agreed on in advance of contracting—no empty promises; funding must be timely; liaison between contractor and military should be day-to-day—trust is critical; access by outsiders is to be severely restricted; base employee compensation on results, not number of persons supervised.

These rules and practices facilitated the creation of such breakthrough aircraft as the U-2 "spy plane" for the CIA in 1955. The aircraft was needed rapidly for covert overflights above the Soviet Union. Accordingly, it was based on an existing Lockheed experimental aircraft, the XF-104, but with the addition of very long, very slender wings, which allowed it to reach the high altitudes required for covert surveillance, to conserve fuel for flights of long duration, and to operate very quietly. It was, in fact, a paradigm-shattering jet-powered glider.

The U-2 was built to serve an immediate need while Kelly and his team worked on an entirely new reconnaissance aircraft, the SR-71 Blackbird. First flown in 1966, it was—and it remains—the fastest airplane ever built. Innovations abounded, including radar-detection-defying proto-stealth features in contour and special paint; the use of titanium for the airframe; expansion-joint construction to deal with the tremendous heat generated by friction at Mach 3.2 (3.2 times the speed of sound, or 2455.26 miles per hour), at an unheard-of altitude of 80,000 feet. It flew far too fast and far too high to be hit by surface-to-air missiles, or by anything else.

SKUNK WORKS PROGENY

In recent years—the last twenty or so—Lockheed's Skunk Works has inspired numerous outside-the-center efforts, including Verizon's "Video Services," Google's "X," Amazon's "Lab126," Raytheon's "Bike Shop," Nike's "Innovation Kitchen," Staples's "Velocity Lab," and Xerox's "PARC." None have been more successful, however, than a little Silicon Valley group defined by three letters: M...A...C...

Steve Jobs' Apple was the first corporate client David Morey's company took on, in 1984. Jobs understood that IBM, creator of the PC, was not just the industry incumbent, but the center of its own marketplace. Clearly, Apple was the David to IBM's Goliath, and Jobs saw in IBM's very strength and incumbency its weakness. Personal computing was, by definition, cutting edge. The product of *innovation*, innovation was at the core of *personal* computing's value proposition. Jobs saw that IBM was institutionally averse to the level of disorganized innovation required to deliver on that proposition. Big Blue had become a "center-of-every-bureaucracy" incumbent. On the face of it, of course, this made IBM an incredibly intimidating competitor. After all, the IBM PC was already the standard business desktop computer, and IBM had anointed Microsoft DOS as the operating system software for *the* desktop computer. Moreover, the businesses that were buying IBM's PCs were looking less for innovation than affirmation. "Nobody ever got fired for buying IBM" was a saying universally heard in corporate America during the mainframe epoch, and Big Blue made no bones about carrying it and the ethos it expressed into the era of the desktop. The assumption was that, mainframe or PC, IBM was and would remain the standard, the true market center and incumbent.

As Jobs well knew, IBM's marketplace supremacy came at a cost—not to IBM (at least not immediately), but to the consumer. IBM was a text-based machine using a text-based operating system. This meant that computer users who bought IBM—the machine nobody ever got fired for buying—had to be willing to put in some relatively hard labor to learn the language of the computer (MS-DOS) to communicate with it. Yes, the machine served the person—but only after the person learned how to serve the machine. And if you never got fired for buying IBM, your sentence of service was for life.

In fact, IBM engineers and marketers created and promoted the IBM PC to consumers who had already committed to a life sentence in a corporate environment. Workers on a "cube farm," which had become the standard corporate office space by the end of the 1970s, were what IBM management and marketing envisioned when they closed their eyes. In a corporate environment, especially such a corporate environment, IBM never really intended the desktop "personal" computer to get all that personal. Big Blue saw the so-called "personal computer" as a more autonomous extension of the computer terminals, which had long existed as the portals through which multiple users accessed the mainframe. "Big Iron," which is what Big Blue called the big central mainframe computer, always enthroned in its own air-conditioned room, was what had made IBM's fortune, and even as the PC began to take the marketplace by storm, the mainframe occupied pride of place in the company's strategy. For this reason, the PC was thought of as a machine that existed primarily to connect to bigger and bigger and bigger IBM machines until it hooked into the Big Iron itself, *the* IBM mainframe. Looked at this way, the PC was meant to be used by *many* people serving one really big machine. Moreover, in true twentieth-century corporate fashion, the IBM PC measured the user's output in terms of speed and efficiency—by which IBM meant nothing personal, like fun, creativity, or self-expression.

In almost every way, from its centralized market dominance to its uncompromisingly techie our-way-or-the-highway user interface, IBM reflected what most market leaders embody, namely the overweening arrogance of an incumbent and a nearly flawless model of autocracy. The reality IBM faced is this: The center of the marketplace, center of the organization, and center of your own bureaucracy is, by definition, bloated, slow, cautious, red-tape-obsessed, change-resistant, and more likely to play defense than offense to maintain their power.

Now, look at the little Macintosh at the time David Morey's company began working with that machine's leader and champion. The Mac was not just an example of insurgent, peripheral innovation, it was a born revolutionary. Like the iconic Nike, it was born in a garage. Like Facebook, it might as well have been birthed in a dorm room. Even before he was fired in 1985, Steve Jobs had marched out of Apple in a combination of anger and paranoia about the competition. He was scared. Computing, he realized, was moving away from fun and kids and elementary schools—the territory his company had staked out—to businesses and adults and then to *everything*. Advantage, IBM.

Jobs had a choice. He could get into bed, pull the covers over his head, and await the inevitable end, or he could do what he did, which was to march across the street from Apple HQ and open a modest set of offices in a little business strip mall. Over its flat roof, he raised a black skull-and-crossbones. *This was* the Mac Group, and under its flapping Jolly Roger, Steve Jobs presided over the making of a Macintosh that was different from the IBM PC in every way possible. Paranoia drove innovation—the kind of innovation intended to disorganize the whole corporate mindset IBM fed into even as the innovation itself was fed by this mindset. Text-based MS-DOS was native to machines, but represented a foreign tongue to human beings. Working in their strip mall—literally on the periphery of Apple HQ—Jobs and his team created the anti-text operating system. It was called a graphical user interface (GUI), and instead of requiring the user to learn a language friendly to the machine and input obscure commands via a keyboard, the GUI "talked" to the user—in sign language. The screen served up icons and menus, and users clicked on their choice of action using a new version of something called a mouse.

Take *that*, cube farm world! The GUI upended—disrupted, disorganized—the corporate order IBM had instilled into its machines. Soon, the Mac and its GUI were creating a legion of insurgents, who loved—yes, loved—their Macs and proclaimed that the initials *IBM* stood for Incredibly Boring Machine. Advantage, the outsider. *Machine* serves *man*.

Steve Jobs was a visionary, and he saw a lot, but he didn't see everything. Not satisfied with blowing apart the text-based universe of DOS with the icon-based garden of GUI, he decided to make the personal computer not merely personal, but downright intimate. The first Mac demanded a monogamous relationship with its user. Whereas the IBM PC was old wine in a new bottle—a 1960s terminal given an upgrade in autonomy, but still intended to connect to Big Iron—the Mac, by design, could not connect to anything bigger, even a network. (The Internet did not yet exist, and even Steve Jobs did not imagine it.)

As for measuring the user's output, the Mac metered "work" not in terms of quantifiable productivity, but as creative expansiveness. It symbolized the idea that innovators who work on the periphery cherish an attitude of difference, move faster, and welcome change as opportunity. They embody the recruiting profile of legendary Alabama football coach Bear Bryant, who wanted every one of his players to be "mobile, agile, and hostile."

APPLE'S MAGICAL PARADIGM: MOBILE, AGILE, AND HOSTILE

If you want to be hostile about it (and Jobs wanted to be hostile about it), you could say that if the IBM paradigm was essentially Soviet, the Macintosh was a model of democracy—democracy with an exponent, democracy raised to the power of Flower Power, the ethos of the 1960s during which Jobs and the rest of his pirate crew had come of age. Nothing about anything Steve Jobs did was coincidental. Like an accomplished magician, he left nothing to chance. Everything he said, everything he *did* communicated the very American, democratic, disorganized species of innovation that can be imagined along the periphery. From the defiant Jolly Roger to the Bösendorfer grand piano to the Mac OS to the triumph of the mouse over the keyboard, and to the spectacular public statement that launched it all, everything conveyed a single message of innovation.

That message culminated in the television ad created by the incomparable Lee Clow, then creative director of Apple's ad agency, Chiat Day. The production—and it *was* a production—was called "1984." It was directed by Ridley (*Blade Runner*) Scott, and it was slotted into the stratospherically priced television real estate of that year's Super Bowl. A woman athlete in bright orange running shorts and white tank top bears the image of the Mac in an outline drawing, holding in her hand a brass-headed hammer. She sprints through a gray hall—through the center of some evil bureaucracy—lined with gray people who stare zombie-like at an overwhelming screen from which a gigantic gray Orwellian Big Brother drones a message about "our Unification of Thoughts."

Helmeted Thought Police, clad head to toe in menacing black, give chase as she races toward the screen, and propelled by an unstoppable momentum, hurls her hammer at it. We see Big Brother shatter into shards amid a burst of bright light and smoke. And the voiceover intones, "On January 24, Apple Computer will introduce Macintosh. And you'll see why 1984 won't be like *1984*." The ad was the apotheosis of the Apple Mac's outsider spirit. It established in the most public of forums the Manichean contest of the peripheral insurgent versus the centralized incumbent that was to power every Apple-against-IBM battle and every Apple-against-Microsoft battle to come. To this day, it is the spirit behind the Apple-against-everybody-else battles.

It was at this point that David Morey and business partner Scott Miller took off from everything Jobs had started and developed for him the full pattern of the insurgent/incumbent campaign model. It drew the distinction between "Bigness Leadership," operating at the marketplace center, versus an innovative periphery focused on "Change Leadership."

We said the potentially vulnerable "in-the-center" Bigness Leaders share the following attributes:

- *They literally worship bigness*—size, scope, market share, and gross revenues.

- *They are used to being number one*, and have developed a great deal of arrogance about this position.

- *They are centralized and bureaucratic*, and believe in the hierarchy of the marketplace even as they believe in the hierarchy of their own corporate cube farm.

- *They are excessively formal*—to the point of making every process into a ritual of superstitious behavior ("this is the way we do things because this is the way we do things"). Their culture is a form of corporate religion.

- *They are oh so cautious*. They've got a lot to lose, so why take chances? Incremental gain? They'll take it, no matter how slowly it creeps. After all, they've been the leader forever and intend to remain the leader forevermore.

- *They are driven by heritage*, owing their success mostly to the past, and therefore are driving into the future with their eyes firmly fixed on the rearview mirror. The reverence they feel is for "the good old days."

- *They hate change*. When you are the market leader, you don't want things to change at all. (If you are number one, change means becoming number two. And that's the *best* case.) In fact, the in-the-center incumbents hate disruption, in the marketplace as well as within their own organizations. Therefore, most big companies cannot innovate themselves out of a paper bag— because, what is innovation if not disruption of the *status quo*?

The peripheral innovation of the Macintosh division of Apple Computer became the insurgent template for thousands of start-ups that followed in personal computing hardware and software, the building of the Internet, and the emergence of mobile technology. The Mac model inspired the innovators and led Warren Buffett, when asked why he so firmly believes in America's ability to succeed, to mention the legions of outsiders who work in garages and dorm rooms to invent new products, companies, marketplaces, and industries. These people, we argue, are precisely the opposite of the "in-the-center," bureaucracy-worshipping incumbents. Change Leaders share the following characteristics:

- *They worship better and better*, rather than bigger and bigger.

- *They take chances.* Accustomed to being number zero, they swing for the fences. They are bold. And *why not?* They don't have all that much to lose.

- *They are informal*, working out of flat organizations. Most of them haven't had the chance to create a hierarchy, and few of them ever will. They work as a team toward the revolutionary goal of unseating the incumbent and disorganizing the norm. Their own cultural glue? It's all about being a part of something great.

- *They value speed and mobility* over size. They're okay with errors of commission, but they are horrified by the errors of *omission* that could put them out of the game.

- *They are vision-driven*, focusing on the future, because that's where change is going to take them. The future is where success lives. The past is where nobody lives.

- *They love change*, because to an outsider-insurgent, change means opportunity. When the market's molecules are in motion, everything is up for grabs—and so to the Change Leader, more motion, more disruption, and more change means greater opportunity to increase their share of business and overall value.

A DIFFERENT SET OF RULES

Think different was the Apple motto under Steve Jobs. An even better way to express what Jobs taught those who are outsiders and want to be insurgents is that outsider-insurgents don't just think differently, they play by a different set of rules than in-the-center incumbents. In today's turbulent, instant, digital, surround-sound information environment, the outsider-insurgents have the advantage. From Bernie Sanders's near nomination win, to Brexit, to Rodrigo Duterte's win in the Philippines, to Donald Trump's election in the U.S.—the outsider-insurgents hold the advantage in politics, business, and, for that matter, magic. So here is a different set of rules, rules intended to help you capture the peripherally innovative spirit of the Lockheed Skunk Works, the McBride Magic & Mystery School, or Steve Jobs and the Mac Group. Here are the rules for thinking outside your own center and disorganizing innovation.

1. **STOP THINKING LIKE A "LEADER"**

    ◆   Today, *think more like a magician,* and *make a commitment not to act like an in-the-center incumbent leader*—no matter how overwhelmingly you may dominate your market or business world. What's the old saying…? "Nothing fails like success!" And the only unstoppable leader is the one playing by outsider-insurgent rules. Don't act like a leader. Act like you did on the way to leadership. Act like you are still in the dorm room, or the Silicon Valley Garage, or in McBride's Magic & Mystery School.

    ◆   No law forbids the leader of the center from creating and implementing peripheral-insurgent strategies. On the contrary, our experience says you *must* do this. In business, the companies doing this—Amazon, Starbucks, Facebook, Uber, Alibaba, Airbnb, Twitter, and others—are now market leaders, again, sometimes of markets they themselves literally invented. In magic, the pure creative force of Jeff McBride's water bowls is but one example of a string of creative breakthrough effects that continue to wow his audiences and redefine the art—McBride is magic's creative insurgent, rather than its incumbent leader. And in business, peripheral-insurgent strategies will not only help you continue to gain ground, they will help you develop more satisfied customers and happier, more productive, more totally committed employees.

Behaving like a peripheral-insurgent will not only *keep* you on top, it will *move* you further up, higher and higher.

◆   Evidence of this concept applied to business comes from the 1980s and early 1990s, when Microsoft, absolutely the market leader, insisted on leading from outside its own bureaucratic center. Back then, the company assiduously developed the culture and work ethic of the peripheral-insurgent, the revolutionary underdog. Some say this was the product of founder Bill Gates's natural paranoia, a paranoia that became part of the company's DNA. Maybe so, but the company's peripheral-insurgent strategy back then was always conscious and deliberate, not an accident of "birth" or a quirk of personality.

2.   **THE DANGER OF "WINNING"**

◆   As Tony Robbins says: "We either party or ponder. When we're winning, we party; and when we're losing, we ponder.... and the key is to ponder at the same time [that] we're winning...."[38] In fact, the human body craves sweets, but sweets, they say, are bad for us. They rot the teeth, bulge the belly, and, after a short-lived high, let us down. The danger of sweet, sweet victory comes the moment when the newly winning crew is doing high-fives at their victory party. "No more chasing. Now *we're* the effing leader! In your face, former incumbent. Eat our dust!"

◆   Of course, we admit that at times even David Morey's own clients suffer from sugar highs and have been guilty of declaring victory and abandoning their outsider-insurgent periphery to enjoy all the spoils and privileges of inside-the-center incumbency. Consider Microsoft up until a few years ago, with the constant drumbeat of unhappy investors who have watched the company's stock sit quietly for the last decade in the wake of continual insurgent innovation from Apple,

Google, Facebook, Twitter, and Amazon. We argue, in fact, that the worst problems of Microsoft began when it donned the ermine-trimmed mantle of inside-the-center incumbency and got into the "protection business" instead of the "creating business."

♦ Yes, that's right, "the protection business" is that thing the Mafia developed. Following this, three years ago, the transformation of Microsoft resulted, albeit far too late, in the "retiring" of Steven Ballmer, although his many billions of dollars of Microsoft wealth will provide solace. Ballmer was Gates' longtime number-two. He was a smart, tough leader, very self-confident, and seemingly someone who could lead Microsoft toward Gates's vision. But as we've all learned, he was no Bill Gates.

♦ In the days when Gates was the firm's hands-on chief, when David Morey's company worked for him, the Microsoft founder delivered an annual speech to the employees...each year recommending a new target worth "betting the company." And the company gambled accordingly. Gates meant it. He didn't really care if he lost it all. It was the gamble that made it worth it, not the sizable pot. Poker, after all, was the one thing he had really aced before dropping out of Harvard. And so the company became an indefatigable pursuer of the bets it made—even when it had already managed to run the table. It was creating stuff like crazy back then.

♦ The temptation to stop scrapping and start basking is hard to resist. In magic, for example, the world's most famous magician, David Copperfield, must constantly guard against complacency or simply returning to effects he has already tested and proven. In fact, every year, Copperfield's Las Vegas show is filled with new material, takes on new risks, pursues new experiments, and seeks new discoveries—often working with peripheral-insurgent magical developers who themselves operate outside the incumbent center and invent new magical breakthroughs.

- In business, virtually all market-leading companies tend to develop ponderous or even thuggish tactics when they begin to use their leverage over their market partners and dependents to hold on to what they've won instead of betting on the *next* goal. Protect and you lose, or you lose what you protect. Either way, this is the rule today. Nick Bilton of the *New York Times* has written very well about the issue of protecting versus creating, and we believe nobody writes or speaks or thinks better about it than Clayton Christensen, author of *The Innovator's Dilemma*. Writing about the smartphone market recently, Bilton said this: "That is the thing about 'creative destruction': You never know when you stop creating and get destroyed."[39]

- In fact, we think you *can* know. To paraphrase, Christensen told us: Stop creating and you get disrupted. In fact, in both magic and business, this is the unavoidable gravity that is peripheral insurgency.

- In the business world, an example of Christensen's "stop creating and you get disrupted" adage is Microsoft— Microsoft acting as an in-the-center incumbent. Under Ballmer, everything served Windows, and, presumably, Windows would serve everything, every need of every market. This presumed that Microsoft could dictate the market and the pace of market change. As powerful as Microsoft was, however, nobody is more powerful than the market, and nobody, but nobody is more powerful than change. Think about it: when Steven Ballmer took over at Microsoft, Google was two years old, Facebook was four years from being founded, Twitter six years off, and the release of the iPhone was seven years away. And every one of these outsider-insurgents sneaked up on the in-the-center incumbent Microsoft.

- A federal judge tried to break up Microsoft in 2000, but was thwarted on appeal. And many now speculate that the constituent companies would have done much better had the judgment stuck.

- In trying to extend the domain of Windows, Ballmer was essentially trying to protect Windows. And that just doesn't work anymore. Ballmer next seemed to try to turn Microsoft into a hedge fund, developing follower brands in gaming, search, tablets, and mobile products to hedge against his huge bet on the immortality of Windows. Result, not so good.

- What Microsoft now has is a more peripheral-insurgent leader. CEO Satya Nadella has changed the game since taking the reins on February 24, 2014: potentially marketing and delivering new software and services to everyone, on any device—leveraging Office 360 Cloud, Windows 10, Surface Pro 4 Tablet, and Xbox 360. While nearly doubling the company's stock price and value reflects these accomplishments, this follows the company's 50 percent loss in market value over the preceding thirteen years. So Nadella still has a high mountain to climb in continuing his innovative assault. But his outsider, peripheral, insurgent approach to innovation is so far "winning."

3. **DISRUPT YOUR OWN SOP**

- One reason we love the metaphor of magic applied to business is that it almost automatically disrupts your own status quo—by its nature, magic challenges your assumptions, shakes your perceptions, and often inspires you to think more creatively and to consider even deeper questions.

- In business today, there is simply too much SOP (Standard Operating Procedures). For example, as much as today's start-ups and upstarts need to harvest their natural advantage as out-on-the-periphery insurgents, today's incumbents must also learn to adopt insurgent strategy. Both challengers *and* incumbents can and will benefit from disrupting their own Standard Operating Procedures and thereby disorganizing their own innovation.

♦ Why do most "in-the-center" businesses need to behave more like insurgents? One reason is the seismic changes that have been taking place in U.S. and most global markets. For most of the last century, the assumption was that a natural tendency toward stability ruled all markets. Some called it the principle of "regression toward the mean," or, in finance, "mean reversion"—the idea that instability is temporary, and a mere prelude to long-term stability. Well into the twenty-first century, however, nobody is talking much about long-term stability anymore. Instead, the talk is all about change, because change, driven by the ongoing Information Revolution, rules, and instability is the constant.

♦ Therefore, the companies and business leaders most comfortable with disrupting themselves and disorganizing their own innovation will win—and they can borrow lessons from the truly great magicians, who are absolute experts at continuing to disrupt themselves and adapting, or better yet, leading the forces of change within their art.

4. **REMEMBER THE "COOL SACRED CENTER" HATES DISRUPTION**

♦ To know is to change. To know infinitely more and know it instantly is to change profoundly. This is what rules the markets of magic and business today. Change rules. And the rules of change greatly favor the peripheral-insurgent, because they embrace change and love change. By contrast, the in-the-center incumbent hates change, because change is a threat. Too damn bad. To swim against change these days is to flail against a riptide, even as you take in more and more saltwater through mouth and nostrils. As we've said, these are *very* tough times for in-the-center incumbents—at least for those who cannot bring themselves to act like peripheral-insurgents.

- In business, it's true that most in-the-center incumbents either don't understand this or refuse to believe it. Again, as Clayton Christensen writes and proves, market leaders hate disruption. The concept that made them great exists in what Robert Shapiro, former client and CEO of Monsanto, and now change agent leader of Sandbox Industries, calls "[t]he cool sacred center of the corporation."[40] This is where the incumbent's truth lives. Therefore, again, innovation invariably happens on the periphery of the marketplace rather than in the center of large, bureaucratic, incumbent organizations. In this cool sacred center, disruption is not tolerated, and change is the enemy.

5. BUILD YOUR OWN PERIPHERAL INNOVATION TEAM

- Ask David Copperfield about the all-star magical team he surrounds himself with to assist his process of imagination, creation, and innovation. Today, the first rule of creativity and innovation is that no one single person does it—because it takes a widely diverse team to succeed. Innovation, in fact, happens not just outside bureaucracies—it also happens *inside* teams; it's not the province of solitary geniuses. Steve Jobs may have been brilliant, but remember, he didn't invent the Macintosh. He didn't even originate the Macintosh project; Jef Raskin started it. As above, a team of brilliant technicians, engineers and software writers did the actual work via the Mac Group. True, Jobs was a brilliant visionary who knew what he wanted and knew how to direct his team to get there. But it was the Mac Group that turned this disruptive technology into reality.

- Successful peripheral innovation teams are as remarkably diverse as a group of today's most successful magicians—

each expresses their creativity and innovation from different perspectives. For example, the computer pioneers' honor roll includes an extraordinarily wide assortment of characters from an amazing variety of backgrounds. In the nineteenth century, there was the team of Charles Babbage, polymath and inventor; Joseph Clement, the genius mechanic from the wrong side of the class divide; and Ada, Countess of Lovelace, who figured out what a computer could do and how to program it. Babbage and Clement, history shows, never actually built the complex calculating machine that Babbage had designed, but the plans and fragments they left behind influenced later innovators; and Ada's writings are still read today.

♦   Another working group that is a great example of a remarkably diverse peripheral innovation team helped defeat the Nazis. As captured in the 2014 movie, *The Imitation Game*, which was set during World War II, mathematician Alan Turing helped design Colossus, the first all-electronic partially programmable computer, as part of the project to break the German codes. And the computer and code-breaking teams included mathematicians, engineers, electronics experts, classics professors, linguists, chess champions, and crossword puzzle experts. Sound familiar?

♦   Perhaps the strangest peripheral innovation team consisted of Lee Felsenstein, an electrical engineer, community organizer, and war protester, who got together with political activist Fred Moore and engineer Gordon French to start the Homebrew Computer Club on March 5, 1975. At subsequent meetings of the club, two young computer hobbyists, Steve Wozniak and Steve Jobs, demonstrated their latest invention: the Apple I. "Without computer clubs," Wozniak later admitted, "there would probably be no Apple computers."

Client, Microsoft founder, and Gates Foundation creator Bill Gates needed to get away to stay ahead of the pack back in the heyday of his company. Beginning in the 1980s and ending in 2008, Gates began what he called "Think Week"—once or twice a year, Gates needed to retreat from the world of centralized bureaucracy and SOP and literally get away...out into the periphery to focus on the all-critical topics facing Microsoft. Often spending the week in a cottage in the woods where family and friends were banned, Gates would spend his days reading extensive briefing papers, thinking, daydreaming, receiving no incoming e-mails, and only playing offense: hitting send and delivering outbound edicts to his Microsoft troops.

It was during one of these retreats, for example, that Gates decided the company must pivot toward, not away, from the Internet, writing his now-famous May 26, 1995, "Internet Tidal Wave" memo. Here, from his cottage in the woods, Gates gave the go-ahead for the highly profitable Xbox Live, imagined his first book, *The Road Ahead*, and repeatedly re-focused his company's strategic direction. "I really wanted to be alone, just reading," Gates told David A. Kaplan in an interview in 2012.[41]

Gates—at times a professorial CEO—was in some ways returning to a childhood where he freely and intensely read and thought; often, during "Think Week," he would read fifteen pages or longer papers, then step back, think, and provide game-changing feedback or instruction. This was innovation recharged: "In one *Wall Street Journal* article, a Microsoft manager described 'Think Week' as 'the world's coolest suggestion box.'"[42] And today, Gates continues mini-versions of "Think Week" at his foundation by attending "invention sessions" at a private investment and invention laboratory.

APPLICATIONS

◆ Innovation is listed today as among the top worries on the minds of every CEO—often "lack of innovation" is the answer David Morey gets when he asks business leaders the telling question, "What keeps you up at night?" In fact, businesses today are hungry for magical inspiration and innovation on the periphery. Examples include companies David Morey has recently helped to creatively disrupt and disorganize—sometimes using magical effects as metaphors for challenging assumptions, thinking out of the box, inspiring innovation, planning further ahead, moving to the offense, or reaching deeper inside to find new sources of boldness. Client examples include such companies as American Express, General Electric, Pepsi, AVG Technologies, CVS, Merck, Blue Cross Blue Shield, BMW, NBC, TD Ameritrade, Travelport, Utilidata, Aga Group, Xingda, and Zhaotai. From developing new and even breakthrough insights into customer perceptions, to refocusing and re-energizing organizational aspirations, to imagining new destinations and definitions of "success," to disorganizing their own innovation efforts—these and other companies have moved their thinking further outside the box, and they continue to borrow from magical lessons and apply them to their own unique business challenges. By thinking like magicians, by thinking differently, they've advanced their own strategies and tactics and driven innovation forward and one step ahead of their own status quo.

◆ This strategy has focused on the power of creating outposts for innovation like Skunk Works. As discussed, whether it's the garages that gave birth to companies like HP, Nike, and Apple, the kitchen that cooked up Xerox, or the dorm room that spawned Facebook, the truth is that the magic of innovation does not exist inside the center of America's hallowed corporate hallways. In fact, this kind of innovation must be *disorganized*— disrupted and formed outside and along the periphery, where technologists, marketers, and entrepreneurs think less like business people and more like magicians.

♦ So, pulling this all together, how to set up your own disruption? Below are five big and magical ways to mobilize the kind of peripheral disorganization your business needs to win.

1. **GET AWAY**

   The secret: We authors sneak away several times a year to magic conventions, or to the McBride Magic & Mystery School, to create our own "Think Week"—we surround ourselves with the creative and inspirational force of magic to think differently about our own challenges and businesses. So, follow the Bill Gates example yourself. Twice a year, find your cottage in the woods and imitate Gates during Microsoft's apex. Bring the work on which you need to catch up, segmented by the prioritized, the most forward-thinking, and the most important—and forget the tyranny of the most urgent and the less strategically valuable. In other words, focus on the more strategically important parts of your business, your career, and your next rung up the success ladder. As far as family and friends, lie, hide, or tell them you've been kidnapped, and like Jeff McBride, unplug your television... and get away and out along your own periphery to think, focus, strategize, create, and above all, to play offense.

2. **SKUNK WORKS YOURSELF**

   Follow David Copperfield's example and build your own Skunk Works of magical inventors from outside the periphery. In business, as in magic, disorganizing innovation means building your own Skunk Works—become part of, or anoint your own, outsider team...including a well-chosen and small team of misfits, of disrupters, the folks who can create but also sometimes get bogged down—in fact, put several of your very best talents alongside your most creative people. Insist they go away—to another place, another city, or even another country to escape your own organizational center. Tell them to think like magicians and go invent something bolder than can be imagined.

3. **CONTINUALLY FIND NEW MENTORS, ANGLES, INPUTS, AND IDEAS**

   Find and subscribe to your own version of the McBride Magic & Mystery School, and go there and think, create, and play more and more offense. Go find new and different-thinking mentors. As Vice President and New York Governor Nelson Rockefeller used to ask his staff, "Who's the expert?"[43] Seek out the best, most knowledgeable, and even better, the magical mentor who has previously *done* what you want to do—become their apprentice, and visit the periphery with them as they help disrupt your life.

4. **RUN A RED TEAM**

   In magic, as detailed in the next strategy, planning one step ahead about what can go wrong is critically important—because what can go wrong, will go wrong, and what can be missed in planning, will be missed in planning. So in business, follow the experience of John McLaughlin and the learning of the U.S. intelligence community and run your own Red Team exercises. A Red Team is an independent group that challenges your organizational status quo to improve effectiveness. These Red Teams, for example, can be tasked with exploring new and cutting-edge strategies or breakthrough technologies; they can test your cybersecurity systems; or they can write articles about alternative futures—even creating the newspaper headline that sums up what success will look like for your organization several years from today.

   For example, a 2003 Defense Science Review Board recommended Red Team exercises in preventing the kind of attack that occurred on September 11, 2001, to assist in adopting the enemy's mindset, testing vulnerabilities, and challenging assumptions. Today, more and more companies are borrowing, and should borrow, this methodology to disrupt in-the-center status quo thinking and over-confidence.

5. **FOCUS YOUR MAGICIAN "META-FRAME"**

A "meta-frame" is a guide or reference point, as well as an overall focus or direction that gives meaning to any interaction. At the core of this book is the belief that thinking like a great magician, thinking differently, provides new and creative power to any business interaction. The next strategies will argue that the magician as a meta-frame is inside all of us—that he or she is clever, commanding, and bold, looks at things anew, and is ready to creatively problem-solve through magical lenses.... We will argue that this magician meta-frame focuses on delivering value to people, i.e., audiences, and in the tradition of the ancient shaman, healing where we can heal. If magic is good medicine, then magicians are good healers—so begin warming up your "magician meta-frame," and begin awakening, accessing, and thinking like your inner magician, because this meta-frame or point of view will help you lead, disorganize, and disrupt your way to new levels of success.

THE FIFTH STRATEGY
CHEAT PREEMPTIVELY

"Losers react, leaders anticipate."

—Tony Robbins

S cene: *Recall the story of Max Malini, told in the introduction. It really happened. Back in the 1920s, Malini, a world-famous magician especially renowned for his "spontaneous" close-up magic, stunned a U.S. senator who asked him to "do a trick" at a formal dinner party.*

Protesting that he is completely unprepared, Malini at last gives in to the repeated entreaties of the senator and his entourage. He asks if anyone happens to have a deck of cards. No one does, of course, but—fortunately—the magician carries a deck. He withdraws it from his pocket, shuffles it, then "forces" a card on the senator's wife. When Malini then asks her to return it to the deck, the card turns up missing. Visibly annoyed, Malini half apologizes. "This is very unusual," he protests.

Then he asks if anyone is carrying a knife. Of course not. Fortunately, however, Malini has one. Brandishing it toward the senator, he begs his indulgence while he deftly cuts through the astonished man's tuxedo jacket and down to the silken lining where he finds...the very card!

In all of Washington—in all the universe—how could this particular card turn up in this particular jacket worn by this particular man?

Over the course of the preceding two years, Max Malini had systematically bribed a well-known Washington tailor to sew a certain playing card into the suit and tux jackets of several senators. When one of them at long last happened to request the "spontaneous" performance of a miracle of magic, Malini was 100 percent prepared.

The perception that something a magician does onstage is real *magic* as opposed to a "trick" or "illusion" depends on the audience understanding a fact of life as grim as it is universal: there is very little in your world that you can control. You cannot control the weather. You cannot control the idiot driving in the lane next to you. You cannot control what your business competitors do. And you cannot control whether you will win or lose. Gloucester put it this way in Act 4 of *King Lear*: "As flies to wanton boys are we to th' gods / They kill us for their sport."

Okay, it's not always quite that bad. But the only reason that it isn't quite that bad is because you *can* take steps to boost your "luck" and at least position yourself for the win. As Branch Rickey, the great general manager of the Brooklyn Dodgers, famously said, "Luck is the residue of design." Prepare before you roll the dice. If you want to be polite about it, you could say this strategy is about preparation. We prefer to call it what it is: preemptive cheating.

PREPARE TO CHEAT, CHEAT TO PREPARE

We keep hearing business leaders say: "Hope is not a strategy." The phrase is tired, but they're right to say it. We find ourselves telling them, "Luck is not a strategy, either." As the example of Max Malini demonstrates, no successful magician relies on luck. Likewise, no successful entrepreneur, business leader, or creative professional puts herself out there to be the sport of Shakespeare's vision of downright sadistic deities. Success is the product of hard work and meticulous preparation.

Albert Einstein was one of the most innovative thinkers in history, but he long resisted quantum mechanics, with its concept of quantum entanglement, by which one subatomic particle of an entangled pair of subatomic particles appears to influence the behavior of the other particle of the pair, regardless of distance and without any means of communication between the particles. Einstein mocked this concept as "spooky action at a distance," and even more famously, declared, "God does not play dice with the universe." Not too long before he died, however, Einstein began to be won over by quantum mechanics. So maybe we should all prepare ourselves for the possibility that God does play dice with the universe. This being the case, the best move is to gain some control over the reality that lies beyond you by loading the dice.

Don't cheat in response to defeat. Cheat preemptively. A coin flipped one hundred times will probably come up heads fifty times, more or less. If you are betting on heads, weight the coin.

Anyone who makes a living by reliably making magic—whether it's Max Malini or Steve Jobs—cheats preemptively by preparing the universe in some way. In the case of magicians, "success" is defined as the ability to reliably perform effects that non-magicians believe to be impossible. To achieve success so defined requires preparation, which involves first taking control of what you yourself can control. Magicians prepare long before their audience is looking. They relentlessly script, practice, and rehearse. They strain their imaginations to anticipate and plan around every possible mode of failure. Without question, preparation includes practicing to perfect a technique. Even more important, however, preparation is about creating a unique frame of reference that will become reality for the audience. As Einstein demonstrated with his theories of relativity, the reality human beings perceive as *absolute* is in fact *relative*. It is a condition defined by a particular frame of reference. Magicians know this, and so do successful business and political leaders. They all prepare a frame of reference in which they believe their effects, their ideas, their projects, their products, their dreams, and/or their candidacy will gain acceptance. The cheat here is that none of them goes out of their way to explain to the audience, the prospect, the consumer, or the voter that the reality being offered is a relative frame of reference and not the universe beyond the frame.

The quotation "I find the harder I work, the luckier I get" has been attributed to at least three great innovators: Thomas Jefferson, Thomas Edison, and Samuel Goldwyn. Doubtless there are more suspects—not to mention the authors of variations, such as the one attributed to golf champion Gary Player: "The harder I practice, the luckier I get." Maybe an American founding father, our nation's most iconic inventor, a movie mogul, and a champion golfer *all* really did say it—and said it for the simple reason that their experience proved it to be true.

The ancients had a proverbial saying, *Audentes Fortuna Juvat*, which found its way with a slight variation into Virgil's Aeneid (Book X, line 344): Audentis Fortuna Juvat, "Fortune favors the brave" or "Fortune favors the bold." It has since been used as a motto by any number of military organizations. Whatever the motto's effect on martial morale, we believe there is considerable empirical truth to it. We are convinced that those who are brave—or bold—enough to roll up their sleeves and fully engage with the universe have an advantage over those who passively allow the universe to do with them what it will. All other things being equal, aggressively and proactively playing offense brings more success than meekly and reactively playing defense. Bravery and boldness are a big part of a successful magician's success. The audience is attracted to—and juiced by—risk.

The beauty of the *Audentes Fortuna Juvat* approach is that it can be combined with thoughtful preparation. Indeed, there is yet another variation on the Latin proverb which was spoken in 1854 by the remarkable Dr. Louis Pasteur, the inventor of food "pasteurization" (a name, by the way, which others, rather than Pasteur himself, gave to it), along with vaccines for anthrax and rabies. On December 7 of that year, Pasteur was lecturing at the University of Lille and remarked, *"Dans les champs de l'observation le hasard ne favorise que les esprits préparés"*—"In the fields of observation, chance favors only the prepared mind." Since this was first spoken, others have boiled it down to a motto: "Fortune favors the prepared mind."

Pasteur was speaking in the context of experimentation, but what he said applies to any innovator. His subject was "accidental" discovery—scientific epiphanies, revelations. "Did you ever observe to whom such accidents happen?" Pasteur asked his audience. "They happen to those whose minds are prepared to recognize them. It is because in the fields of observation, fortune favors the prepared mind."

In magic, the principle of the prepared mind is both powerful and simple. It is called *"one ahead."* If the magician can somehow move himself just one step, one article, one minute, or one piece of information *ahead* of his audience, he can reframe their frame of reference such that it transforms their reality. Recall the familiar parable, "In the land of the blind, the one-eyed man is king," which is attributed to the Renaissance scholar Desiderius Erasmus, but dates at least conceptually to the New Testament, as in Matthew 15:14: "If a blind man leads a blind man, both will fall into the pit," and in Luke 6:39: "Can a blind man lead a blind man? Will they not both fall into a pit?" The magician is not superhuman, but his imperfect knowledge is the one eye that allows him to stay a step ahead of his relatively blind audience. In short, magicians use the *one ahead* principle to create and operate within a reality different from that of their audience. It allows them to reorganize their own universe, their own stage, their own show, or even their own battlefield on their own terms for their own magical advantage. Within a well-prepared frame of reference, the magician can shift time, information, and objects to a different dimension, which he or she controls.

Magicians also use the *one ahead* principle to prepare their minds not just to create the frame of reference they want, but also to be ready when an effect does not go as intended. As Lance Burton, former Las Vegas headliner and one of the most successful magicians of the last hundred years, puts it, "You can tell how good a magician is by how they look when things go wrong."[44] And since magic is for those brave and bold enough to repeatedly confront the high bar of having to create an alternative reality to our known universe, plenty can and does go wrong. As magician and former Society of American Magicians President Ice McDonald said in an inspirational lecture to fellow magicians, "Murphy hates magic!" In other words, per Murphy's Law, what can go wrong, will—someday—go wrong, *especially* in magic.

PUTTING THE PREEMPTIVE CHEAT TO WORK

Drawing below on magical and athletic inspirations, our argument is that the *one ahead* principle not only allows magicians to change their audience's reality and to preplan what to do when things go wrong, but properly applied, can help businesses and business leaders inject a new kind of strategic proactivity into what they do. In fact, this kind of *one ahead* thinking is among the most powerful crossover lessons from magic to business, particularly in today's overloaded age, when even the best of businesses find themselves in the predicament of perpetually reacting to whatever is coming at them. Getting *one ahead* is a powerful way to regain control of today's unique *leadership challenges.*

GET THE RACKET BACK EARLY

With the principle of preemptive cheating now fully in mind, just how do we go about getting ourselves, our company, and our business *one ahead*? Consider the following masters.

For two years, as he was training for the decathlon in college, David Morey worked in Florida for the legendary Australian-born tennis coach Harry Hopman, a man who could rightfully have claimed the title of the Obi-Wan Kenobi of *one ahead* in tennis. Indeed, Hopman literally wrote the book on how to win tennis matches using superior strategy. The title of his 1975 classic, *Lobbing into the Sun*, gives away one of the best tactics of strategic tennis. If you lob the ball high into the air, aiming at the sun's highest point, you will blind your opponent and disrupt their retaliatory shot. Think tennis is just about two players on a rectangular court? For Hopman, tennis was an occasion to recruit the solar system itself as an ally.

Hopman truly did redefine first Australian tennis and then U.S. and global tennis. In his early years as an athlete, when he was supporting himself as a journalist, he and his wife won four Australian mixed doubles titles, and in 1935, went on to become the first husband-wife team to reach the Wimbledon finals. Overall, Hopman coached twenty-two winning Australian Davis Cup teams, and later, such greats as Lew Hoad, Ken Rosewall, Rod Laver, John Newcombe, Tony Roache, Vitas Gerulaitis, and John McEnroe.

Hopman relished his well-deserved nickname of the Old Fox, and he once flew his entire tennis squad from one Australian city to another after hearing an all-day rain weather forecast for his home city. His objective was to gain one extra day of practice against the local competition. This truly is thinking *one ahead*, but of all the *one ahead* advice Hopman gave to his tennis protégées, Morey most remembers the simple adage he taught his youngest players: "As soon as you read backhand or forehand, get the racket back early...immediately...earlier than at first feels comfortable." With this, Hopman taught future tennis stars, players like John McEnroe, not to react, but to anticipate, to position themselves before they must. Doing this alters reality by reducing the number of variables while also positioning the player to hit a winning shot. "Get the racket back early," he would say again and again.

MAGIC GOES TO WAR

It is September 1856, a period of "tribal unrest" and resistance against French rule in what was then the colony of Algeria. As part of its response, as legend has it, the French government recruits the man to whose name Harry Houdini—born Erich Weisz—paid homage in choosing his own stage name. Jean-Eugène Robert-Houdin, the greatest magician of the nineteenth century, is persuaded to eschew retirement and secretly help put down the native revolt.

The challenge: France needs to suppress popular uprisings being led by holy men, or marabouts (religious teachers), who use traditional fakir tricks such as walking across fire and charming snakes to bolster their claims of being prophets of Allah. French colonial administrators, deciding to fight magic with magic, call on the father of modern magic to outdo individuals they consider politically dangerous spiritual pretenders.

In fact, Robert-Houdin has been preparing for this assignment his entire career without knowing it. He begins a performance before gathered chieftains and their followers by producing bouquets and cannonballs from a hat, throwing coins high into the air to see them appear in a crystal box hoisted over the heads of the onlookers, and miraculously filling an ornate punch bowl with steaming coffee as a gift for the java-loving Arabs. Next, he moves to the psychological plane. Producing a strongbox, the magician asks a volunteer to come onstage and lift the box. In response, a particularly strong man comes up, and in front of all, grabs a ring atop the chest and easily lifts it. Suddenly, Robert-Houdin waves his magic wand and proclaims the strong man "weaker than a woman." Asked to lift the box again, the strong man fails, and fails again and again. Sweating, straining, he simply cannot do it. At last, falling to his knees screaming, he suddenly yanks his hand from the ring and flees the stage, crying out for Allah to save him.

These spectacles, however, are but overtures to even more real magic. Robert-Houdin catches a marked bullet in an apple. Oh…and then he makes an audience member vanish.

But he is still not finished. After the show, Robert-Houdin comes clean to his audience. He admits to them he has used tricks—just as the marabouts do. None of what he or they do is supernatural, he says. (Magicians today know that Robert-Houdin prepared a powerful electromagnet under the stage to keep the strongbox in place, and an electrical shock to the box's handle was all it took to administer the coup de grâce to the unhappy strongman.) Three days after the exhibition, the chieftains honor Robert-Houdin. They praise his art, and they re-pledge their allegiance to France.

Eighty or so years after Robert-Houdin's show and "confession," World War II is raging. Jon Latimer's *Deceptions in War* and David Fisher's *The War Magician* recount how conjurer Jasper Maskelyne taught British military planners how to apply the way magicians think to create a set of tactical illusions that materially contributed to winning the war. Maskelyne's lifelong study of the principles of illusion enabled him to create large-scale deceptions that made military vehicles, aircraft, and buildings virtually invisible to aerial reconnaissance.[45]

The magician took the concept of camouflage to a new level. Working with what Maskelyne calls his "Magic Gang" of fourteen talented assistants, he hid real weaponry and installations from the enemy's prying eyes. Maskelyne was particularly successful with a device called the "Sun Shield." This was a folding contraption that enveloped a tank and made it appear from the air to be just a truck—very much the kind of thing a magician might do in a stage illusion. Along with this, he developed a broom-like gadget that dragged along behind tanks and obscured the tread marks that they make. And he also created light-weight canvas tanks that could be lifted by two men, as well as a fire-resisting cream that aided in firefighting and fire-proofing clothing and equipment.

Later in the war, as part of Operation Fortitude in the run-up to the Normandy landings of D-Day (June 6, 1944), the British and Americans called on filmmakers, set designers, and scenic artists to create new magical deceptions. The Allies understood the Germans occupying France would assume that the British, Americans, and Canadians planned to invade the Continent via the Pas de Calais, the closest point across the English Channel from Dover. With the objective of reinforcing the Germans' very reasonable assumption—*their* perception of reality—the Allies deployed inflatable rubber tanks and other mock vehicles and aircraft in and around Dover. They augmented this deception by creating fake track marks in the ground and manufacturing a continual stream of fake radio communications. This illusion deceived the enemy into believing that their vision of reality was accurate, that the Allies were going to invade at the logical, expected place, far to the north of Normandy.

Much of British deception in World War II was the work of Dudley Clarke, the brilliant officer who headed a deception unit called the A Force. It is surely no accident that Clarke was the grandson of Sidney Clark, an accomplished amateur magician who was one of the founders of Britain's legendary Magic Circle, perhaps the most exclusive magic society in the world.

THE FIRST CASUALTY OF WAR AND THE SEVEN LAWS OF MAGIC

Most authorities believe that the oft-cited maxim "The first casualty of war is the truth" was coined by Hiram W. Johnson, the staunchly isolationist Republican senator from California who said in 1917 or 1918, "The first casualty when war comes is truth." It also happens that the British politician Arthur Ponsonby, 1st Baron Ponsonby of Shulbrede, said something very like this in 1928—"When war is declared, truth is the first casualty"—and in 1758, Samuel Johnson put it rather more elaborately in one of his *Idler* essays: "Among the calamities of war may be jointly numbered the diminution of the love of truth by the falsehoods which interest dictates and credulity encourages."[46]

Whatever the truth is or whoever said it first, the maxim reveals why magic proved to be so effective a weapon in war. For not only is truth the first casualty of war, it is also the first casualty of magic.

Now, we do not mean to say that magic is a lie. In fact, if truth is the first casualty of magic, lying is the second. For what magic reveals is that what people call the truth or *call* a lie depends on their frame of reference at any given time and place. The magical wartime deceptions of Jasper Maskelyne altered neither truth nor falsehood, but greatly impacted perception based on frames of reference created (mostly) by experience and expectation. The non-speaking half of the magical team of Penn & Teller, originally named Raymond Joseph Teller, is one of today's most famous and successful magicians and is widely admired by fellow magicians as among the most creative thinkers in magic. In "Teller Reveals His Secrets," published in *Smithsonian Magazine* (March 2012), and in "Magic Shows," published in *Lapham's Quarterly* (5:3, Summer 2012), Teller writes about what he calls his "Seven Laws of Magic." As you read below the summary of the seven, please take note that none of them has anything to do with truth or lies, and all have everything to do with frames and perceptions.

1. *Exploit pattern recognition*: People grope for patterns, and we magicians take every possible advantage in managing our audience's perceptions.

2. *Make the secret a lot more trouble than the trick seems worth*: Audiences are fooled by something if it involves more time, money, and practice than they would be willing to or expect others to invest.

3. *It is hard to think critically if you are laughing*: A joke eats up valuable mental bandwidth and makes it hard for our audiences to backtrack rationally when they are laughing.

4. *Keep the trickery outside the frame*: Use innocent gestures or objects and move the real method of deception outside the audience's area of focus.

5. *To fool the mind, combine at least two tricks*: For example, when a magician levitates an object and then also passes it through a hoop.

6. *Nothing fools you better than the lie you tell yourself*: Teller recounts the way Omaha's legendary magician, David P. Abbott, fooled people way back in 1907 with a floating ball illusion like the one Teller performs on his Las Vegas stage every night, "After the show, Abbott would absentmindedly leave the ball on a bookshelf while he went to the kitchen for refreshments. Guests would sneak over, heft the ball, and find it was much heavier than a thread could support. So, they were mystified. But the ball

the audience had seen floating weighed only five ounces. The one on the bookshelf was a heavy duplicate, left out to entice the curious."

7. *If you are given a choice, you believe you have acted freely*: The magician and only the magician knows where the effect will end, so unbeknownst to the audience, he or she can organize their own reality to get to this ending point. The magician knows how the effect ends. The audience does not.

These Seven Laws of Magic are the basis of much of the greatest magic performed over the last hundred years or so. They are the basis of Maskelyne's combat deceptions, and they are available to us all as we face today's business challenges. Take, for example, Teller's Second Law of Magic: *Make the secret a lot more trouble than the trick seems worth*. This is at the heart of the opening story of Max Malini's extraordinary *one ahead step* of hiding, over a period of years, a playing card in the linings of various senators' tuxedos to prepare for a moment that just *might* come up somewhere sometime.

Who does such a thing?!

Who, indeed? That is precisely the point. That is what Teller is illuminating. The audience, which may perhaps be saner than some of magic's greatest performers, simply has a very hard time even imagining the remarkable preparation that preceded the witnessed event. Precisely because they cannot imagine such preparation—and who could?—the event appears miraculous. Truth to tell, it is miraculous—as long as you don't venture outside of the common frame of reference and into the extraordinary frame occupied by a Malini.

John McLaughlin recalls a time when he and another U.S. government official were meeting with Carlos Menem, then President of Argentina. During such meetings, it was no secret that McLaughlin was an amateur magician and therefore not unusual for this subject to come up in casual conversation. Sure enough, someone mentioned this, and President Menem asked if McLaughlin could show him a trick. Prior to this, McLaughlin, thinking *one ahead*, had noted that Argentina was having some serious economic problems: a Malini-like opportunity to be ready with an effect involving money, just in case a trick was requested. So, borrowing a $1 bill from someone in the meeting, McLaughlin folded it several times, and upon unfolding it, the $1 bill transformed into a Benjamin—a $100 bill! Jokingly, McLaughlin suggested that Argentina could benefit from this technique. Well, a few weeks later, a cable arrived from the U.S. Embassy in Buenos Aires indicating that President Menem was prepared to offer McLaughlin his Finance Ministry (in jest, of course).

Now, turning a $1 bill into a $100 bill is not something the average person, or the average magician, does spontaneously. It requires preparation. Who goes to such trouble, with no assurance the occasion will even arise? Answer: someone following Teller's Second Law of Magic, in terms of going to more trouble than the average person would contemplate—trouble that might never even pay off—just on the chance that a miraculous opportunity may present itself.

Our friend, the amazing performer and teacher Jeff McBride, who is perhaps the most influential magician of the last fifty years or more, tells a wonderful story about how he spent months learning the power of memorized systems. For example, he trained with the mnemonic frameworks outlined in magician Harry Lorayne's memory books.[47] McBride had just finished a long cruise ship engagement over several weeks, during which he used his downtime to commit the latest *Time* magazine to memory for his performances. A few weeks later, picture McBride being asked to meet with Time Warner's senior executives about a potential show.

While sitting in their waiting room, he takes note of the very same *Time* magazine he'd already committed to memory by sheer chance lying among the other waiting room publications: *National Geographic, People, Fortune, The New Yorker*, and so on.

Talk about a *one ahead* opportunity!

At length, the senior executives summon McBride into the large conference room to discuss his potential performance. The conversation begins. The conversation progresses. Like Malini, McBride bides his time. Unlike Malini, he does not bide it for two years, but for just twenty minutes. Twenty minutes into the meeting, one executive asks if McBride can show them something. *This* is what the magician has been waiting for—but he gives a demonstration of reluctance and demurral that would have made Max Malini proud. At last, he relents—only cautioning his audience that he's certainly "not prepared."

Taking a breath, Jeff McBride asks the execs if they happen to have a magazine handy. Sure enough, one eager suit says, "Of course," and they all follow him out into *their* waiting room to retrieve *their* copy of *Time* magazine, which McBride has casually (in other words, deliberately) tossed on the top of the heap, skewed just enough to draw attention to it. What follows is one of the most astounding displays of mentalism ever seen by any audience anywhere as McBride quotes whole stories and describes photographs he has—presumably—never seen. Without question, he gets his show.

KNOW THE ANSWER

Getting *one ahead* can be valuable in just about any situation because it conveys the impression that you have more control over the world than any ordinary human being enjoys. Essential to getting *one ahead* is rigorous adherence to the time-honored trial lawyer's adage: "Never ask a question to which you don't know the answer," or "Never ask a witness a question if you don't know how she will answer it." It's a matter of preparation and research, getting *one ahead* of where your witness, your audience, or your client or competitor is. Forget asking OJ if he can try on the glove. You know beforehand he will convince the jury that it just doesn't fit.

Like magicians, businesspeople need to use the power of research and the Internet to study and get *one ahead* of their industry's trends, vendors, competitors, and customers, not to mention their customer's network of contacts, employees, and, well, *everyone*. This means being willing to prepare earlier and even to stay *one ahead* of your own marketplace. Take the example of IBM and its legendary CEO, Thomas Watson, Sr. It is the mid-1930s, the Great Depression. As the American economy falls to its knees, amid plummeting sales, bottomed-out stock prices, and vanishing employee retirement accounts, Watson bucks the trend by ensuring that IBM keeps its factories running and its employees working even as sales continue to decline.

Is he too stupid, stubborn, or deluded to cut his losses—as everyone else is doing? Or does he know something the others don't know?

It is the latter—or, more precisely, a version of the latter. For it is not that Watson knows some crucial fact that has been kept secret from everyone else. It is that he sees a connection that no one else sees between a well-known current event and the future of his company. Just as important, he possesses the steel nerves to continue risking a full—and costly—operating level until the time is right for that connection to bear fruit.

Like anyone else who reads a newspaper, Watson knows the monumental Social Security Act is being debated in the halls of Congress. There is no certainty it will pass, but he knows FDR's predecessor, Herbert Hoover, failed to take bold, innovative action after the Crash of 1929, and that this failure cost him reelection. Watson reasons that with the Depression still oppressively bearing down, neither the President nor a majority of Congress will risk losing their jobs. He therefore believes Social Security will indeed become law, and he wants his company to be ready when it does. The unique reality Thomas Watson recognizes is that IBM and IBM alone makes the "business machines" necessary to do the enormous math- and data-intensive work the Social Security Administration will need to do. Passage and implementation of the Social Security Act, when it comes, will be a bonanza for IBM—provided the company is operating at full capacity. Watson is therefore willing to undertake the high-risk, high-endurance work necessary to prepare to be *one ahead* and thereby take advantage of what, to the rest of the world, will appear to be a remarkable stroke of great good luck and wonderful timing for his company. To Watson, however, this "luck" is neither more nor less than the residue of design.

THE MAN WHO GOT *ONE AHEAD* OF THE SOFT SOAP REVOLUTION

It is an early morning in 1977, and inventor and Minnetonka Corporation CEO Robert Taylor is driving to work. His eyes watch the road ahead, even as his imagination drifts to a strange vision. It is like a movie montage featuring messy bars of soap sitting atop sinks, one sink after the other, across our great republic. Oozing, melting, sticking, and getting slimy, dirty, discolored, and gritty. It is an unattractive vision that Taylor wishes to purge not only from his own mind's eye, but from the American landscape itself.

On he drives.

What, he asks himself, what if he could create an entirely new kind of soap, a liquid soap, a hand soap not locked in a cakelike "bar," but obediently waiting to be dispensed from a pump bottle? What if he could create Softsoap?

Well, this is a great idea. Forget that some form of liquid soap was invented in 1865. Taylor has a great idea—except that giants like Procter & Gamble, Armour-Dial, and Colgate Palmolive are bound to treat whatever Taylor does as a mere prototype; they are bound to latch onto it, imitate, and come to market with a similar and cheaper product almost instantly.

Taylor is no pessimist. But the thing is, he's had this experience before. Back in 1964, after founding his own company with nothing more than $3,000 and an idea, Taylor began selling upscale, nicely packaged gift soap. He soon expanded into body lotions, scented candles, bubble baths, everything nice, clean, and luxury priced. In the span of a single spring, Taylor launched no fewer than seventy-eight new products. And his company grew.

But there was trouble in paradise. Taylor noticed that as soon as he innovated a new product, big incumbent competitors were there, nipping at his heels with a cheaper, more widely distributed, yet strikingly similar alternative. They were slip-streaming him, riding in his wake. Clairol and Gillette, for instance, knocked off his hot-selling fruit-scented shampoo.

Taylor did not give up. He put his mad scientist development team to work to create a liquid soap incorporating emollients in a shampoo-like formula. Beginning with larger, more wholesale products, he slowly started to see that this Softsoap product could take hold of a mass market. In the late 1970s, the U.S. soap market totaled about $1.5 billion in annual sales—cornered by big incumbents, such as Dial from Armour-Dial; Ivory and Zest from Proctor & Gamble; Dove from Lever Brothers, the U.S. subsidiary of Unilever; and Irish Spring, made by Colgate-Palmolive, owner of Irish Spring. Softsoap was a little man in a bar fight against a gang of bigger adversaries. Nevertheless, Softsoap sales soared to $39 million in annual sales.

Taylor is still worried. He *knows* the bigger players are coming at him. He can feel their hot breath on the back of his neck, and his experience teaches him they will work hard to imitate, underprice, and crowd Softsoap right out of its own category.

That's when Taylor has his *one ahead* brainstorm.

What if Minnetonka buys virtually all the plastic pumps that suppliers can turn out? He calculates he will have to order and pay for as many as 100 million pumps to preempt and block every competitor. It's not an unprecedented move. Back in the early 1900s, no less than John D. Rockefeller bought the company that made most of the iron rings used to manufacture oil barrels. Suddenly, his competitors in the oil business could not get barrels. And, for that matter, this kind of world-shaping *one ahead* tactic would be employed again in business, this time by Steve Jobs in the early 2000s. Repeatedly, Jobs identified the key components in key devices and then locked up the supply. Take, for example, the flash drive memory used in Apple's iPods. Without a flash drive, there is no iPod—or iPod wannabe.

Find a key bottleneck, an indispensable part, a pinch point in the system, and then jump all over it. Prepare. Preempt. Block. Do these things, and you are *one ahead*. You have changed reality—at least for now, at least long enough to claim that all-important first-entry advantage. The problem is that for a small company, buying 100 million pumps is no small undertaking. In fact, it is a huge risk. No one wants "His Company Died Under the Weight of 100 Million Plastic Pumps" on their tombstone. But it works. Taylor gets *one ahead* by creating a world without pumps—for anyone but him, that is.

This is also a world in which little Minnetonka can hold and expand its leadership position in Softsoap sales—within the rapidly growing liquid soap marketplace his company is itself creating. Innovating at hyperspeed, Taylor wastes no time before he starts spinning off other liquid soap products—for the shower, for the workplace, and for medical facilities. It will take until 1983 before behemoth Procter & Gamble finally overtakes Minnetonka's Softsoap with its Ivory Brand. By then, however, Minnetonka can reposition itself by cutting costs and dropping prices to fight its way back to number one on the strength of its founder brand identity. The company soon reemerges as the top brand, with 36 percent of sales in a $100 million liquid soap marketplace.

Years later, Taylor will introduce "Check-Up," the first anti-plaque toothpaste in the U.S. to be retailed in a pump dispenser rather than a tube. In 1987, he sells his beloved Softsoap to Colgate-Palmolive for $75 million. A few years later, he sells his entire company to a Unilever subsidiary for $376.5 million. You want magic? Robert Taylor takes $3,000 and turns it into $376.5 million. All this requires is changing an ugly vision of soap bars into a paradise of pumps—and then changing the world just enough to make this vision real.

SCRIPT, PRACTICE, REHEARSE

While there are differences in how great magicians prepare versus the best business leaders, the similarities are far more profound.[48] This means borrowing from the great magicians' approach, discipline, and key steps, a topic we will return to in the Sixth Strategy, and moving to a more strategic, proactive, and get-more-control approach: First, develop a script, the precise magic words you will use to move your audience; second, practice exactly what you will do, even the seemingly small and unimportant elements; and third, rehearse, rehearse, and then rehearse some more.

SCRIPT

Scripts change the world by replacing spontaneity with certainty. The truth is that you cannot prepare for a presentation—or a show—before you have a script. This does not always have to be a fully composed narrative. In many cases, it is even more effective simply to outline the three key points you want to make. We call this the power of the "3 x 5 Card," which David Morey and his business partner Scott Miller developed for every political campaign on which they consulted. This 3 x 5 Card is the simple summary of the three key messages a political candidate—or magician or CEO—must deliver to win a campaign. The communicator must make all three of these key points, whether they are speaking for thirty seconds or three hours.

Another key communications tool is the "Stump Speech." This is an eight- to fifteen-minute version of the candidate's (magician's, or CEO's) 3 x 5 Card. It is a speech defining who they are, why voters should support them, and what the future will look like under their leadership. As powerful as these messaging tools are, simply reading from a 3 x 5 Card or a Stump Speech script is not sufficient to frame reality as you want reality framed. Both forms of communication need to be internalized and memorized, so that the message becomes second nature—*your* second nature. Only this level of authenticity makes for a presentation persuasive enough to seem like a vision of reality. Work diligently at this. No matter how exhausted you may be, you can work through an internalized Stump Speech at any time and under any conditions. David Morey's clients—from former South Korean President Kim Dae Jung to U.S. President Barack Obama—all used some form of a 3 x 5 Card and Stump Speech. These formed the spine of their communications.

What is true in politics and business regarding internalized 3 x 5 Card and Stump Speech messaging is true in the world of entertainment. The late great George Carlin always seemed like a fresh and spontaneous performer. But review YouTube videos of his shows, and you see something amazing. Carlin says almost the same exact thing at each stop across any one tour. This is because his performances always begin as a script. He writes it. He refines it. He memorizes it. And he comes to understand it so deeply that it becomes a part of him. When he performs, the internalized script materializes as the reality he creates for his audience. Watch *any single* performance in a tour, and you will be convinced that Carlin is making it all up as he goes along. It is immediate in its impact. Watch a *series* of his performances on any one tour, and you discover that what he presents every time is an incredibly well-rehearsed show.

Magicians, the best of them, work virtually 100 percent from a script—allowing them the luxury of going off script to react and extemporize, only to return to the planned spin of their communication. As Eugene Burger argues, "You can't practice before you have a script." After the conceptual development of a new piece of magic, the first and most critical step is to create a script. Whether you are a magician, a consultant, or a CEO, do not make the mistake of dashing off a few notes and calling the result a script. Notes are an important means of internalizing your thoughts, but essentially, they are neither more nor less than a record of the very spontaneity on which you are trying to get "*one ahead*." A first draft of a script is a little cleaner record of this spontaneity. But the truth is, as Eugene Burger always said, *good* writing is *rewriting*. Indeed, the opportunity to rewrite is one of the most important sources of the timeless power of the written word. How often do you wish you had the opportunity to do something over or make a spur-of-the-moment remark wittier? When you create a script, you have this opportunity—and you have it over and over again. The sequence of writing and rewriting lets you remake and redo reality until it's perfect. And who *wouldn't* take advantage of that opportunity?

PRACTICE

Having written and rewritten a script, the second step is to *practice*—as in piano. The concert pianist spends many hours a day practicing to achieve the realistic appearance of spontaneity. Basic techniques are worked and reworked. There are many possible ways to move the fingers from one set of notes to the next. And the diligent pianist practices to find the *one* way that is best for what she wants to achieve.

For the magician, practice involves the secret stuff the audience does not see. For the business leader, practice involves the preparation, staging, and blocking that Apple CEO Steve Jobs worked on so compulsively before every introduction of every new blockbuster product—those apparently spontaneous presentations in which the most important revelation almost always came at the end and was introduced by a phrase that became something of a Jobs trademark: "And one more thing...." Nothing is more spontaneous than an afterthought—especially an afterthought so meticulously rehearsed that it really does look and sound spontaneous.

Learn from Tony Clark, one of the world's top magicians, magic producers, and magic directors. He employs something he calls the "Rehearsal Ritual 100." He developed it with the infinitely meticulous Tony Slydini, and it is a complete strategy for achieving what could be called "performance preparedness." A master magic teacher and one of the greatest sleight-of-hand performers magic has ever known, Slydini would, for his lucky students, break down his own magical effects step by step, and teach each step, one at a time. He insisted that one step be mastered flawlessly before the student could go on to the next. His students never performed an effect in public until each step became seamlessly flawless.

After each teaching session with Slydini, Clark spent hours practicing. First, he visualized every step-by-step move. Next—immediately, while it was all fresh in his mind—he began his own Rehearsal Ritual 100, practicing for a minimum of four hours, performing each step at least one hundred times until perfect, and then integrating and doing the full routine at least eighteen times. Clark's goal was to practice each step, or "move," at least one hundred times, because, he reasoned, if you do something one hundred times, it becomes second nature to you. A key to his practice sessions was breaking them into manageable chunks.[49]

REHEARSE

Practice is not the same as *rehearsal*, which is the third and separate step beyond scripting and practicing. The greatest magicians and performers rehearse the reality they want to create. In contrast to practicing, this means running through their entire show, live, stopping for nothing as if it were the real show. And the best magicians record each rehearsal on video and review the results ruthlessly.

Winston Churchill was prime minister of Great Britain and not a magician, but he also followed the scripting, practicing, rehearsing sequence, progressively sharpening and refining both his language and his delivery.

Script, practice, rehearse. What could possibly go wrong?

When President Bill Clinton began his 1993 address to a Joint Session of Congress—live, on national TV—to promote his health care plan, he quickly realized the wrong speech has been loaded into the teleprompter. Never mind that it took aides an interminable seven minutes to load up the correct speech, the President chose to wing it. Having been deeply involved in reviewing drafts of the speech, Clinton knew exactly where he was heading, and he extemporized the opening for seven minutes until the problem was fixed. Indeed, some felt Clinton was at his best when he extemporized without a script. Judge for yourself at: https://www.youtube.com/watch?v=cJ56eOT3YA0. (Link active at publication).

Watch yourself. It seems self-evident that speaking is a verbal medium. In fact, audience research shows that a mere 7 percent of a speaker's credibility and persuasiveness has anything to do with the actual words spoken. A whopping 38 percent comes from how the voice is used, and most of a speaker's impact, 55 percent, is pure body language.[50] Each of these elements—words, voice, and body language—can be trained with video workshops, either self-conducted or led by experts. In our experience, the average improvement in performance that results from work with video is not small. Typically, it is in the 20 to 30 percent range. Video training confers a powerful, indeed magical, advantage on business leaders, especially given research showing that these days, a company's brand and reputation are 49 percent attributable to the way its leader communicates.

Why not just practice in front of a mirror?

Real time is the enemy. In real time, we tend to see what we want to see. As we go through the motions, we look for affirmation more than we hunt for problems. We are inside ourselves, looking out. In contrast to looking in a mirror, watching a recording is observing history, accomplished fact. It is, therefore, much harder to lie to ourselves—or even to unconsciously misperceive. The video camera is a magician's secret weapon, and it is ruthlessly, relentlessly honest, showing us where we "flash" or expose something and where we are awkward. Video shows us how to smooth out our miracles.

Prepare your "outs." Bill Clinton survived—indeed, triumphed over—his teleprompter snafu because he came before his audience with an "out," namely the ability to extemporize on a subject with which he had made himself very familiar. In the world of magic, some seventy-seven years ago, Charles H. Hopkins published a seventy-nine-page pamphlet that has found a secret place on the bookshelves of the world's greatest magicians. Indeed, most have tucked the best parts into the recesses of their memory. As Hopkins saw it, rehearsal was the ideal time to prepare and learn your outs.

Published in 1940, *"OUTS" Precautions and Challenges: For Ambitious Card Workers* was written out of a deep understanding that all magicians operate along the very narrow and very high wire of doing the impossible each time they perform. No wonder "Murphy hates magic!" If something can go wrong, it will go wrong—in magic. In fact, something goes wrong in *most* magic performances. Mishap comes with the territory. So, if—or, rather, when—things go wrong, Hopkins counsels, don't panic and don't confess. Anticipate mishaps by planning and rehearsing your "outs," so the audience will not notice you did not intend to go where you just went. Remember, *your* conception of your reality gives you a huge advantage over the members of your audience, who know nothing of *your* reality until they see it.

Like the business leader making a pitch, the magician knows what the ending should look like. The audience does not. Make the most of your advantage. Recall Teller's Seventh Law of Magic: *If you are given a choice, you believe you have acted freely.* Only you, the magician, knows where the effect will end. This means that you can organize your own reality to get to this ending point. You and you alone possess the map.

Hopkins makes it his business to "pre-think" every possible way a given card effect or mind-reading miracle can go south. He reveals ways to turn each mishap back into the miracle you hoped it would be. For a magician, Hopkins' pamphlet is a book of nightmares: What if you lose control of the card? What if the spectator forgets her card? What if the spectator decides he doesn't want to tell you his card? What if you miss your "force" on the spectator and fail to make her pick the card you want her to choose? What if the spectator challenges you? Heckles you? Or what if you, the mind reader, draw a blank at precisely the wrong moment?

Hopkins offers an architecture of recovery and triumph that should be the envy of every business crisis manager and consultant. He plans, trains, practices, and rehearses each step along the way, determined to be ready for anything Murphy throws at him.

Years ago, David Morey performed at the Magic Castle before what started out as a small crowd, but quickly became a large crowd, hovering around a close-up table. At the time, he was just returning to magic. He was working on a "Spectator Cuts the Aces" effect when to his unspoken horror, the spectator—actually, the magician—missed the fourth ace to botch the climax of the routine.

But Morey had prepared his luck and came equipped with an out, a quick change for the errant three of spades to the ace of clubs. And the audience absolutely loved the "fix." They smiled knowingly: The magician *must* have been heading here all along! In fact, the reaction was so strong that today, Morey goes out of his way to miss the fourth ace. In using his out, he produced a more magical ending.

If you ever go to see the very top magicians in Las Vegas, take note that some of their funniest or most effective moments derive from something that goes "wrong" in their show and that they fix magically with an "out" or even a joke. The idea is that magicians and business leaders alike need to practice not just for success, but also for failure. Do this, and you will be *one ahead*.

The best outs are those you prepare for nightmare scenarios. All magicians have nightmares about losing their luggage—and, backing these up, they have real-world war stories about actually losing their luggage. Picture this: You have nothing, everything is lost, but you must put ninety minutes of performance together for 500 people on a cruise ship. You have the next two hours to make it happen. The best magicians really do practice losing their luggage. For example, they study a wonderful presentation by the extraordinary Max Maven, one of history's greatest mentalists, featured in our Seventh and Eighth Strategies. Max's presentation shows magicians and mentalists step by step how to buy what you need at a convenience store two hours before you must step on stage, and how to assemble, practice, and refine extraordinary mind-reading effects with everyday objects. Some magicians even keep "ninety minutes" inside a small plastic bag inside the carry-on luggage your airline simply cannot lose. Others apply the so-called "Starbucks rule" for presenters. If you had to, could you go to Starbucks to deliver the presentation that corporate terrorists just stole from your computer bag? In other words, do you have the emergency or "guerrilla" version of this presentation on a sheet of paper, on an index card, or inside your head? Just in case, could you deliver the very basic version of this presentation without your fancy computer or demo reel or PowerPoint...and still make your case?

FORTUNE FAVORS THE PREPARED

Remember the great Pasteur: "Fortune favors the prepared." In today's hyper-competitive and swiftly shifting marketplace, prepare internally, script, practice, and rehearse. Don't forget to put together your outs. Do this, and you will put yourself one ahead. If you are prepping for the meeting as you ride up the elevator, it's too late to be one ahead, and that means that you will be stuck with everyone else's reality. Good luck with that.

THE SIXTH STRATEGY
REDIRECT YOUR AUDIENCE

"Start the fire in the east; attack in the west."

—Sun Tzu

S cene: *This really happened[51] (http://www.youtube. com/watch?v=x5lGwhbvANo; http://www.youtube.com/ watch?v=FW6oQZc_c80). Tony Slydini, born Quintino Marucci in Italy in 1900, learned the rudiments of magic from his amateur magician father. The boy was never much interested in grand props and great stages, but focused instead on the proscenium within his own mind. Early on, he mastered a sleight of hand technique founded on precise timing and so-called misdirection. In fact, it was* <u>direction</u> *that Slydini practiced, honed, and perfected, creating a style of close-up magic that was entirely new.*

Traditional effects relied on theatrical conventions, including a certain distance between the magician and the audience. Traditional magicians, accordingly, developed a repertoire of grand, if often stagey, gestures. Not Slydini. His magic invited close inspection. It never sought to evade reality, but to embrace it. Nor did he create about himself a phony aura of wizardly remoteness from his audience. Instead, he welcomed them, inviting them to move in closer and closer. He eschewed rigidly set programs, in which the scale of effects typically rises in a crescendo of you-ain't-seen-nuthin'-yet showmanship. Instead, he engaged with his audience, apparently following their lead while directing them to inspire the direction of his show.

All the while, Slydini was very quietly very much in charge. Within the intimate sphere of the reality he shared with his audience, coins appeared and disappeared, paper balls floated over the head of an oblivious spectator. The TV talk show host Dick Cavett, himself an avid amateur magician (just like his friend Johnny Carson), was utterly astounded when Slydini performed on his program. And when Cavett asked the legendary Dai Vernon if any magician out there could still fool him, the sleight-of-hand master reflexively answered: "Slydini."

The great Tony Slydini performed all kinds of magic, but he is best known for what the public calls sleight of hand or close-up magic. Close-up typically uses the simplest and most familiar of props—the metaphors of mundane reality itself—to disrupt the status quo of our perceptions. At its best, sleight of hand is based on the intimate bond a master close-up artist creates with an audience, whose members collaborate in the performance even as the magician subtly directs them throughout. If David Copperfield practices magic on the level of a great choral symphony, the likes of Tony Slydini and the legendary Dai Vernon performed string quartets, the chamber music of the mind. By getting inside heads, they guided their audiences to "think different."

This phrase—*think different*—is, of course, associated with the late Steve Jobs, who along with the brilliant TBWA/Chiat Day and Lee Clow and his team, ultimately worked on and approved it for a 1997 ad campaign featuring a montage of such figures as Albert Einstein, Bob Dylan, Dr. Martin Luther King, Jr., John Lennon and Yoko Ono, Buckminster Fuller, Thomas Edison, Muhammad Ali, Ted Turner, Maria Callas, Mohandas Gandhi, Amelia Earhart, Alfred Hitchcock, Martha Graham, Jim Henson, Frank Lloyd Wright, and Pablo Picasso. The voiceover narrator—originally Jobs himself, but actor Richard Dreyfuss in the version that finally aired—identifies them as "the crazy ones, the misfits, the rebels, the troublemakers, the round pegs in the square holes, the ones who see things differently. They're not fond of rules, and they have no respect for the status quo.... They change things, they push the human race forward.... While some may see them as the crazy ones, we see genius. Because the people who are crazy enough to think they can change the world are the ones who do."[52]

The campaign was brilliant, but the two-word phrase was genius. Like close-up magic, it depends on the most intimate of details. Casual critics carp that Think different is bad English. Think is a verb, which of course calls for an adverb—*differently*—and not the adjective Jobs supported and approved. What they miss is the magic of the exhortation. Jobs is not telling his audience to "think differently," but to think *different*. He is redirecting them from a mere thought process to an act of conjuring. "Different," in his two-word sentence, is not the adjective it is *supposed* to be, but the noun Jobs wants it to be. He is proposing to his audience that they use their brains to conjure up—like a magician pulling a rabbit from a silk top hat—*different*, a new reality, a new reality on a par with what Einstein created, or Picasso, or Maria Callas....

What is more, Steve Jobs just happens to be in the business of creating tools that empower people to *think different*. In the case of the Mac, *different* was the ability to manipulate a visual (graphical) reality directly and viscerally, using the physical motions of hand on mouse, finger on button, instead of indirectly and cerebrally, by means of arcane words and symbols typed on a keyboard. Later, in the case of the iPhone, it was the ability to make anyone anywhere in the world present to you wherever you happen to be at the time—by touching a small glass screen framed by an aluminum bezel.

MAGIC USED TO BE EASIER

Every great magician invites us to think different. When Max Malini cut into the jacket lining of a United States Senator to pull the one card in the universe that was the right card, he persuaded onlookers that the laws of physics pertaining to time and space—not to mention the laws of common sense and God Himself—constituted a reality that could be *thought different*, that is, changed utterly and profoundly through the mere will of the magician. In their own way, Jesus, Moses, Muhammad, and Buddha each invited the world to *think different*. Whether for a magician or a holy man, achieving this was never easy. But it was easier the less an audience knew and used technology. Jeff Bezos has not attempted the biblical feat of turning water into wine, but he has provided a vital link in the handheld technology that allows anyone with a finger, or a voice, to order a bottle, a case, or a cellar of wine from almost anywhere in the world.

To the concern or even despair of magicians everywhere, again, novelists Arthur C. Clarke wrote, "Any sufficiently advanced technology is indistinguishable from magic."[53] And this is perfectly true—to the degree that most people can explain neither what the magician does nor what the electrical engineer or software developer does. In fact, we understand there are specific sets of human beings—magicians and technicians—who know how to do magic and technology, respectively. We may not share in their knowledge, but we know it exists and that there are people who know how to use it. Even in the absence of our possessing the knowledge to perform magic or create a killer app, the presence of this knowledge in others is sufficient to attenuate both the magic of magic and the magic of technology.

Let us just agree, then, that the progress of technology has not rendered magic obsolete. It has just upped the ante by complicating the magician's task. Today, the magician must persuade her audience that her effects are not the product of technology. In other words, she must convince them that the different reality she presents comes from her "supernatural" abilities. Indeed, in an important sense, the everyday miracles of today's technology create a new frame of reference that enhances the performance of magic. While others must rely on readily available technology to communicate with some distant person, the magician can do so without any technology at all. The person who apparently possesses the powers of an iPhone within himself is a magician indeed.

The six-shooter revolver that Samuel Colt perfected and mass-marketed in the nineteenth century was dubbed the "great equalizer." At one time, a strong man could be counted on to defeat a weak man. A weak man with a gun can defeat a much stronger unarmed man. Put a Colt in the hands of both the strong man and the weak man, and their chances of victory become pretty much equal. Introduce Superman into the equation, and the Colt become irrelevant.

Of course, Superman is a product of comic book fiction. But our civilization is built on any number of men and women who are capable of consistently performing in ways that elevate them to the status of Supermen and Wonder Women. Steve Jobs, again, was an example. He always put himself out front of the technology he presented. Like a skilled magician, he projected himself as the master of all his company invented. As a marketer, he never served the technology. He commanded the technology, and his offer to consumers was a share in that command. Even more, he never married himself to any one product. He was not selling the Mac, the iPod, the iPhone, but the promise of these and even greater technology merchandise to come. He was selling a share in future miracles, and he did it with such conviction and credibility that a large fraction of the consumer public became loyal followers who were willing to line up for hours in advance for the privilege of being among the first to acquire a new item—even though they well knew this item was to be mass-produced in virtually inexhaustible quantities.

Envious rival marketers regarded this as "marketing magic." And there is more truth to this assessment than they know. As discussed, recent studies reveal that 49 percent of a company's brand and reputation emanate from the CEO.[54] In the case of Steve Jobs, this may well have been even higher. Make no mistake, Jobs launched great, truly innovative products into the market. The ad industry giant David Ogilvy said, "Nothing kills a bad product faster than good advertising." He was not quite right. Our version? "Nothing kills a bad product faster than great marketing." This said, the converse is also true: "Nothing kills a good product faster than poor marketing."

It is the job of a CEO to ensure that the company creates great products, and it is also the CEO's job to direct the attention of consumers to the same place that the best magicians direct the attention of their audience: namely, just where they want it to be.

Like Steve Jobs, magicians with sufficient skill to get into our mental space invite us to *think different*. They sell their illusions in the same way that master marketers sell their firm's wares. They convey *relevant differentiation*—the quality of a product, service, or business that combines innovation with relevance to the needs, desires, and aspirations of the consumer—and that separates it uniquely from that consumer's perceived competitive set.

The real trick here is to recognize that not all innovation is relevant to consumers' needs. Thomas Edison's first patent was for an electric vote recorder in 1868. The invention was a technical success, but a commercial failure. Edison invented it with the intention of selling it to local, state, and federal legislative bodies, having simply assumed these customers would welcome a quick and efficient way of recording the many votes they took in their governmental work. When Edison sought to market the device in the best way he knew how—by demonstrating it—he quickly discovered the very last thing legislators wanted was a quick and efficient means of voting. Instead, they needed the laborious and antiquated process of the roll call vote, which provided ample time for last-minute cajoling and the marshaling of desired votes. From this initial "failure," Edison drew a valuable lesson. He learned that while innovation is *necessary* to the inventor's trade, it is not *sufficient*. No innovation is successful unless consumers find it relevant. Edison decided he must take steps to determine the existence of a market before embarking on his next invention.

The interface separating *crazy* from *genius* is membrane-thin. In 1973, Arthur Fry, a new-product developer for 3M, attended a talk given by another 3M scientist, Spencer Silver, who in 1968 had developed an adhesive with an unusual molecular structure that was strong enough to adhere to a wide variety of objects, yet weak enough to allow a temporary bond. After five years, no one had been able to come up with a commercial use for the product. After all, adhesives were marketed for their permanence and strength. And Silver's breakthrough appeared to be a classic instance of innovation without relevance. Had Silver relentlessly tried to force this product to market, he would, at some point, have been deemed crazy—or, at least, unemployable. Instead, he put it back on the shelf, until he talked about it in 1973. It just so happened that Fry sang in his church choir—and he marked his place in the hymnal with loose scraps of paper, which, of course, frequently fell out. It occurred to Fry that Silver's temporary adhesive might be the answer to his prayers. He asked Silver for a sample of the adhesive, and applied it to one edge of his bookmarks, since he did not want the exposed portion of the paper to be sticky. The

Post-it note was born, and Silver's innovation found its relevance in a spectacularly marketable product.

For magicians, dexterity and a library of magic books are helpful, but the ability to manipulate cards and objects is not enough to create a "market," an audience. The successful magicians prepare and work from an internal script that is crafted to control the dialogue within the imagination of their audience. They look for ways to be different and stand out, and to ensure that all the small elements of their effect, act, and show all move in the same magical direction. A great magician does not push or prod the audience. Through a well-crafted step, he directs them to precisely the mental place he needs them to go. Like great magicians, skilled communicators and leaders in business, politics, education, and other creative fields internalize their scripts for a similar purpose. Their objective is to create a frame of reference that corresponds to their vision of reality and then to direct their audience into this reality.

COMMUNICATIONS DISCIPLINE

Here we present the three key elements of *communications discipline*. Each is critical to winning any high-stakes campaign, whether it is for election to the office of President of the United States, converting a prospect into a customer, or transforming an audience into believers in magic:

1. **Control the Dialogue**: Put to work your own well-developed, memorized, and internalized script.

2. **Focus Where You Want Your Audience to Focus:** Direct, redirect, or misdirect your audience's attention to your *own* answer to the most important question in business today, namely: *How are you different, special, and better than anyone else?*

3. **Remember, Everything Communicates:** Align even the smallest details in the *same* direction, so that each focuses, reinforces, and leverages your key themes and essential message.

CONTROL THE DIALOGUE

When David Morey delivers a keynote, he sometimes begins by saying he will give the audience a single word. Next, he asks the audience to clear their minds. Then he asks that, after he gives them his word, they yell out the first word that comes to mind.

"Volvo," Morey calls out.

After a short pause, three thousand yell back in almost perfect unison: "SAFETY!"

How does this happen? How, over many decades, does a company get people who are not even their own customers to focus on one word—in the case of Volvo, "Safety!" As brand expert Al Ries advises, "If you want to build a brand, you must focus your efforts on owning a word in the prospects' mind. A word nobody else owns."

Go back in time to Sweden, 1940. Nearly eighty years ago, Volvo was already obsessed with safety as a key point of difference in the auto marketplace. Jump to 1958, and Volvo is inventing the three-point seat belt. The company even shares this breakthrough technology with its competitors, so strongly does Volvo believe in its importance. Later, through the 1960s, when no one is even wearing seatbelts, Volvo is still all about safety. Steadily, the market begins to catch up to the company. Volvo *believes* in safety. This is no magic trick, no slick advertising slogan. It is the company's core ethos and focus.

In the late 1980s, Volvo released a series of TV ads in which crash-test dummies assumed animate humanoid life to demonstrate to us all how

Volvo was taking ownership of safety. In one ad, a "family" of dummies climbs into a Volvo 340, buckles in, turns the ignition, shifts into gear, and drives through a third-story plate-glass window, so that the car lands nose down on the concrete below. The vehicle settles back on its wheels, the dummies unbuckle, open the doors, and walk out. *Voiceover*: "The Volvo 340—tested by dummies, driven by the intelligent."

Step forward to the 1990s, when Volvo continues to define the word safety to its own industry by introducing airbags and side airbags. Now move into the twenty-first century, today, as the company continues, even across uneven sales and new ownership, to set industry standards and win Insurance Institute of Highway Safety (IIHS) awards. Across all these decades, Volvo's focus is relentless: *"No one should die or be seriously injured in a Volvo."* It is a focus not on messaging alone, but on the creation of each new iteration of the product. Here are Volvo's firsts:

1944 Safety cage

1944 Laminated windshield

1957 Anchor points for 2-point front safety belts

1958 Anchor points for 2-point rear safety belts

1959 3-point front safety belts standard

1964 First rear-facing child safety seat prototype tested

1966 Crumple zones front and rear

1966 Safety door locks

1969 Inertia reel safety belts

1971 Reminder safety belts

1972 3-point safety belts—rear

1972 Rear-facing child safety seat

1974 Multistage impact-absorbing steering column

1974 Bulb integrity sensor, to warn of burned-out and non-functioning lights

1975 Braking system with a stepped-bore master cylinder that supplies more brake fluid when the driver hits the brake hard, as in a panic stop

1978 Child safety booster cushion

1982 "Anti-submarining" protection, to prevent passengers from being propelled under their lap belt in a crash

1986 Three-point safety belt—center-rear seat

1990 Integrated child safety cushion in center-rear seat

1991 Side Impact Protection System

1991 Automatic height-adjusting safety belts

1992 Reinforced rear seats in station wagon models

1995 Integrated child safety cushion—outer rear seats

1997 Roll Over Protection System

1998 Whiplash Protection System

1998 Inflatable Curtain airbags

2001 Volvo safety concept car

2002 Roll Stability Control

2003 New front structure called Volvo Intelligent Vehicle Architecture

2003 Rear seat belt reminders

2003 Intelligent Driver Information System

2003 Inauguration of Volvo's Traffic Accident Research Team in Bangkok

2004 Blind Spot Information System

2005 Door-mounted inflatable curtain

2006 Personal Car Communicator (PCC) remote control

2006 Collision warning with brake support

2007 Power parking brake

2007 Driver Alert Control (DAC)—alerts the driver when driving
becomes inconsistent (as when driver begins to fall asleep)

2009 City Safety—automatically stops car at speeds below 19 mph
(31 km/h) if obstruction is detected in front of car

2010 Pedestrian Detection with auto brake

2012 Pedestrian airbag

How can you achieve the level of control over the dialogue that companies like Volvo create? How do you control the dialogue in your own business and your own marketplace, or within your own organization? How do you get people focused on the *one word* that sums up your brand?

In the world of magic, building on the "Script, Practice, and Rehearse" sequence presented in the previous strategy, our colleague, philosopher, magician, and current Dean of the McBride Magic & Mystery School, Dr. Larry Hass, details in his superb new book, *Inspirations: Performing Magic with Excellence*, the steps successful magicians use to take a new piece of magic from "the cradle to the stage":

The first step is to find or create excellent material. Just as a company needs superior products, services, or strategic focus, a performer needs superb effects to transport his audiences.

The second step is to practice the parts. Work through the separate business pieces, the mechanics, displays, metaphors, just as magicians master the individual sleights or moves in an effect. Steve Jobs spent weeks achieving this mastery before every new major product launch. Frédéric Chopin was always a meticulous craftsman, but he lavished the most painstaking attention on the four solo piano works he called "Impromptus." Chopin understood that achieving the effect of impromptu spontaneity required careful thought, brilliant composition, a great deal of rewriting and revision, and endless hours of preperformance rehearsal.

The third step is to create good words. Unless you are a super-rare, touched-by-the-finger-of-God exception, again, you must thoroughly script your own "3x5 Card" messaging and "Stump Speech" to lead and to do so effectively. When you have the good words in place, internalize them as what they are: What you and your company believe, an expression of your leadership values, an explanation of how you are relevant and different in your marketplace, and how your organization defines the future of its industry.

The fourth step is to memorize your good words. Business leaders, like magicians, must internalize their good words so they truly own them. The script must become part of you, accessible and within your grasp 24/7, no matter how exhausted you are, what new pressures you face, or how many times you've repeated the same words.

The fifth step is to rehearse the whole thing. To ensure that the whole emerges as greater than the sum of its parts, the entire presentation or performance or event must be rehearsed in dress-rehearsal fashion, as if it is the real live show. Such rehearsal must be repeated over and over again... until it has the appearance of spontaneity.

The sixth step is on with the show. Unless you give the speech or present the performance again and again, you are not ready. Ronald Reagan, Barack Obama, and Donald Trump all gave stump speeches over several decades in each of their careers both inside and outside of politics. Note that one of the greatest magicians of the last hundred years, Lance Burton, always answers the question *Who is the best magician?* the same way: "The one who performs the most." Truth be told, the more you perform, the better performer you become.

The seventh step is to go back and revise the work at previous stages as necessary. Whether it is a product launch, an articulation of a major strategic shift, or the framing of the company's new vision, you need to work through every part to master the whole. This is what great magicians do. Their secret: follow all these steps, and the magic will *look* easy and impossible.[55]

FOCUS WHERE YOU WANT YOUR AUDIENCE TO FOCUS

Let's dive deeper into how a marketer can employ message discipline to direct or redirect consumers' attention—exactly as magicians focus the attention of their audience—to *precisely* where they want it to be. As the great Chinese military strategist Sun Tzu advised: "Start the fire in the east; attack in the west." Or drawing from a more recent source, director-producer George Lucas: "Always remember, your focus determines your reality."

If you've seen Martin Scorsese's 2013 movie *The Wolf of Wall Street*, you are familiar with super-salesman Jordan Belfort, who in the late 1980s founded his own brokerage firm, which he called Stratton Oakmont—a name he pulled out...of thin air. Stratton Oakmont's product was every penny stock and questionable investment floating around the marketplace. And the core of Stratton Oakmont was its super-secret *Training Manual*. Here is what the manual says about qualifying your prospect and rebutting whatever objections the prospect offers:

QUALIFYING CALL...

"...Very simply, sir, with your permission, all I would like to do is introduce myself and my firm, forward you a complimentary issue of our

monthly research report, and at a later date, perhaps get back to you with our latest recommendations. Fair enough?"

HAPPY WITH BROKER...

"...That's great. Believe me, we're not looking to run your portfolio. Stratton Oakmont is a boutique investment banking firm making only a handful of recommendations a year. I am only asking that when I share an idea that can make you money, you would have an open ear. Fair enough?"

BROTHER/FRIEND/COUSIN...

"Don't let your personal relationships interfere with your ability to make money in the market. Stratton Oakmont makes only a handful of recommendations a year, so you won't be hearing from me too often. Very simply, when we're moving on our next investment opportunity, I'd like to be able to call you and run it by you. Fair enough?"[56]

Fair enough? You get the idea. Or do you? Reflect on how you feel when you read these excerpts. We find ourselves wanting to agree with the imagined "Stratton Oakmont" salesperson on the other end of the phone. In fact, these scripts are designed to trick the prospect—and not in a good way. By relentless focus, they move the prospect back to where the salesperson wants them to focus. To quote Al Koran, one of history's greatest mentalists, "It's the words that fool."

And these Training Manual words were designed to fool—again, not in a good way. Specifically, their objective is to redirect, or *pivot*. By contrast, as we argue repeatedly, the world's greatest magicians, including Al Koran, are not out to fool or trick people, but rather to transport them, to entertain them, and, at their very best, to take them to a place of bigger dreams. But there is nevertheless a valuable lesson to be learned in the *pivot*. During 2016-2017, both David Morey and John McLaughlin made many appearances on national cable shows, commenting on current events, crises, and the latest political improbability. As Morey began preparing for such appearances by working with a former journalist and top media coach, he was fascinated to learn how compressed and accelerated the television medium has become over recent years. "Bill O'Reilly will interrupt you within the first five seconds if your opening isn't strong," advised the media coach. The lesson: You need to *pre*-think and even *pre*-practice the three key points you'll make, as well as your sound bite—ideally pithy, insightful, and memorable—and be ready to pivot to the answer you want to give. Always be ready to pivot. Be prepared to bridge to the three points you've *pre*-prepared. Henry Kissinger often asked reporters gathered around him at State Department briefings in the 1970s, "Do you have any questions today for my three answers?"

When he was advising the 2008 Obama campaign, David Morey often worked to pull the strategy toward an insurgent "we're-still-behind" mentality. By resisting over-confidence, he worked to focus the campaign's energy on striving to control the dialogue at every turn, in order to control every kind of definition the campaign could possibly control. In early 2008, however, the campaign moved into the kind of crisis that looked familiar to Morey. It was the kind of crisis that makes or breaks a candidate, along with his or her election. Besieged by negative media concerning Obama's former and beyond-impolitic minister, Reverend James Wright, the campaign headquarters in Chicago was suddenly infected by a kind of institutional cautiousness and hunker-down-for-the-hurricane mentality. Amid the newly prevailing attitude of "let's-just-wait-it-out," one single person emerged with a very different approach. His instinct was to pivot straight into the headwinds.

That insurgent dissenter from his own campaign was Barack Obama.
He wrote—personally wrote—and delivered one of the greatest speeches
in a lifetime of great speeches, in which he demonstrated the power of
an honest pivot—not a misdirection, but a redirection, the kind that
transcends. On March 18, 2008, in Philadelphia, candidate Obama offered:

> I am the son of a black man from Kenya and a white woman from
> Kansas. I was raised with the help of a white grandfather who
> survived a Depression to serve in Patton's Army during World War II
> and a white grandmother who worked on a bomber assembly line at
> Fort Leavenworth while he was overseas. I've gone to some of the best
> schools in America and lived in one of the world's poorest nations.
> I am married to a black American who carries within her the blood
> of slaves and slaveowners—an inheritance we pass on to our two
> precious daughters. I have brothers, sisters, nieces, nephews, uncles,
> and cousins, of every race and every hue, scattered across three
> continents, and for as long as I live, I will never forget that in no other
> country on earth is my story even possible. It's a story that hasn't
> made me the most conventional candidate. But it is a story that has
> seared into my genetic makeup the idea that this nation is more than
> the sum of its parts—that out of many, we are truly one...."[57]

Senator Barack Obama's courageous approach to redirecting the debate
recalled the speech Senator John Kennedy had made nearly fifty years
earlier in Texas, tackling head-on the issue of his Catholicism. Like JFK's,
Obama's courageous speech redirected the course of the 2008 presidential
campaign. This is the kind of magisterial political and historical example
David Morey's company uses in advising political candidates as well
as business leaders. Good debate prep, preparation that facilitates a
productive pivot from the hostile question, can win a campaign. To be

sure, the absence of such preparation can just as easily lose a campaign. Control the dialogue by moving the conversation to the territory you want to own. Define yourself, your opponent, and the future. Fail to make these definitions, and your opposition will.

Controlling the dialogue is a prime objective of all great magicians. For example, magicians study the work of Dariel Fitzkee, who in the third volume of his 1945 trilogy, *Magic by Misdirection*, details the psychology of deception as applied to magic. The magician's options for the pivot include:

Disguise

Alternative control

Simulation

Dissimulation

Interpretation

Maneuver

Pretense

Ruse

Anticipation

Diversion

Monotony

Premature consummation

Confusion

Suggestion

You get the idea. There is a surprisingly long list of ways the magician can redirect his audience, pivoting their attention to exactly where the magician wants them to focus.

Another example from the world of magic: summon to mind Teller's "Seven Laws of Magic," discussed in the Fifth Strategy, and focus on Laws 1, 3, and 4:

- **Law 1: Exploit pattern recognition**. People grasp for patterns, and we magicians take every possible advantage in managing our audience's perceptions—people stop paying close attention following repetition.

- **Law 3: It is hard to think critically if you are laughing**. A joke eats up valuable mental bandwidth and makes it hard for our audiences to backtrack rationally when they are laughing—following a good joke, we magicians can do secretly magical things.

- **Law 4: Keep the trickery outside the frame**. Use innocent gestures or objects and move the real method of deception outside the audience's area of focus—keep the audience focused on the magic, not the method.

These are powerful tools of redirection for magicians, political candidates, and business leaders. We all follow, consciously and unconsciously, the patterns that we see, because we expect them to continue. We all put away our engineering degrees when we laugh. Each of us can focus only on one major frame at a time.

One of the greatest magicians and magical thinkers of our time, Spain's Juan Tamariz (1942–present), analyzed the magician's tools for directing the focus of an audience to the frame on which the magician wants them to focus for the duration of the performance. In his classic work, *The Five Points in Magic*, Tamariz details the most effective ways the magician can create focus by using:

- The Eyes
- The Voice

- ◆ The Hands
- ◆ The Body
- ◆ The Feet

These are all God-given weapons in the battle for control over the frame of reference that the audience accepts as reality. And consider one of Tamariz's magic formulas, which he calls "Crossing the Gaze."[58] Using this, a magician can switch an object undetectably by controlling where he or she looks, which, done skillfully, controls where the audience looks. Tamariz instructs:

- ◆ First, don't look at your own sleight of hand, but rather look at the audience.

- ◆ Second, shift your gaze—and the audience will follow your focus.

- ◆ Third, cross this gaze—move it in the opposite direction and across where the audience is now looking—and the spectators will forget where the potential sleight of hand may have originated.

These are all powerful principles of misdirection, redirection, or pivoting. As master magician Marc DeSouza points out, whatever you call the concept, it comes down less to misdirecting an audience and more to affirmatively *directing* an audience. Or, to paraphrase John Ramsay, one of history's greatest magicians and sleight-of-hand masters: If you want people to look at you, look at them. If you want them to look at something, look at it yourself.[59] This is all about focusing in ways that create the frame of reference you need to create. Recall from the First Strategy the oft-cited example of the gorilla no one saw—the literal 800-pound gorilla in the room. That effect was part of a psychological experiment, but Derren Brown, one of the world's top mentalists, recreates something like it every night in front of his live audiences. Trust us: There is no chance you will see the gorilla stealing a banana under the bright light near the center of the stage, even though Brown has repeatedly warned you it will happen.

Classic close-up geniuses Tony Slydini and Dai Vernon were among the world's greatest magicians, who use every possible element to direct the attention of the audience, to get it focused where *they* want it focused, and to control everything the audience sees and experiences. Magicians of all kinds direct and redirect by exploiting the off-beat, using surprise, asking a question, delivering a joke, getting an audience to relax, creating the illusion that something is finished before it's even begun, looking at something, breaking the theatrical "fourth wall" by moving into the audience, creating deliberate confusion or even mild discomfort among the audience, and finally, by offering a word, an object, a look, or (in the case of President Donald Trump) a Tweet of greater interest to the audience than whatever they are focusing on now.

By far the most powerful frame to which you can direct the focus of an audience or a set of consumers is the frame that defines how what you offer is different from the pack—different and better than the reality others create. In the 1990s, David Morey and business partner Scott Miller worked for Visa with the company's marketing guru, John Bennett, and Vice President for Advertising and Marketing Communications Jan Soderstrom to develop insurgent branding strategies against American Express and other credit card incumbents. In the 1970s and 1980s, American Express had advertised and communicated the benefits of its "membership" by spotlighting such famous cardholders as Stephen King, Thomas P. "Tip" O'Neill, and Ella Fitzgerald, who turned to viewers and asked rhetorically: "Do you know me?" The message was clear: You, too, can be a member of this elite group.

Beginning in the mid-1980s and through the 1990s, Visa began fighting back with a *focused* marketing and advertising campaign ostensibly targeted against American Express. The campaign was bolstered by Visa's

Olympic, Super Bowl, and U.S. Decathlon Team sponsorships and was built around one core theme: *"Visa. It's Everywhere You Want to Be."*

Focusing on "accessibility" rather than exclusivity, the campaign appeared to be directed solely against American Express. In fact, it was a masterpiece of redirection as misdirection. At the time, credit cards were commodities, one pretty much like another. Visa certainly had no real or relevant differentiation in the credit card marketplace—and specifically, there was nothing substantial that separated Visa from Mastercard. In many ways, Visa was seen to be the same as Mastercard, different in name only. And so Visa's strategy was to elevate its position by getting into an argument with the far more distinctive and visible American Express and to do so on the issue of acceptance.

The Visa campaign was launched across all channels, and it was focused on small establishments such as Rosalie's restaurant in Marblehead, Massachusetts. All the time, the ads made the point that at Rosalie's, they welcome Visa...but don't bother bringing your American Express card. Visa began loading serious money into this campaign—for example, $92 million annually in the very late 1980s, with television ads like this one, directed at people planning to attend the Winter Olympic Games: "Bring your camera and your Visa card. Because the Olympics don't take place all the time, and this time, the Olympics don't take American Express." A print version of the ad carried the headline: "At the 1988 Winter Olympics, they will honor speed, stamina and skill. But not American Express." Thanks to its new campaign, there was a 25 to 45 percent shift in card volume from American Express to Visa, a shift that roughly remains in effect today as measured by purchase volume per card network and U.S. card circulation. The point: this was driven by a relentless focus on relevant *differentiation*.

Take another less familiar example. Joel McCleary was a pioneer of "functional beverages" with his forerunner company, Drinks That Work. McCleary and his mastermind mixologist, Brian Lovejoy, developed the first energy shooter, "UpShot." Since its U.S. entrance in 1997, Red Bull had opened the minds of consumers and convenience retailers to "true" functional beverages, drinks that were genuinely differentiated from the mainstream beverages, Coke and Pepsi. Red Bull did this based on performance and personal brand experience, as opposed to brand imagery. You drank it, you felt it.

Across the 2000s, Red Bull shoved open the door for other energy drinks like Monster and a cooler-full of wannabe brands. McCleary and Lovejoy were obsessed with product effect, however, and they developed a tiny concentrated shot of energy: Upshot, which sold consumers a perceptible performance boost while offering retailers shelf stability, so that the product could be displayed near the counter or cash register in a convenience store, not in a cooler or back among the other merchandise. Moreover, Lovejoy's home was in gnarly Santa Cruz, California, so his product got a quick foothold in the surfer community. UpShot was a way of maxing energy without taking too much time off the board.

But this foothold was about all that McCleary and Drinks That Work could afford at the time. Other little shooters began popping up, particularly in convenience stores and gas-and-diesel stations along the interstate highways. The appeal was being made to long-haul truck drivers, who, by the way, had been the original foothold market for Red Bull in Asia. And then it happened.

Along came a product with enough money to *make* its difference make a difference in the marketplace. It was led by the revolutionary Manoj Bhargava, a Princeton dropout who had spent twelve years in a monastery in India before returning to the States. Back home, he became a serial entrepreneur, finally founding Living Essentials as a supplement company and then quickly following with 5-Hour Energy, his own energy shooter entry. He constantly played Big Casino, positioning 5-Hour Energy not against its direct energy shooter competitors, but instead against Red Bull and the 8.3-ounce to 16-ounce energy drinks. What is more, he invested heavily in advertising, principally on Sirius/XM Radio, which has a heavy trucker audience.

Throughout, Bhargava made his relevant differentiation clear. Other energy drinks got a lot of their boost from sugar. The energy high was a quick upturn—and then a dead drop. By contrast, 5-Hour Energy's name was based on how it was different from the energy market leaders. 5-Hour's energy boost didn't depend on sugar. It was different, so different that it lasted five hours—long enough for an eighteen-wheeler to traverse I-80 westbound from Rock Island, Illinois, to Omaha, Nebraska, with a half hour left over to pick up another 5-Hour. As Bhargava's Living Essentials continued to plough every penny of revenue back into marketing, his shooter nonchalantly nudged all other shooters, McCleary's Upshot included, off the shelf. Forbes recently estimated the former monk's wealth at $4 billion and rising.

5-Hour Energy was an exercise in self-definition as self-differentiation. Bhargava might as well have borrowed from the magician's playbook. He focused, redirected, and controlled every definition related to his product. In the next two strategies, we'll be talking quite a bit more about definition, but it is so closely related to focus and redirection that some basics are important to deal with right here and now.

First, define yourself. Over the three-plus decades David Morey has been creating strategy, he's never seen a global political campaign win with a candidate who stays predominantly on the defensive. To be on the defensive is to relinquish control of your own self-definition. In politics and business, successful leaders define their own character, personality, and values. Fail to do so, and others will define these attributes for you. And you can count on their definitions not being to *your* advantage.

Second, define change. Falling behind the forces of change puts an organization and its leader in reactive mode—permanently on the defensive. As the 1932 Roosevelt campaign, the 1980 Reagan campaign, and the 2008 Obama campaign have shown us, there is only one consistently effective competitive strategy: to lead change. Consider Trump vs. Clinton in 2016: At almost every key juncture, Donald Trump stood for change and Hillary Clinton for a form of the status quo. Change won. And change wins. This has never been more urgently the case than it is today.

Third, define the future and differentiate. In politics, the candidate who has best defined the future for voters in ways that are compelling and credible to *them* has won nearly every free and fair (genuinely "democratic") election in history. In the same way, successful CEOs must define the future of their own industry and business in compelling and credible ways. Going forward, create ways to articulate your vision and define your brand as different and better than the others.

Building on our "Category of One" approach in the Third Strategy, differentiation—defining how you are different from the others—is key to adding business value. Not surprisingly, it is also key when it comes to separating the world's greatest magicians from the magical status quo of their day. Consider:

- In the 1910s and 1920s, Harry Houdini broke away from the prevailing paradigm of magic by escaping from anything and everything, by accepting and defeating all challenges, and later, by exposing fraudulent mediums, charlatans who claimed they could speak to their patron's loved ones who had passed to the next world.

◆ Fifty years after Houdini, Doug Henning broke from the magical pack by channeling an intense love of wonder and a childlike excitement about the miracles before him. He performed on TV and Broadway in *The Magic Show* and *Merlin*, respectively.

◆ A few years after Henning, David Copperfield separated away from the magical paradigm of his day by combining story, romance, and theater, creating award-winning TV specials with celebrity participants, and as we detailed in the Third Strategy, doing big things far bigger than anyone—from vanishing the Statue of Liberty to walking through the Great Wall of China.

◆ At about the same time that Copperfield began his career, mentalist Uri Geller broke another aspect of the contemporary magical mold by mysteriously using his mind to know what others were thinking; by psychokinesis—bending spoons and other objects with his mind, live and just inches before the eyes of his audience; and by predicting the unpredictable.

◆ A decade after Copperfield and Geller's early years, David Blaine invented yet another radically different magical direction via television specials filmed in the streets, with coverage that focused on audience reactions. Later, borrowing from Houdini, Blaine performed various feats of superhuman endurance, defying heat, starvation, gravity, and air, and even holding his breath underwater after breathing pure oxygen for a world record seventeen minutes and four seconds.

◆ Following hard on Blaine's heels, Criss Angel took his own differentiation into another direction by injecting a kind of goth rock character into his "Mindfreak" TV specials, focusing on anything out-of-the-ordinary in magic. Today, he produces and headlines a highly successful Las Vegas magic show.

Without difference, there is no paradigm shift, no fame, and no historical success in magic, nor is there any enduring value in business. Warren Buffett's phrase *economic moat* refers to a "competitive advantage that is instrumental for a company's overall prosperity." Buffett never invests unless both he and the company's customers understand the firm's "competitive advantage": what makes the company different, special, and better. As David Morey's former client and one of history's greatest business leaders, Roberto Goizueta, Chairman and CEO of The Coca-Cola Company, once said, "Be different—or be damned!"

Forget damnation. Value today is created by relevant differentiation, for the basic economic reason that value is created by scarcity. Think about it: A brand can be *cheaper*. It can be *better*. But, best of all, it can be *different*. (Worst of all? It can be out of *business*.)

Different, it turns out, is the most powerful brand positioning possible, and it is the best way to create real as well as perceived value. Today, most markets are dominated by the undifferentiated and implicit brand positioning of "me too!" as companies seek to imitate the success of others. Most companies are very content to accept the category-defined benefits of usage. But you must redirect, pivot, and differentiate if you want to disrupt the status quo of your own marketplace. This relevant differentiation, moreover, must be clearly apparent. The more obscure your brand is, the louder these differences need to scream. For example:

- ◆ It's 1933, and the weight of the Great Depression is oppressive everywhere. Three brothers running two shoe stores are asking themselves not only how they can survive, but how they can stand apart from everyone else who is fighting for survival.

- ◆ *The answer:* Institute a policy that will break the dominant paradigm and challenge retailing history—*Allow customer returns with no questions asked!* The company in question soon becomes Nordstrom, and the legend is that a customer once returned a tire or tires (no one is sure how many) for a cash refund. Nordstrom never sold tires. No matter, the store issued the refund—and it's still being talked about today. What set Nordstrom apart and transformed retailing was a relentless and differentiating focus on putting customers first, period.[60]

- It's 1997, and Steve Jobs has returned to the company he founded and from which he was fired a decade earlier. Looking to jump-start what needs to be the greatest corporate turnaround in business history, how can Jobs re-energize and transform his then-failing company?

- *The answer*: He does all kinds of things to reclaim the company's relevant differentiation, including reminding Apple loyalists and employees that what makes them special is their unique ability to "Think Different." Jobs also pulls key Apple executives into an all-day strategy meeting to focus them on "core" questions about where the company is going. And he does one more simple and cheap thing. At a time when all computers are beige, Jobs produces iMac computers in attractive colors! The result: mothers and grandmothers want—and keep asking their husbands or grown-up kids to get them—one of "those nice-looking Macintoshes."

- It's 1999, at the height of the dot.com boom, and new companies are sprouting every hour to overcrowd an already crowded marketplace. Seemingly, everyone has a new "dotcom" idea, along with the sense that there's gold in them hills. So what does a little company that sells woman's shoes online called Zappos do to stand out and apart from all this Web-fueled craziness?

- *The answer*: The founders make a single desperate decision to define some point of difference. They decide to offer free shipping and free returns—unheard of at the time. Soon, this allows the company's leadership to realize that what makes them special is not price, but rather a fanatical attention to over-servicing their customers. Zappos realizes that online business is not so much about websites as it is about the entire retail value chain: From the warehouse, to the way orders are filled, to shipping—across every detail and up and down this supply chain. Today, Zappos, now owned by Amazon, continues to break molds. And it is no accident that nine out of ten retailers offer free shipping over the holiday season. These competitors are simply following in the footsteps of Zappos' differentiation while searching for their own success.

Today, the rules of leadership, business, and communications have completely changed. The old rules are gone, and today's consumers are empowered with instant and ubiquitous information produced by an interconnected network of sources. This is true for all categories of consumers—consumers of information as well as customers, employees, investors, voters, or audiences seeking the latest in magic. All consumers have infinitely more choices, brands have infinitely more competition, and all of us are consumed in a tsunami of data, with the crassly trivial and critically important swirling together in one crushing, never-ending wave. No wonder consumers feel overloaded. They *are* overloaded. And yet they compulsively continue to seek even more data. Your only chance to break through is to define your relevant *differentiation*. Be different or be damned!

In our era of intensively interactive communication, the tried-and-true rules of mass marketing, which were developed in and for the era of non-networked, one-way broadcast mass media, are still being tried, but they are no longer true. Greater and greater marketing investments are yielding lesser and lesser results. And this new reality has created a need for a new, truly magical model for business leadership, a model centered on controlling the dialogue, on defining one's relevant differentiation, and on a cardinal rule of leadership today: *everything communicates.*

REMEMBER, EVERYTHING COMMUNICATES

David Morey and business partner Scott Miller learned this simple adage from their work on political campaigns. If anything, it applies even more powerfully to business: *everything communicates.*

Every successful magician agrees. Control every element of the show, down to the smallest. Do this, and you create an experience for the audience that is far bigger than the sum of its parts. In politics, business, and magic, every detail counts. In a political campaign, everything the candidate says and does—even what the candidate *fails* to say or do (think Hillary Clinton's e-mails)—is important. To today's presentation-savvy voters, consumers, and audiences, no detail is minor. In our crowded and competitive marketplaces, every detail is either selling or un-selling. Nothing is neutral or unimportant.

Consider brand development: everything communicates. Product, package, distribution, sales, placement, promotion and merchandising, pricing, advertising, Web and social or mobile media, employees, and loyalist consumers—all communicate the details of brand meaning. Everything communicates, and everything must align to create a coherent meaning. In fact, alignment just may be the most important element in today's hyper-cluttered communications environment. Alignment of all details amounts to consistency of what marketers call the "brand communication." It's all about focusing everything in the *same* direction.

Go back to 1943, World War II in North Africa, and things are not going well for the American army, which is making its combat debut in this theater of the war. Lieutenant General George S. Patton—one of our favorite insurgent commanders—is summoned to take charge of the U.S. II Corps, which has just suffered a grimly humiliating defeat at the Kasserine Pass in Tunisia in the very first contest between the U.S. Army and the vaunted German Afrika Korps under General Erwin Rommel, "The Desert Fox." Arriving at II Corps headquarters unannounced, at a point when American military confidence has been shattered, Patton immediately sizes up the unit's problem as one of leadership—or, more accurately, lack thereof. The troops look sloppy and dispirited. They are more rabble than army. Just when there is an urgent need for them to function as soldiers, they have stopped caring.

So, Patton acts. He immediately decrees a regimen aimed at achieving perfect discipline through attention to every last detail. He begins by enforcing regulations governing uniforms, including what will become infamous in army lore as the "Necktie Order"—requiring all soldiers, including frontline soldiers, to wear leggings, helmets, and neckties... always. Why? General Omar N. Bradley, Patton's second-in-command at the time, understood why; because everything communicates. "Each time a soldier knotted his necktie, threaded his leggings, and buckled on his heavy steel helmet," Bradley later wrote, "he was forcibly reminded that Patton had come to command the II Corps, that the pre-Kasserine days had ended, and that a tough new era had begun."[61]

CEOs like Disney's Bob Iger understand what Patton understood and what the world's greatest magicians understand. Absolutely *everything* matters because absolutely *everything* communicates. For II Corps, perfectly knotted neckties were a first step toward making defeated men feel like soldiers, so they then performed like soldiers. In fact, in a remarkably short time, a defeated and defeatist mob became a battle-winning army. In Dennis Snow's book, *Lessons from the Mouse*, the former Disney executive sums it up this way: "Never let backstage come onstage." In other words, control every element and image and detail. Control everything. This is the only way Disney is "show ready" and able to produce magic every day at every park and ride and movie and experience around the world.

For the great magician, as for the great business leader, perfection is in the details and in using each detail to create a result that is *just right*— and is therefore far "greater than the sum of its parts." Look at your own organization or brand through the lens of what we can call an "Everything Communicates Audit." Examine everything, and ask what it says about you, your organization, your values, and your products. If it does not say what you want it to say, change it or dump it. If it says something negative, dump it now. If it doesn't say anything at all, dump it now as well.

The old saying goes, "The devil is in the details." We far prefer the version coined by the great architect Mies van der Rohe, an apostle of clarity and simplicity in architecture. He liked to say: "God is in the details." So go ahead. Embark on a journey of exploration, probing the intimate relationship between a winning strategy and every single sacred, holy, and magically communicative detail of your company, your people, your product, your brand, and yourself. Put the dynamism of focused definition, differentiation, and details to work—relentlessly.

PART THREE

EMPOWER

THE SEVENTH STRATEGY
GRAB THE DIALOGUE

"Whoever plays offense first wins."

—Bill Clinton

S cene: *This really happened[62] (https://www.youtube.com/ watch?v=ksXbsFzdzFY). Like most sons, Harry Blackstone Jr. imagines following in his father's footsteps. Three decades before, the father, Harry Blackstone Sr., had made a borrowed handkerchief dance impossibly and mischievously alongside his audience's imagination.*

Now, it's 1987. The son enters the stage to reach for a light bulb in a lamp held by his lovely wife. It's hot. He waits, cooling, and now almost magically removes the still-lit bulb and admits:

"Of course, it's impossible...that's why we do it."

The bulb continues to burn brightly, alive again in the magician's hand, and now, this is the moment it begins slowly to float, never mind the small hoop that Blackstone Jr., passes around the light bulb to prove there are no threads, no suspension, and no tricks, and then:

"Just a moment, someone says they could not see it. Who was that? You? Well, here...."

Blackstone Jr., in control, breaks the proverbial fourth wall and walks into his transfixed audience, where he asks a lady, then a man, to hold the light bulb and look at it. Then, taking it back, it floats yet again... now he walks back to the stage and turns:

"But you...out in the far rows, you haven't seen it yet, so look, but do not touch...."

Blackstone Jr. seems to throw the magical light bulb just over his audience's heads: It's flying outward now, into and well past the middle of his audience, then it flies over to people in the back... This is real magic... And then it quickly boomerangs back to its magical owner, its master, its magician, again through that same small hoop and away from anything but pure magic. Blackstone Jr. has a kind of magical relationship with this brightly burning light bulb.

A few magicians who watch this famous piece of magic think the father, Blackstone Sr., must be looking down with pride upon his son, Blackstone Jr. The son is not just performing a levitation, he's doing something far bigger than a magical effect. In this theater, we all see the light, and it somehow centers us. All the time, it ignites our hearts and our imaginations.

"In the beginning was the Word," the Gospel of John proclaims, "and the Word was with God, and the Word was God." The simple and creative power, the force of imagination and creation, is fused into the power of language, of speech, of dialogue. Like other spiritual messengers, John knew this and put the principle into action. Magicians, shamans, priests, and political as well as cultural and business leaders perpetually search for the right words—the good words, the magic words—necessary to move people and create change.

The greatest magic "tricks" are scripted. Whether spoken or unspoken, there is always a story behind any magic effect that endures. One of the true modern masters of magical storytelling is David Copperfield. Born David Seth Kotkin, this magician took his very name from the most famous novel of the master storyteller of the Victorian Age, Charles Dickens.

It is 2012, and we're onstage at the MGM Theater, Las Vegas, special guests of David Copperfield, who has just been honored as "Magician of the Century." The audience is warming to a story the magician tells. Coming from a performer known for large-scale theatrics, it is an uncommonly intimate narrative about his family and his desire and his pain. Suddenly, almost imperceptibly, the room begins living the story, entering, as it were, into a dialogue with Copperfield. Truly, in the beginning was the word.

As the audience bears witness to the transformation onstage, Copperfield, without breaking tone or cadence, tells of his father's early dreams of becoming an actor and how he was "talked out of it" by the magician's grandfather, who wanted his son to "earn money." Copperfield's narrative now transitions into his own self-discovery. We see him as David Seth Kotkin, a gawky Jewish kid from Metuchen, New Jersey, who happens to love magic.

That's one part of the discovery. The other?

Magic turns out to be a very good way for a shy boy to meet girls. He reveals his discoveries to his grandfather, who responds by trying to nip this dream in the bud, much as he had the acting ambitions of his son. David, however, protests that he is good with tricks. No matter, his grandfather predicts that he will fail if he goes into magic.

And so, the magician confesses to the audience: "We would never speak again.... My grandfather was stubborn...and his stubbornness made me stubborn..."

This revelation is a slap in the face. It brings the audience down, even as their human empathy draws them ever more deeply into the unfolding story. The shared sadness has transformed a monologue into an emotional dialogue between David Copperfield, uncharacteristically seated quietly on a stool, and his listeners.

The storyteller continues. He tells the audience how years passed, and in those years, despite his grandfather's prediction, he has achieved remarkable success and started performing in his first Broadway show. Always connecting with his audience, even on Broadway, Copperfield looks up and sees an old man, the very image of his grandfather, seated way in the back of the theater. Later, when David walks out into the audience, he heads for the back. But the old man is gone.

Most likely, David admits, he had only imagined that it was his grandfather.... And so he tells his Las Vegas audience that even more years passed, and with them, his grandfather passed as well. The magician never even had a chance to say goodbye.

The audience is with him. They understand, and, on the fulcrum of this understanding, Copperfield suddenly lifts the pace. In rapidly accelerating tempo, he interacts with audience members and brings some onstage, including David Morey. Copperfield asks them to volunteer some random numbers. They do. In the meantime, he recalls that his grandfather had a dream, too. He dreamed for the longest time of owning a 1949 Lincoln. Of course, he also dreamed of winning the lottery....

At this point, an image of a 1949 Lincoln flashes on a screen behind the magician. With this, Copperfield points to a box that's been sitting onstage throughout the entire narrative. It is padlocked shut. He now asks for more numbers, random numbers, and they come flying up from the audience both onstage and in the seats. Someone's favorite number...a birthday. The audience is throwing numbers at him, and he records them with increasing velocity on a blackboard.

In the end, there are eight numbers. And now it is the dialogue and the experience that accelerate...Copperfield describes how the whole family helped to clean out his grandfather's attic after he died. In an old dresser drawer, he says, they found a ticket stub. It was for his grandson's Broadway debut.

So the old man was there after all.

The revelation slows Copperfield's pace as he lets it sink in. He hopes his grandfather is watching now, he says.

And having said it, he opens the padlocked box, the box that has been there onstage with him and his audience all along. Inside is a slip of paper. He draws it out, revealing the same eight numbers the audience had just moments ago tossed randomly to him.

And there is more. Much more. But as fellow magicians, we can't reveal the spectacular ending to this beautiful effect—we can only urge you to go see David Copperfield's extraordinary show to be fully, completely, and totally amazed, and to watch this wonderful tribute to dreams, to dreams of fathers and sons, to dreams of magic.

THE THREE STAGES

Harry Blackstone Jr. and David Copperfield, the first in tribute to his father, the second in a beautifully structured evocation of his grandfather, both expand the traditional *abracadabra* into a personal memoir that summons followers, and leads them into the magical dreams most personal to them. The narrative pushed the magic into the minds and hearts of the audience.

There are three stages to every great magical effect. Every great magician knows them and traverses them:

- First, **take over** the stage: *magic first*
- Second, **transfer** ownership: *use story as strategy*
- Third, **transcend**: *context is everything*

These principles are key to grabbing the dialogue in stage magic, in a movie, in a speech, in a corporate turnaround, or in your leadership and market dialogue with your business's key audiences. So we show below how to apply all three of these principles to your strategic and transactional dialogues with customers, investors, stakeholders, employees, voters, and whoever else you need to move.

TAKE OVER THE STAGE: MAGIC FIRST

Along with author Eugene Burger, our magic teacher Jeff McBride argues that a magician is best when applying the principle of "Magic First!" Begin with magic. Deploy your strongest opening, your most powerful way of grabbing hold of your audience or your customers. McBride calls this the *Opener*, and it must define you instantly, pull in the audience—the customer—and command further attention.

Tony Clark, master magician, magic producer, and one of David Morey's teachers, references this takeover concept in the very first chapter of his recent book, *Insider Secrets: Mastering the Craft, Show & Business of Magic*. He calls it the "Takeover the Stage Principle." The title of his first chapter is "The Fifteen-Second Secret: Win Over and Hold Your Audience, or Else!" It begins with a story about watching old tapes of magicians appearing on the famed *Tonight Show* in the days of the legendary Johnny Carson. Clark notes how the pace was more leisurely in the 1980s than it is today— though the polyester sports jackets were much more colorful, especially when seen on the smeary color video of the era. Yes, today we move faster— and more smoothly, in hi def. Our audiences and customers are also faster and smoother. Bombarded by information and choice, they need us to pull them in very, very quickly. Or they move on.

In 1999, Tony Clark was working with the late television producer Gary Ouellet on a new show for NBC: *The World's Most Dangerous Magic*. Clark plans to close the show with an effect that risks his life. He must find one among one hundred different keys and use it to release himself from a chain locked firmly around his waist, and in so doing, avoid the car that is barreling toward a container filled with a flammable substance sure to explode and kill him on national TV.

Yes, the prospect of instant death *must* be the "closer."

But the producer knows better. "This is the *opener,* the hook!" Ouellet exclaims; "If you don't grab them at the beginning, they'll never watch to the end."

Whether you are an entrepreneur or a stage magician, you must grab them at the get-go. The great Lance Burton tells a story from early in his career, when he put in his Gladwellian "10,000 Hours" (the principle that 10,000 hours of deliberate practice are needed to become world-class in any field) at a strip bar off the Sunset Strip in Los Angeles. His opener, Burton told us, had to be awfully good. So, one of the greatest magicians of the last century threw a gigantic flame out over the heads of his audience, only to hear the collective *Ahhhh!* as the fire turned into a beautiful white dove, which flew back into the master's waiting hand.

It earned attention. And as Tony Clark reminds us, "First impressions are the key to your success." The late Roger Ailes, controversial political consultant and founder of Fox News, wrote a book about this principle in 1988, *You Are the Message.* Way back then, he was preaching a version of the "15 Seconds Secret"—which is about as long it takes any audience to gauge a person's body language, voice, and words before they decide whether they understand, believe, or have any interest in you and what you're selling. This is not because people are shallow. The instantaneous computer that is a subconscious feature within us all evolved over thousands and thousands of years to help us distinguish predator from friend, enemy from leader, and charlatan from godlike mage.

One of the greatest mentalists and magical thinkers in history, our friend Max Maven, has another framework for this. He thinks of it as three questions and adds an additional fifteen seconds. Max argues that any audience, like any customer, asks and answers three questions across this short half-minute:

- Who is this person?
- What story are they trying to tell me?
- Why should I care?

In our instant-on age of information, all-day television, and 24/7/365 social media bombardment, ask these three questions about whatever you are presenting. Then be sure to embody the answers in your "opener." That is the *Magic First!* approach.

So much for the first fifteen to thirty seconds of whatever you are doing. If you do manage to hook your audience, your customer, your prospect, you've got a good deal more time to fill. Recent research shows that the greatest magicians, like the greatest business leaders, can't let the initial hook do all the work. They need to add new—and relevant—information every fifteen seconds or so to refresh their argument or change up the pace. Think Bruce Springsteen in one of his legendary three-hour concerts. Three hours—all the time keeping an audience rapt and dancing! No problem—*if* you hook them with your opener and then change up your song or the frame or story that goes with your song. Better yet, call some songs on the spot. Think like a Super Bowl quarterback who, seeing his receiver open, calls an audible and changes the play near the end zone because he is inside the moment. You need to change up the pace to ensure that you are continually giving your audience or your customer a refreshed definition of who you are, what story you are telling, and above all, why they should care.

Before you make your next pitch, be certain you can answer the following two questions: What's my hook? How can I do magic first? Every great business leader answers these time after time. Not long ago, David Morey delivered a speech on "insurgent military strategy" to an elite group of senior American and Filipino military leaders in Manila's officer training academy. At an early point in the speech, by way of illustrating the "Perceptions Rule" concept, David performed a quick piece of mentalism, reading the most senior general's mind. He watched the entire room transform. Gone was any stiffness or distance between Morey and the generals, both American and Filipino. As happens in every context and for every audience, the "Magic First" principle changed the room's dynamic from formal to friendly. Decorated officers became grown-up kids, returning to a world of childhood imagination, of the mind wide open, of a realm of magic and the possibilities magic represents.

John McLaughlin discovered the utility of the *Magic First* principle when dealing with foreign intelligence services. Such services come in many varieties and with varied histories in terms of their relations with the United States. Particularly with services that for whatever reason were reluctant to work with American intelligence or had a history of tensions with the United States, it was important to break the ice, change the room from formal to friendly, and reduce the distance between the U.S. side and its hosts—as in the situation David Morey faced in the Philippines. Nothing worked better than a little magic to accomplish this. In a restaurant in a city that must remain nameless, McLaughlin recalls breaking the ice in an awkward and formal situation with his counterparts by calling for a deck of cards and doing a classic effect called the "Ambitious Card"—causing the host's chosen card to rise repeatedly and defiantly to the top of the deck, a subtle way of expressing respect for the magician's influence. Soon, the two sides, having shared a laugh and the experience of wonder, were far more able to communicate on a human level and in a much warmer and more cooperative manner. Magic to the rescue.

Back in 2010, David Morey was appearing in Washington, D.C., in *A Magical Way of Thinking*, a one-man play on magic and life. To fine-tune the show, he flew to Quebec and worked for four days with legendary Broadway and magic director Bob Fitch. David planned on opening the ninety-minute play with a beautiful rose production that splits into two roses, in about thirty seconds of magic. Toward the end of the second day of working with Fitch, he noted to the famous director that they were still refining the first half-minute of the play, that beautiful rose production. Without skipping a beat, Fitch, who, some believe, has appeared in more Broadway plays than any other actor, singer, or dancer in history, and has directed both David Copperfield and David Blaine, offered: "We must get this first piece right, because it sets the tone for the next eighty-nine and a half minutes."

In magic as in business, starting out bold wins. Play offense to take control of your audience, your marketplace, and your future. Harry Blackstone Jr. and David Copperfield, like other great magicians, control every detail of their presentation and communication, especially their opener. The world's greatest magicians fashion the words to create the perception that trumps reality. They begin, frame, and shape their story, their narrative, to influence participants—magicians call them "humans"—onstage. "Be bold," Goethe wrote, "for there is genius, power, and magic in it!" For magicians, this means *Be Bold* from the moment they begin their well-rehearsed entrance to their opener. The only acceptable objective is to *use magic first* and take over the stage.

TRANSFER OWNERSHIP: USE STORY AS STRATEGY

Everything that follows the opener needs to be dialogue that transfers ownership of the "magic" from the magician or business leader to the audience or the customer. Magic is marketing, in that it is most powerful when the magician succeeds in transferring ownership of choice and decision from himself to his audience. In commerce, the great brands are those consumers *themselves* choose again and again, led irresistibly, at their own pace and in their own way, to the decision the marketer wants them to make. This is exactly why the world's greatest magicians and history's greatest magic effects transfer the magic into the hands of the audience, empowering them by casting them in the role of magicians. For a moment, one or two spectators hold Blackstone Jr.'s light bulb in *their* hands, and then it floats upwards from *their* hands. Onstage in Las Vegas, Copperfield brings a dozen spectators up on stage to witness the final miracle we can't tell you about. The most powerful magic, as with the most powerful marketing, happens in the spectator's hands, minds, and hearts. Magic and marketing share this power of transference.

Most significantly, in magic and in marketing, the transfer is catalyzed by certain words that create a psychological, albeit subconscious, advantage. Again, as Al Koran advised: "It's the words that fool." And what the great mentalist meant was not just that words can trick our minds or eyes, but that the words are a key part of this package of the impossible that breaks through our barriers, our doubts, and our cynicism. Importantly, these words of transference are not intended to deceive, but rather to lead audiences—consumers, voters—into the deeper and more exhilarating concepts of mystery and possibility.

In fact, today, no great magic or great marketing is possible without a dialogue, a two-way conversation between performer and audience, between business leader and customer. One-way monologues only work from Chairman of the Worker's Party Kim Jong-un in totalitarian North Korea. Today, communications are empowered by two-way conversation—where the great magician, like the great marketer, listens to and is seen to care about his audience. This is called *The Outward Mindset*, which is also the title of a recent book by the Arbinger Institute. It is about seeing outward—seeing others more than yourself. It is about dialoguing with people, audiences, or customers. Both magic and marketing die when they slip into anything close to a self-focused argument or an egocentric performance.

Doubtless you are familiar with the "charismatic" charm of some of the most memorable U.S. politicians. They are masters at acknowledging the people they are meeting, listening, or appearing to listen, and creating a sense of relationship even when they are speaking to a packed room. Consider Ronald Reagan, who seemed to be talking to all Americans in the manner of the friendly grandfather we either had or wished we had. He was trusted, leading us by the twinkle in his eye and the wisdom in his voice. There was Bill Clinton, who was seen as "feeling your pain." Those who have met the former President or have heard him speak in person report that he "looked right at me" or say that he "was talking to me." Barack Obama may be a former law professor and a super-charged intellectual, more comfortable with logic than displaying emotion, but watch this former President work a room and look deep into the eyes of each person he meets and whose hand he holds and shakes. It may be for a grand total of five seconds, but it is five seconds of meaningful communication. It is charisma.

The magic of transference is the creation of a palpable connection and real dialogue, even for a matter of seconds. The height of this magic is the ability to do this with every audience, customer, and person the magician, marketer, or President of the United States meets.

The magic of charisma is amplified and elaborated by the story a leader tells. Whether it is the CEO of a company talking about how they arrived where they are, what makes them great, and where they are going, or a president or candidate for president defining him or herself, the story is the way we all take in our side of a dialogue. Without story, there is no vision, no strategy, no chance of implementation. Since before Old Testament times, story has been the vehicle of all great communications.

Consider that some of the greatest CEOs in history—from Jobs to Goizueta, from Welch to Gerstner, from Bezos to Zuckerberg, and from Musk to Buffet—are each able to tell a hell of a good story. It is no historical accident that the forty-fourth and the forty-fifth presidents of the United States, as vastly different as they are from one another, were elected in significant measure on the strength of extraordinary stories they told about themselves.

For all the books that have been written about business leaders and politicians, not to mention the learned analyses of history's great works of literature, remarkably little analytic attention has been devoted to discovering the elements of effective storytelling. One man who has dived into the subject is Robert McKee. Back in the early 2000s, when David Morey attended his renowned four-day "Story Seminar," he realized that McKee was the English professor you wished you had in college: no notes, wearing all black, each sentence emerging as if it had just been very carefully written as he delivered long, smart, soaring paragraphs.

McKee, born in 1941, began teaching at USC; the seminar grew from this work and now runs twice a year in New York City, Los Angeles, and London, along with a few other cities at different times. This is the code-breaking, cult-popular course that has helped inspire 63 Academy Award winners, 164 Emmy Award winners, 30 Writers Guild of America Award winners, and 26 Directors Guild of America Award winners. McKee looks and sounds like he knows the secret to story. This does not, however, mean *that he and his* students look at the mechanics of story, but rather into the deeper elements that make narrative work—what makes a compelling story compelling. Sitting in the audience, David was struck by how this fits into his own work in developing strategies for candidates and companies. In fact, McKee went on to consult for the likes of Microsoft, Nike, Hewlett-Packard, Time Warner, and Siemens on the use of "story in business."

McKee's best-known book, *Story: Substance, Structure, and the Principles of Screenwriting,* is to the telling of a compelling story what Sun Tzu's *The Art of War* is to fighting a victorious battle. It gets you to the fundamentals of holding an audience's attention or pulling your company's employees, stakeholders, and customers along with you with your narrative and the dialogue it creates. Consider McKee's aphoristic explanation of why one of the greatest films in the history of film works first and last as story. He writes of Crisis, Climax, and Resolution, imploring storytellers to "Give the audience what they want, but not the way they want it." In light of this, read for yourself the penultimate scene of *Casablanca,* part of fifteen minutes of climactic, non-stop action, as Rick puts Ilsa on that "plane to Lisbon" with Victor Laszlo:

RICK. If you don't mind, you fill in the names. That will make it even more official.

RENAULT. You think of everything, don't you?

RICK. (Quietly) And the names are Mr. and Mrs. Victor Laszlo.

Renault stops dead in his tracks and turns around. Both Ilsa and Renault look at Rick with astonishment.

ILSA. But why my name, Richard?

RICK. Because you're getting on that plane.

ILSA. (Confused) I don't understand. What about you?

RICK. I'm staying here with him 'til the plane gets safely away.

Rick's intention suddenly dawns on Ilsa.

ILSA. No, Richard, no. What has happened to you? Last night we said—

RICK. Last night we said a great many things. You said I was to do the thinking for both of us. Well, I've done a lot of it since then, and it all adds up to one thing. You're getting on that plane with Victor where you belong.

ILSA. (Protesting) But Richard, no, I, I—

RICK. You've got to listen to me. Do you have any idea what you'd have to look forward to if you stayed here? Nine chances out of ten we'd both be in a concentration camp. Isn't that true, Louis?

Renault countersigns the papers.

RENAULT. I'm afraid Major Strasser would insist...

ILSA. You're saying this only to make me go.

RICK. I'm saying it because it's true. Inside of us we both know you belong with Victor. You're part of his work, the thing that keeps him going. If that plane leaves the ground, and you're not with him, you'll regret it.

ILSA. No.

RICK. Maybe not today, maybe not tomorrow, but soon, and for the rest of your life.

ILSA. But what about us?

RICK. We'll always have Paris. We didn't have it, we'd lost it, until you came to Casablanca. We got it back last night.

ILSA. And I said I would never leave you!

RICK. And you never will. But I've got a job to do, too. Where I'm going, you can't follow. What I've got to do you can't be any part of. Ilsa, I'm no good at being noble, but it doesn't take much to see that the problems of three little people don't amount to a hill of beans in this crazy world. Someday you'll understand that. Now, now...

Ilsa's eyes well up with tears. Rick puts his hand to her chin and raises her face to meet his own.

RICK. Here's looking at you, kid.

...And cut to: *"Give the audience what they want. But not the way they want it."*

Think about it: We all want Rick to rise above who he is, to defeat his own demons, to find "Paris" again, and to live happily ever after, we think with Ilsa, but even better—now, as a hero, at once saving Ilsa from life in a concentration camp and helping to save humanity. This is our surprise: Rick rises to and above the moment. He is the real hero now, sacrificing true love for the greater good. He *gives us what we want. But not in the way we want it....*

In so many ways, strategy is story—well-told story. It's about giving audiences, voters, or consumers what they want, but not necessarily the way they want it. One striking lesson in studying military, political, and business strategy is that the best and most exponentially effective examples of strategy can be told very simply as stories, in a series of steps that pull you in.

- There is an opening, Once upon a time…
- A dialogue, seemingly with the leader of strategy… or a series of steps
- And a context that rises above the ordinary tactics of the status quo.

In his *Inspirations*, Larry Hass writes about the power of "The Frame" in the context of great magicians. He cites some famous magicians' effects and the simple frame, or "story," they represent:

- Jeff McBride's masterful Linking Rings routine
  The Frame: Kabuki Theater
- Lance Burton's world championship-winning Dove and Candle act
  The Frame: European elegance
- David Copperfield's awe-inspiring Flying
  The Frame: Childhood wish

Eugene Burger modernized the concept of the presentational-frame in magic, which can be applied equally well to business—or to any occasion on which you must communicate and communicate well. As for the qualities of an effective frame, Hass tells us to "Keep it strong; keep it small; keep it good." This means, again, as Eugene Burger constantly taught in refining scripts for magic, "Cut, cut, cut, cut…." Or as Eugene also put it, "I think that good writing is always the result of rewriting." That is why Eugene always advised his magic students to audio record every show. Doing so helps ensure their presentations are entertaining and magically powerful at the level of simply listening. He admonished us all to cut, cut, cut, to rewrite and hone the script, and to continually evolve it so that it becomes more and more magical. This is precisely what all speakers, performers, and leaders must do: record, edit, and raise the power of every single spoken word.

We equate chance and spontaneity with reality and sincerity, yet the stories that feel most real and sincere are those that are so perfectly scripted that they represent spontaneity in a manner that seems far more spontaneous than actual spontaneity. Magic is not an escape from reality. It is a form of "super" reality. As discussed in the preceding strategy, that is why Larry Hass advises magicians to break in a new piece of material in seven meticulous and painstaking steps:

- First, find excellent material.
- Second, practice the parts.
- Third, create good words.
- Fourth, memorize these words.
- Fifth, rehearse the whole.
- Sixth, perform it.
- Seventh, at every step, go back and revise the work at previous stages as necessary.

Again, as Larry Hass teaches us, if you don't have a script, you cannot rehearse. As magician Pete McCabe explains, you need to rehearse every move to ensure that you pull your audience in, take over the stage, transfer ownership of your dialogue to your audience, and make them a part of the magic. You cannot rely on spontaneity and chance to accomplish this complex series of actions. Dai Vernon, the magician who has built some of conjuring's greatest routines and has developed some of magic's most intricate and ingenious details of sleight of hand, advised: "Learn to do the sleight or secret move to perfection, then spend hours on *what to say.*"

The creative arsenals of the world's greatest magicians are powerful models for today's business leaders. Magicians:

◆ Break through the "fourth wall" by going out into the audience, acknowledging them, and speaking with them. The best stage magicians are like the most enduring giants of popular song. Performers as diverse as Diana Ross and Tom Jones connect with the audience, change up the pace of their shows, and ensure that everyone is with them.

◆ Script to recreate the best of what happens by accident in a show. This is what the fantastic magician and Las Vegas headliner Mac King does. During one show, a woman accidentally signed her name on the *back* of her selected card, making it rather easy for King to find it as he looked through all the backs of the cards. Today, when you go to King's Vegas show, you are sure to see this funny moment. It was too good to leave to chance, so King wrote it in.

◆ Or study David Copperfield's Vegas show. Copperfield tapes and reviews every performance to capture what really worked so that it can be repeated, and to capture what failed so that it will never happen again. During one show, a man entered late, and Copperfield found himself, to the delight of his audience, summarizing in a few funny lines what had just happened in the first few minutes of his performance. Now, he makes sure this happens the same way every night. Erase anything bad. Enshrine anything good.

◆ Edit the memory of the audience, as the great master Juan Tamariz teaches. For example, in the magician's recap, the show lives on, and audiences repeat and tell one another exactly what the magician wants them to remember. The details, true or edited, are controlled by the magician, who transfers the details to his audience in precisely the way he wishes.

Business leaders can also break the fourth wall and go out into their "audience"—to speak with employees, customers, and key allies. They can also make sure mistakes never happen again, even as they stay on the lookout for what works so that they can repeat it, refine it, and script it.

They can also learn to summarize every story they tell in whatever context they want their audiences to remember them.

Recall the following example of a business leader who broke through the fourth wall. Suit jacket off, the balding CEO explains: "After twenty years, he fired us. He said he didn't know us anymore." Now, the CEO admits the company has in fact lost touch not only with this single "old friend" and customer, but with all its customers, relying too much on fax and phone and not enough on old-fashioned face-to-face dialogue. Then cue to a solo piano and Gershwin's familiar *Rhapsody in Blue* as the CEO's secretary begins handing out plane tickets with a United Airlines logo on each. "We're going to set out for a little face-to-face chat with every customer we have," the CEO announces. "But Ben," one executive objects, "that's got to be over two hundred cities." Mr. CEO retorts: "I don't care," adding that he will personally visit the "old friend who fired us this morning."

This United Airlines TV ad aired in 1990, but it still sticks today—other than the part about "too much fax"—but given our technological dependence, obsession, and disconnection, this ad is even more relevant now than it was nearly three decades ago.

Three years after this ad first aired, another CEO faced the same problem. "We're going to set out for a little face-to-face chat with every customer we have," Louis Gerstner announced, having just taken the reins of a beleaguered IBM—a computing giant that had lost control of its own face-to-face customer dialogue.

IBM was in trouble in 1993. Big Blue was losing money and market share and was out of touch with the new trends moving the world toward personal computing and away from IBM mainframes. Gerstner was a former McKinsey consultant and an RJR Nabisco and American Express CEO. Many assumed that he had been brought in by IBM to break up a company more valuable for its constituent parts than put together. But Gerstner soon had a different idea for his first one hundred days. In a real-life flashback to that United Airlines commercial of three years earlier, he embarked on what IBMers called "Operation Bear Hug." It was time to get reengaged and get the company's customer dialogue under control again. It was time to listen.

Soon, Gerstner and his key executives were flying to more than 200 cities to listen to and talk with key customers. In the end, "Operation Bear Hug" shifted the ailing company's destiny and set it back on the way to being what it once had been: one of the world's most valuable companies.

Opening face-to-face dialogue gave birth to a cavalcade of destiny-changing decisions based on what the CEO and his team *heard*: Cut mainframe prices, sell unproductive assets, keep IBM together, and build a consulting arm to help integrate the technological mishmash customers told Gerstner they were forced to deal with every day.

In 1993, as Gerstner took the new leadership role, IBM's stock had lost over 70 percent of its value over the preceding six years. In his 1993 book, *Big Blue: The Unmaking of IBM*, Paul Carroll went through the litany of bad decisions that disconnected the company from its customers. It is an anatomy of losing touch. Gerstner—an avid computer user himself and, at American Express, a technology buyer—saw this immediately. As he offered in his own 2002 book, *Who Says Elephants Can't Dance?*: "I began by telling my audiences that a customer was now running IBM."

It didn't happen overnight, but over several decades, Big Blue had managed to lose its customer focus and the dialogue so vital to understanding consumer wants, needs, and dreams. By the 1990s, it hardly mattered that back in the 1960s, IBM had created the gold standard for customer service. What mattered in 1993 was that its gold standard had turned to lead. Gerstner helped to remold the leadership model for an incumbent company by listening more closely to its customers. In one meeting of IBM's top fifty executives, the CEO insisted they each visit a minimum of five big customers over ninety days. Their direct reports—some totaling two hundred executives—were to do the same. Their assignment? Listen.

Like the fictional "Ben" in the United Airlines commercial, Gerstner saved some of the key customer face-to-face dialogues for himself—people like Intel's Andy Grove, Lotus's Jim Manzi, and Microsoft's Bill Gates. Across Operation Bear Hug, brief one- and two-page reports were delivered to Gerstner about each visit. Gerstner also shared these with anyone at IBM who might learn from them. By pulling IBM back to its customer focus, Operation Bear Hug rebooted the company, setting a new change-focused trajectory that proved IBM made more sense together than apart. It cemented IBM's new reputation as a "full-solutions" company. Over the next decade, IBM shifted its strategic trajectory to providing "high margin" solutions for its clients, now back in touch and back in control of its two-way customer dialogue, transferring the ownership of customers' ideas into the story of its own strategy.

TRANSCEND: CONTEXT IS EVERYTHING

Perhaps the most powerful appeal of magic is its ability to rise above our everyday clatter and controversy. This was the great lesson of Houdini, remember. His most memorable effects were escapes, "miracles" of transcendence. And for these, he is justly regarded as the icon, the archetype of the modern magician. Ask just about anyone to name the first magician who comes to mind, and "Houdini" is the likely response.

Transcendence is also one of the most powerful positions in business, leadership, and politics. In addition to transferring ownership to your audience and using story as strategy, it is imperative today for anyone who aspires to leadership to *transcend*. Since transcendence is the stock in trade of the great magicians, magic is the obvious model to emulate.

Today and historically, each successful magic effect rises to heights above the everyday, and, most importantly, magicians lift their audience along with them. They achieve this not by producing sensation alone, but by staying totally alive, awake, and in the moment during every single performance. Contrary to cliché, magicians don't cast a spell or put their audience in a trance. They command the heightened attention of the audience by the power of their own heightened awareness onstage. Demonstrating supreme aliveness and wakefulness is infectious. It makes an impression. It molds the collective memory of the audience so that they leave the theater with an enduring and exaggerated recall that disrupts their everyday reality. When they recount to others their experience of the show, it is not a summary or a faded copy, but a transcription of the event, augmented. It is reality heightened. In a magical context, this means the best magicians lift their audiences above their own everyday reality. And the greatest magicians help these audiences dream bigger dreams. It is analogous, in a business and marketing context, to the process of transforming consumers into fans, loyalists, and champions.

As Eugene Burger taught, "All magic is about transformation. What the greatest magicians are telling you is that you are the magician in your own life. *YOU* are the agent of transformation, your own transformation." Eugene went on to argue, "Magic is the only art form that is always forever and ever concerned about transcendence. True, other art forms get there— novels, poetry, painting. But they don't need to get there and sometimes don't want to. By contrast, magic is always about transcending the human condition. And I think that's one of the powers of magic and why it's been here so long."[63]

Another of the greatest masters of magic, Dai Vernon, described magic in 1994 as a process by which "the mind is led on, step by step, to defeat its own logic." This elaborates on Eugene's concept of magical transformation as transcendence. Magic works and magic endures because of the power of a transformation that supersedes our own everyday logic. Magic appears to transform the everyday reality that appears to reside outside of us. In fact, it enables us to transcend our own inner logic-as-usual. This is the very essence of what yet another master of master magicians, Juan Tamariz, does when he recaps and edits the very memory of his audience, or when he applies to them his "theory of false solution." putting himself in the audience's thinking and memory, and once there, directing and editing it, and by so doing, keeping disbelief suspended during as well as long after the performance.[64]

Today more than ever before, business leaders, to be great business leaders, must take over, transfer, and transcend. After thirty years as a political and business consultant, during which he advised eighteen winning global presidential campaigns, David Morey developed a set of strategic axes that govern the way business leaders and political candidates must position themselves to lead greatly. They need to put themselves on the right side—the right-hand side—of these dualities:

- ◆ FRAGMENTER vs. UNIFIER: Neither businesses nor nations can afford leaders who divide, and who seek to thrive by pulling organizations apart. The greatest leaders, both historically and today, bring us together and unite us.

- ◆ POLITICAL vs. MORAL: Employees, stakeholders, and customers almost instantly sense business leaders who are in it for themselves, who are all ego and willing to play one faction against another. The same is true of political leaders. Those who win today are those seen to be capable of transcendence, those who rise above politics, infighting, and division and who lead to higher levels of success.

◆ PAST vs. FUTURE: All great business and political leaders today
focus more on the future than the past. Failed leaders keep
looking backward, repeatedly recounting votes and the size of
inaugural crowds, as if to settle old grudges or replay old feuds.
Transcendent leaders, by contrast, aim their audiences forward
into a future about which they have only as yet dreamed.

Business leaders do well by positioning or repositioning toward the
right side of all three of these axes. They succeed by following the lead of
the world's greatest magicians and magical thinkers, pulling the audience
together into one transcendent magical experience; telling a story with
important and enduring meaning; and aiming the audience, aiming us all,
forward toward bigger dreams.

Let's get down to an actual case of transcendence in business. If you have
any interest in the "great outdoors," you are probably familiar with REI—
Recreational Equipment Incorporated. Venture into an REI store, and you
receive a crystal-clear message that rises above the high-end clothing and
equipment that is being sold on the store shelves:

"YOUR NEXT ADVENTURE"

Rising above the everyday retail grind, REI sets the context for where *you*
are going: from a wintery cross-country skiing expedition in Yellowstone,
to a midsummer trek across the Sonora Desert, to a quiet afternoon
hike in a local park. Customers purchase the REI context along with its
merchandise. In 2016, REI sales were $2.56 billion, up from $2.42 billion in
2015, with total assets of $1.56 billion—and, by the way, no debt.

This is a long way from the origins of REI in 1938, when a group of Pacific
Northwest mountain climbers formed a cooperative to import European
climbing gear for themselves and their friends. The first REI retail store
opened six years later—if, that is, you consider three shelves in the back

of a gas station to be a "store." Today, REI is 152 stores, a global website, a mail-order catalogue business, an adventure travel firm, and an online sale-and-discount outlet—all within the transcendent context of "YOUR NEXT ADVENTURE."

In a retail sector littered with casualties ranging from the walking wounded to dead as a door nail, REI is doing just fine, thank you. What's the secret? How does the "YOUR NEXT ADVENTURE" context and transcendent messaging contribute to REI's success?

First, REI's management team knows what to tell their customers, because they *are* their customers. From the company's earliest days, REI's employees have been outdoor enthusiasts. Today, by the way, REI is *still* a cooperative, with over six million members.

REI, moreover, is different from other "outdoorsy" retailers such as L.L. Bean or Eddie Bauer. REI does not offer casual clothing or weekend wear. No, it is the real thing—that is, a store of, by, and for outdoor adventurers. This is the message that rises above all else, that defines and transcends the outdoor adventure marketplace. As you enter an REI store, notice displays of top-of-Everest-looking hiking boots, climbing gear, and rows of mountain bikes hanging from above. This is not a place for pretenders. This is where real adventurers come to buy their gear.

Second, REI's transcendent messaging is embodied in more than its merchandising. It is reflected in REI programs like the one that celebrated the centennial of the National Parks with special products co-designed with the National Park Service, and with an app that maps all the National Parks in the contiguous United States. The parks are a cause to which REI dedicates its considerable philanthropic support. Moreover, for anyone who wants to visit one of the parks, but is unsure of the difference between a tent-peg and a carabiner, REI offers in-store classes, day trips, and adventure vacations. You can visit a National Park near where you live—or travel to Kilimanjaro, Antarctica, or Everest.

Third, REI goes further in defining the context of "YOUR NEXT ADVENTURE." In a store committee brainstorming session in February 2015, someone proposed the ludicrous idea of closing all REI stores on Black Friday—the day after Thanksgiving, the year's heaviest shopping day. The proposal was, in effect, a vote against a stressful occasion that celebrates crass commercialism and connects cynically with the "spirit" of the holiday season.

Management went the proposal one better. As a form of symbolic protest, it was decided to give REI employees a paid holiday on Black Friday, so they could all go outdoors. Cooperative members, customers, and the public are all now invited to spend Black Friday outdoors, too. The hashtag #OptOutside expresses this transcendent message.

REI announced the #OptOutside plan in October 2015, and the campaign quickly went viral. By Black Friday, November 27, 2015, the Sierra Club and 170 other organizations had joined the movement; 1.4 million people posted the #OptOutside hashtag; and 1,000 parks provided free admission for the day. Altogether, #OptOutside got 8 billion social media and news impressions, REI attracted a million new members, and in the fourth quarter of 2015, there was a record 90 percent increase in job applications of people hoping to work for REI. Today, the #OptOutside campaign continues to define REI's core values and transcend the company's own marketplace, allowing REI to literally rise higher and perform above its competition.

TAKE OVER, TRANSFER, TRANSCEND

To grab the dialogue is the objective of any great magical effect and any great business. The grab is a three-phase gesture.

Take over by using Magic First, bringing out your most disruptive effect or proposition the very moment you stride the stage, engage, or get that customer on the phone. You dedicate yourself to adding new interest and excitement to everything you do, continually refreshing your own leadership brand and your company's brand.

Transfer ownership of what you sell—whether it is a magical effect, a new idea, or a product or service—by using story as strategy. Begin by listening, by putting your customers in a big, friendly, two-way Operation Bear Hug. Perpetuate this relationship with the fuel of your undivided attention. Keep listening. Answer the three questions that are on the mind of every audience member or customer: *Who is this person? What story are they trying to tell me? Why should I care?* In crafting your answers, continually frame, script, practice, rehearse, and tell the story you want to tell and only the story you want to tell.

Transcend by continually finding ways to rise higher as you lead. Remember, today more than ever before, the only way to lead is to stand above the ordinary and rise to higher callings for change.

Your objective is nothing less than transformation. It is the subject of the next two strategies. It what all magic is about. Indeed, transformation is the real magic inside us all.

THE EIGHTH STRATEGY
OVERCOME AND PREVAIL

"Never, never, never give up."

—Winston Churchill

*S*cene: *This really happened[65] (http://www.youtube.com/ watch?v=4S4pJzhmmMs). Lance Burton achieved the accolade reserved for the greatest of Las Vegas headliners: his own stage in his own theater. The first American to win the Gold Medal awarded by the Fédération Internationale des Sociétés Magiques—the "Olympics of Magic"—in 1982, Burton is performing on his stage in his theater at the Monte Carlo Hotel, when suddenly one of his comely assistants is menaced by what can only be described as a man-monster.*

The masked being brandishes a sword—prompting Burton to interrupt his show, grab his own trusty blade, and engage in an apparently impromptu Errol Flynn-style duel. There is thrusting, parrying, and the discordant clash of real steel against real steel. Clearly, Burton is battling for his theatrical life, conducting a brave fighting retreat up a staircase and taking his stand at the top.

"What do you want?" he demands of the apparition. "Why are you here?"

With this, Burton covers himself with a floor-length cloth, through which we still hear him asking questions.

Unimpressed, the man-monster viciously stabs through the cloth several times. He then pulls his sword back, looks around, and finds— well, nothing at all. In obvious confusion, the masked apparition turns to the audience, as if appealing to them for the explanation he cannot discover on his own.

He glares at the audience through his mask. At length, his hand reaches for it, and slowly, ever so slowly, he removes it to reveal at last the answer to the magician's final question: "Who are you?"

He is Lance Burton, who has overcome and prevailed against—and changed places with—evil incarnate.

As for the audience, it is transformed into one great eruption. And the legendary magician Jay Marshall, who appeared on The Ed Sullivan Show no fewer than fourteen times, pronounced it "[t]he best one-man illusion in the history of magic."

Lance Burton displayed the power of overcoming opposition within his magic performance while creating remarkable theater. But the truth is every performance of magic is about facing and confronting the laws of nature and overcoming them by creating the impossible. This deep fact about magic performance—that every performance overcomes reality itself—is part of why great magic feels so inexplicably powerful. Whether it is when David Copperfield defies the laws of gravity and flies, or when Harry Houdini escapes from any kind of bondage and elemental stress thrown at him, or when Max Maven defies the veiling of his sight by a blindfold to see what cannot be seen, great magic is about defeating challenge, adversity, or an enemy.

As The Coca-Cola Company's legendary leader—and David Morey's late client—Roberto Goizueta once said, "Without an enemy, there can be no war." (Remember: Coke never tired of taking on Pepsi!) And a sure way to make a display of theatrical magic truly magical is to get the audience rooting for you, the magician, wishing and hoping that you will overcome and prevail against an enemy—or even against everyday reality itself.

"With friends like that, who needs enemies?" The question is rhetorical, of course, but it turns out that the answer is crucial. You need enemies— or at least one. An enemy makes you important. Every god requires a devil, and a miracle-working magician has no less a need for an evil foil. For some, it is a masked man in monster's garb. For others, it is simply the mundane—the dreary presence of a quotidian reality that denies the possibility of the miraculous and magical. Great theatrical magic, like all great drama, needs an antagonist to represent opposing forces, good versus evil, us versus them, the magician versus...whatever. You need a villain against whom you must fight. Over the decades, great magical performances have pitted the magician against a "water torture cell," against bondage and oppression, against gravity, against the limits of human endurance, and so on.

KEEP YOUR FRIENDS CLOSE—AND YOUR ENEMIES CLOSER

Finding Goizueta's proverbial "enemy" is even more important in politics and business than it is in magic. Such an enemy, along with the fight you wage against it, is often key to how you define yourself as a candidate, a nation, a brand, or a leader. In 1997, when David Morey was advising the presidential campaign of South Korea's Kim Dae Jung, his company conducted a study as the future Nobel laureate was poised to take office amid his nation's worst financial crisis since the Korean War. David wanted to identify those leaders who were most successful over their first one hundred days, those who had begun their terms in office with the best running start and had ultimately used this great beginning to define a positive historical legacy.

David and his staff looked hard for examples. If the search were being conducted today, by the way, Donald Trump would not make the cut. His first one hundred days and beyond were marked by multiple legislative setbacks, dropping approval ratings, and a cascade of self-inflicted wounds, culminating in the appointment of a special investigator—and all this in the context of a Congress controlled by his own party. But back in the late 1990s, if you recall, President Bill Clinton also suffered mishaps in dealing with the issue of gays in the military and a string of nomination disasters. Other leaders squandered their first one hundred days and never regained critical momentum in defining themselves and their legacies. So, after some hard thought, the list was narrowed to a top three: President Franklin Roosevelt (the originator of the "Hundred Days" metric), Prime Minister Margaret Thatcher, and President Ronald Reagan. All three enjoyed relatively high levels of popularity following their first one hundred days in office, and all three cemented their places in history from extraordinarily strong beginnings. From this early platform, all three defined themselves and largely managed to control the entire process of creating this definition. They played offense and played it well, controlling the dialogue, staying focused and disciplined, and steadily adding to their support—rather than subtracting from it, as the current occupant of 1600 Pennsylvania Avenue has done.

The three leaders were very different in many ways, and they faced very different problems, but they had one tactic in common. They all set their sights on an "enemy" to sharpen their own definition of themselves, to define the causes for which they stood, and to define what ultimate success will look like. During Roosevelt's first Hundred Days, the enemy was a group of "uncaring, mindless bureaucrats." For Thatcher—again, at the commencement of her administration—it was "socialist over-spenders." For Reagan, from the get-go it was supporters of "big government." The enemies varied, but they were all enemies. And thus, these three very different leaders energized their own definitions of themselves and of success by defining the people they were against.

Now, in business, consider the clarity that insurgents, or "change" leaders, bring to a marketplace competition by defining themselves against a big, bloated, bureaucracy-loving incumbent—or against a marketplace "enemy." Pepsi found its enemy in Coke, Apple in IBM. But even a great and iconic company like Microsoft can lose focus until it finds the right enemy—the enemy it needs. As David Morey and Scott Miller chronicled in their 2004 book *The Underdog Advantage: Using the Power of Insurgent Strategy to Put Your Business on Top*, way back in 1994, Microsoft's enemy was Novell. In 1995 and 1996, it was Netscape. In 1997 and 1998, it was Sun Microsystems. Later, Microsoft's enemy was Linux and the so-called open-source systems. By the way, Microsoft's infamous twenty-one-year legal battle against antitrust rulings was a great example of choosing the *wrong* enemy. What consumer has sympathy for—and will offer loyalty to—a company fighting for its rights as a monopolist?

If you are looking to infuse your company with a winning culture, you need to lead your organization against an opponent you define. This enemy defines who and what they must fight and defeat. Importantly, this struggle can never be about blind hatred. On the contrary, it must be a calculated, chess-champion-like strategy concerning your competition. Do not overestimate or underestimate your enemy's strengths, and never "dis" the foe. Teach the people you lead to respect the competitor and to learn from his strengths—even as they exploit his weaknesses.

In business, defining the enemy is often quite simple, especially if you don't happen to be number one in the marketplace. In such a case, the most obvious candidates for enemy are the market leader or the next competitor up the ladder from you. Pick one rather than blur your organization's focus by taking on everybody at once. As President Lincoln told his Cabinet in response to Secretary of State William H. Seward's suggestion of a declaration of war against England while the Union was fighting the Confederacy: "One war at a time, gentlemen." It was very good advice. Yet even worse than taking on multiple enemies or a vaguely defined foe is the more usual mistake company leadership makes when it declares, "We don't really have competition for what we do."

In fact, if you do not have competition, you need to create it. You need an enemy. In business, instead of denying the existence of competitors, define some other enemy. The most effective candidate for villain is a problem that consumers face in the marketplace. It may be a problem that innovation will solve; it may be a problem that consumer education will solve; it may be stagnation of choice, a problem created by one or two big players' marketplace domination.

As detailed in the First Strategy, the benefit consumers most urgently want is control. Fail to define a marketplace with elements that they can control, and your appeal is doomed to meet with indifference. Earlier, we referenced the visionary mission Bill Gates defined for Microsoft in 1975: "A computer on every desk and in every home." To be sure, this mission was motivated by its focus on creating a need for the company's product, operating system software, but the underlying conviction was that the information revolution was on the march and ready to make *all* people's lives better. In this context, the enemy was those people or forces that might somehow oppose the democratizing, equalizing, and liberating benefits of the revolution. Allowed to win, these people or forces will prevent the improvement in life. A secondary enemy was implied as well. Call it complacency. Allow the anti-democratic forces to win, and you will be left behind in the march of progress. And being left behind brings the doom of irrelevance.

Finding, creating, defining, overcoming, and prevailing against an enemy works just as magically in the corporate world as it does in politics. There is tremendous power in defining a marketplace antagonist or villain. To take another Microsoft example, consider that the company's spreadsheet application, Excel, currently owns about 76 percent of the spreadsheet market, with an astounding three-quarters of a billion users worldwide. This was not always the case.

Back in the early 1990s, when Microsoft was a client of David Morey's firm, the unquestioned spreadsheet market leader was a product called Lotus 1-2-3. At that time, Hank Vigil, Microsoft's senior VP for strategy and partnership, vowed to unseat 1-2-3. He made defeating this enemy— yes, *enemy*—his focus, and in an act as daring as anything Harry Houdini ever did, Vigil launched his anti-1-2-3 campaign with a strategy meeting held not at the Redmond, Washington, headquarters of Microsoft, but in Cambridge, Massachusetts, home of the Lotus corporation. He summoned his magician-generals not merely to the hometown of Lotus, but he convened them around a table in Michaela's restaurant, at the time located in the very lobby of Lotus corporate headquarters. With seemingly supernatural audacity, these strategic conjurers were eating their fill as they plotted their plans in nothing less than the belly of the beast.

Years later, about a decade ago, Google took an even more ambitiously magical approach. At the time, its two grad student founders, Larry Page and Sergey Brin, asked David and business partner Scott Miller to help them analyze a newspaper-based initiative intended to transform the traditional publishing world's advertising-purchasing model. While doing this work, it became obvious to the consultants that *Google continuously defines and refines its culture* by what it is against. Consider. The company developed a corporate mission proclaimed in a credo that was truly unique in the history of business:

> **Don't be evil.** We believe strongly that in the long term, we will be better served—as shareholders and in all other ways—by a company that does good things for the world, even if we forego some short-term gains.

For Google, the imperative "Don't be evil" meant *fight those who fight change*—and especially fight those who stand in the way of Google's own civilization-changing mission: to help computer users find exactly what they want on the Internet. Ergo, the enemy was the advocates of the status quo, the fat-and-happy opponents of change.

Companies and their leaders are most compelling when they have an enemy. This enemy might be a direct competitor, or it might be the consumer's enemy—what marketers call a consumer "pain"—something they want or need that they are not getting. In either case, the competitive appeal of a company is greatest when its leaders and constituents put the enemy directly in their sights. We earlier mentioned such companies as Uber, Facebook, Alibaba, and Airbnb, which literally created markets that did not exist before and that crafted business models that broke the dominate paradigm of their times. Each of these companies—indeed, every successful start-up company we've worked with—has held a clear-eyed view of the consumer pain they oppose. Their enemy, on behalf of the consumer, is the pain people must shoulder. In the realm of magic, keep Houdini uppermost in mind. We all crave some escape—escape from limitations, escape from a boss, escape from a dreary spouse, escape from quotidian responsibilities, escape from the limitations of our own limited talents. Houdini, time and again, in performance after performance, offered the fulfilled hope of escape. He was like the evangelist who presents dramatic testimonials of answered prayer to his audience.

THE CLOSEST ENEMY OF ALL

If you can't find an enemy, look in the mirror. Quite often, the enemy against which a company must prevail is the company itself. The famous statement of Commodore Oliver Hazard Perry referencing the War of 1812— "We have met the enemy and they are ours"—sourced the derivative phrase of the great American cartoonist Walter Kelly, first on a 1970 Earth Day poster, and later in his famous *Pogo* comic strip: "We have met the enemy and he is us." Kelly died in 1973, but his phrase lives on as a battle cry for all organizations, all businesses, and all governments, to ensure they do battle against their own worst bureaucratic instincts and behavior. In fact, while Roberto Goizueta's "You can't fight a war without an enemy" was directed at Coke's external marketplace, the adage has been used at The Coca-Cola Company and at many other companies to rally against paralyzing over-cautiousness, navel gazing, and an array of "politicized" behaviors, incumbent arrogance, and bureaucratic thinking.

"Get action!" was the wonderfully simple phrase President Theodore Roosevelt admitted was the very definition of his philosophy not just of leadership, but of life itself. *Get action!* was how TR battled against Tammany Hall and Washington bureaucrats, not to mention the challenges in his own life. This simple phrase captures the guiding impulse of some of the great Founder/Performer CEOs we've worked with and studied.

MORE MAGIC

Magicians take a very basic and dramatic approach in their fights. They pit darkness against light, concealment against revelation, deception against truth, and evil against good. In magic, the power of this drama takes place not on the stage, but within the imagination of the audience. In business, it is found not on the factory floor or the product showroom, but within the imagination of consumers. In both venues, the struggle is to disrupt whatever denies us freedom and fulfillment. As it is with the power of great political leaders and great magicians, the power of great companies is most compellingly measured by what they defeat. The company that finds, creates, overcomes, and prevails against an *antagonist* earns the right to define itself as the hero, a *protagonist* deserving the support of consumers and the loyalty of customers and clients.

As mentioned in earlier strategies, our friend Max Maven is one of the top mentalists in magic history. His extraordinary play *Thinking in Person* is appreciated not just by "humans" (i.e., non-magicians), but by top professional magicians as well. In his typical show, Max displays some of the theatrical skills in reading minds that have set him apart from others in the field—taking on a character that is not immediately knowable or even likeable, although that changes as the performance unfolds. From the very beginning, Max is in control of his character and his audience. Introduced, he greets the audience with his unusual widow's peak, long hair pulled back into a pony tail, and a downright overall scary look. Max looks at the audience, pauses, and then delivers an opening line he himself says took him five years to write: "Boo!"

A fan and aficionado of professional wrestling, Max understands the power of antagonist versus protagonist, villain versus hero. Notice the dramatic clarity of good vs. bad in most professional wrestling matches: Vince McMahon, Ric Flair, or Bobby "The Brain" Heenan versus Stone Cold Steve Austin, Hulk Hogan, or The Rock. And if you get a chance to see Max perform, notice the complexity and development of his own character. He appreciates that his audience will be taking a ninety-minute ride during an evening's performance into some of the best mind reading in history, but, at the same time, he knows that they will become even more engaged by trying to figure out whether they like the antagonist he presents himself to be—or if he will eventually become their protagonist, a mind reader they not only admire, but come to feel affection for. Such is the battle between magician and challenge, between mind reader and the impossibility of reading a mind. Such is the challenge that great performers and business leaders must successfully meet.

But exactly how might we apply magical and theatrical examples of successfully overcoming and prevailing against some form of evil to the business world—and to your own leadership? The three-part answer comes straight from the world of magical performance:

First, *prepare internally* to overcome and prevail.

Second, adopt a Founder/Performer mentality.

Third, find ways to hedge against failure by winning with more boldness.

PREPARE INTERNALLY

It is no secret that many of the world's top business experts see economic trouble ahead. This happens to be true just about any time. A long-held theory has it that all economies—as with all companies—move through "seasonal" change, and in so doing, carry businesses and business leaders with them. They begin in spring, enjoy summer, worry through fall, and then suffer in winter—which is followed by the recovery and rebirth that is spring. Tony Robbins, in his excellent "Business Mastery" seminar, describes this as the "10 Stages of the Life Cycle of a Business": birth, infancy, toddler, teenager, young adult, maturity, midlife, aging, institutionalization, and death. Seasonal economic and business theory has proved itself to be far truer than not, and you don't have to be a fan of *Game of Thrones* to understand that someday—and soon— "Winter is coming."

Our best chance of surviving, overcoming, and prevailing in the coming winter is to focus on what we ourselves can control. In magic, this means focusing on our own stage, our own magical performance, our own inner magician. And in business, Tony Robbins convincingly argues in his seminars and recent books that surviving and flourishing today means adopting the attitude of "the Gladiator."

Think about the metaphor. Ultimately, the odds are against all gladiators, because they simply can't win forever. But they can and must prepare and get ready for the next unpredictable battle, preparing themselves internally, if you will, for the life-and-death challenges that will come to them as surely as winter's arrival. Winter, for us, today, is coming.

The greatest magicians and the greatest business leaders never give up. By discipline, pathology, and sheer guts, the greatest magician—or the greatest business leader—rises to the long-term challenge of climbing to and staying at the top of the profession. Each in their own way, these magicians and business leaders practice more, practice smarter, and practice more consciously. They prioritize better. And they make *their* difference make *a* difference. As Eugene Burger puts it: "Great magicians are made one effect at a time." This means they focus on what they can control to get ready for winter—to prepare for the intense and unpredictable challenges of being among the world's greatest magicians and performers.

The greatest magicians find ways to get ready *internally* for the challenges of winter. Typically, they drive to excellence by mastering and differentiating themselves "one effect at a time." Here are some examples: Our teacher Jeff McBride and his famous mask act, Lance Burton and his FISM-winning dove and candle opening act, David Copperfield with his extraordinary dancing cane, and later, with his flying and his bigger-than-big vanishing of the Statue of Liberty, or Uri Geller and his bending metal and other objects by the focus of the mind. You get the idea. These magicians follow Eugene Burger's adage of driving to absolute excellence one step, one effect, and one piece of magic at a time. In the same way, great CEO Founder/Performers build their companies one product, one service, and one brand offering at a time.

David Morey remembers a long conversation with the legendary Channing Pollock, whose remarkable dove act of the 1960s redefined excellence in the art and became the most imitated magic act in the history of magic.[66] While Pollock, with his extraordinarily good looks and charisma, was a gifted performer, he worked as hard as any magician in perfecting his craft—graduating from the Chavez College of Magic, in some ways the Harvard University of the field, and building a picture-perfect seven-minute act that was unforgettable. But one of Pollock's greatest secrets—which he shared with David during their conversation—was what he called "mental practice." Lying in bed after each magic practice and rehearsal, before he went to sleep at night, and upon arising in the morning, Pollock mentally ran through the act as if he were performing live on *The Ed Sullivan Show* or at the Café de Paris, both of which he eventually did. Pollock's secret to overcoming and prevailing was that his best magic came from within, not just from his talented hands, but from his powerful mind.

Skier Jean-Claude Killy, who won all three Olympic gold medals in the alpine category in 1968, once revealed in an interview that while recovering from a terrible downhill accident, he was unable to ski and could only practice mentally. Yet it was this *internal* practice that enabled him to deliver one of his best performances.[67]

Or consider what golf great Jack Nicklaus said about his own use of mental practice and visualization:

> I never hit a shot, not even in practice, without having a very sharp, in-focus picture of it in my head. It's like a color movie. First, I "see" the ball where I want it to finish, nice and white and sitting up high on bright green grass. Then the scene quickly changes, and I "see" the ball going there: its path, trajectory, and shape, even its behavior on landing. Then there is a sort of a fade-out, and the next scene shows me making the kind of swing that will turn the images into reality.[68]

Pollock, Killy, and Nicklaus all practiced inside their own minds, magically visualizing each step toward success—and then, when it counted, their physical bodies followed an internal script they'd built from within. This is related to internal attitude. Beyond any cliché, it really does all begin with *you*. In truth, your own internal way of thinking is the most powerful and magical tool available to you—or to any magician or business leader. In fact, in magic, as Eugene Burger taught: Your audience will never take the magician's magic more seriously than the magician takes his or her magic. How much import do you give your magic? Your audience will never think what you do is more important than you think it is.

Preparing internally to overcome and prevail, to defeat whatever "enemy" you face in business, means taking yourself as seriously as you expect others to take you. Our experience working with top CEOs and presidents of countries is that each of them believes, deep-down, that they are a top CEO or the president of their country. Their own self-image is a powerful driver, filter, and vision, which they continually access, aim, and move toward. Taking their leadership role and success seriously becomes a self-fulfilling and central element of their success.

Some years ago, Eugene Burger told a story about Federal Express losing his one and only copy of a corrected manuscript of a book he had just finished. Eventually, three months later, the errant package would be discovered in the middle of the country. But there was no way of knowing this at the time, and Eugene had to—in the present—re-create the careful, painstaking work he had already completed. Initially feeling hopeless about taking on this task for a second time, Eugene got some interesting advice from a friend: "Here's what you do. Tomorrow morning when you take a shower, say out loud: 'I give myself permission to be powerful.' Say it twenty times, and see how you feel when you say it." Eugene was skeptical, but in the shower the next morning, he found the phrase jumping to mind, and so he began saying it out loud—twenty times. He did this again the next morning. And the next.

It began to work. Steadily, Eugene finished—yet one more time—the painstaking editing job. Years later, he would find himself repeating this same set of "magical words," an inward and empowering song that pulled him into a positive mindset and helped him tackle whatever seemingly impossible task was at hand.

The truth is that you don't need to search too deeply into magic, business, or any part of life to find the power of magical words sung as an inward and empowering song. For some, the tune plays loudly and consistently, helping these lucky people jump over the hurdles we all face in life. Basketball great Michael Jordan was cut from his high school team, failed to be recruited by North Carolina State, the college for which he wanted to play, and was not drafted by the first two NBA teams that could have selected the future greatest-ever-to-play-the-game. Still, he kept playing his own inward and empowering song. He stayed positive, working on his early weaknesses—his defensive game, his ball handling, and his shooting. Jordan's coaches were always surprised about how much harder he worked than anyone else. For Jordan, becoming the greatest at what he had set out to do came down not to his God-given talent, but to the way he prepared internally, to his innate hunger for success, and to his inward and empowering song filled with "magical words." As a former Bulls coach once described Jordan: He's "a genius who constantly wants to upgrade his genius."

Richard Branson says the same thing: In his book *The Virgin Way*, he argues that hard work and a positive attitude help people make their own luck. Branson tells a story about the triangular relationship between hard work, positive attitude, and luck:

> I remember watching the final round of the British Open golf championship on TV and seeing one of the leaders chip out of a deep greenside bunker. His shot was high, but it just clipped the top of the flagpole, and amazingly, the ball dropped right into the hole. One of the British commentary team exclaimed, "Oh my goodness, what a lucky shot!"
>
> Another commentator in the broadcast booth (a retired American champion, as I recall) immediately snapped back with a stinging rebuke, "Lucky! What do you mean 'lucky'? Do you know how many thousands of hours we all spend practicing shots like that? He was trying to put it in the hole and he succeeded. Let me tell you, he worked long and hard on getting that lucky!"[69]

Tony Robbins has a simple three-point framework for preparing internally—focusing on and shifting "State," "Story," and "Strategy."[70] The steps can be performed anywhere at a moment's notice. Internal preparation as an exercise is ready when you need it:

♦ **STATE**: People in a negative "State" see only problems, not solutions. They are trapped inside a negative tunnel vision and are therefore overwhelmed by self-defeating thoughts, which send them into a lowered state of emotion

Solution: Change your State. Work out, meditate, do yoga, drink water, walk, do deep breathing exercises, clear off your desk and clear out your inbox; raise your posture into a powerfully positive position. This is very much like the way magicians prepare to go on stage, transforming their State so that they can face their audience and go to work to produce miracles for them.

♦ **STORY**: People tell the same old self-defeating, endless-loop "Story" of victimhood and negativity, disempowering themselves from a set of actions that might change this Story.

Solution: "Prime" a new Story, one that enables you by transforming victimhood into opportunity. Everyone likes a comeback, a second act, an underdog. Refocusing on this new Story puts you back in control. This is like the way magicians develop their own internal character: inventing the way their onstage character thinks, the character's backstory, and the way he or she reacts to literally anything that comes at the magician during a show.

♦ **STRATEGY**: People don't just stay stuck inside a negative State or endlessly retell a negative Story, they also simply react to what comes at them—to e-mails, incoming calls, requests for favors, or even to fate. They operate across tactical to-do lists that are unprioritized and create more paralysis than forward momentum.

Solution: After you change your State and prime a newly positive Story, think Strategically to become exponentially more effective. Set goals and objectives. Think big ideas. Ruthlessly prioritize the top 20 percent of tactics that can deliver 80 percent of results. And build progress by "chunking" tasks in a way that builds the magic of momentum. The greatest magicians are invariably successful strategic thinkers and therefore highly effective people. Success in magic resembles success in business. There are no accidents. Luck alone is not enough. Success requires a positive State, an empowering Story, and a smart Strategy.

THINK LIKE A "FOUNDER/PERFORMER"

She claims she has been hit by lightning three times. Love or hate Martha Stewart, one must concede she is a fighter, definitely someone we can call a "Founder/Performer." Author of seventy-nine books, Martha sleeps four hours a night and is famous for what might appear to be a pathological drive for control and excellence. It is a "pathology" that has made her a billionaire, helped her survive felony convictions and prison, and may someday make her a billionaire again.

We've grown up watching Stewart's story. Born in 1941, the second of six children, to Polish middle-class parents, Martha Kostyra, later Martha Stewart, displayed the kind of drive that builders of businesses and self-made millionaires and billionaires use as the fuel for their success. The founder of Martha Stewart Living Omnimedia (MSLO), she gained success in publishing, broadcasting, merchandising, and e-commerce—so much success that *New York Magazine* declared her in its May 1995 cover issue "the definitive American woman of our time." Four years later, the IPO of her company made Stewart the first female self-made billionaire in the United States. In 2003, however, this "definitive American woman of our time" was indicted on nine felony counts related to insider trading, including charges of securities fraud and obstruction of justice. Voluntarily stepping down from her own company's leadership, she went to trial in 2004, was found guilty, and was sentenced to a five-month term in a federal correctional facility.

She preferred not to wait for the results of her appeal. Controlling what she could still control, all the while watching the toll her conviction was taking on her company, Stewart reported at 6:15 a.m. on October 8, 2004, to the Federal Prison Camp in Alderson, West Virginia. By all accounts, she was an "ideal" prisoner, admitting in a post-prison interview to rising before other prisoners so that she herself could clean the shower.

Following Stewart's release, and during two years of supervised release, including five months of home confinement with electronic monitoring, the CEO Founder/Performer plotted and began her comeback. It was fueled by her legendary work ethic, which often includes twenty-hour work days. As Stewart served her prison sentence, many predicted the end of her business and the destruction of her brand. How wrong they were. During her actual prison stay, the value of her company's stock more than doubled, after many months on a downward spiral. On paper, she even became a billionaire for the second time in February 2005.

But this was not the end of her battles. Company leadership problems and changes, inflated internal compensation packages—including to herself—and consecutive years of losses all represented challenges to MSLO, as did a partnership and then a legal falling-out with Macy's— mainly over what the retailer argued was Stewart's courting of J.C. Penney during her contractual relationship with Macy's. Today, Stewart's current net worth is roughly $300 million, according to www.bankrate.com. MSLO, along with her blogs, lifestyle website, PBS cooking show, social media presence, meal kit services, and wine brands all continue to drive her empire, and many experts see her well positioned not only to survive today's challenging and hyper-competitive retail environment, but to rise even higher in wealth and success. Martha Stewart is the emblematic woman hit by obstacles she herself helped to create, but who continues to fight, perhaps someday all the way back to her previous billionaire status.

So, what does this woman who says she was hit by lightning three times have in common with a self-described "Shoe Dog," or with the man who built the world's largest fast-food empire?

Phil Knight's 2016 book, *Shoe Dog: A Memoir by the Creator of Nike*, chronicles an extraordinary series of challenges, challenges anyone who has ever entered a "Niketown" and bought something to feel more like a champion either forgot or never knew about. There were legal battles, debt swaps, near bankruptcies, strained credit lines, supplier nightmares, and media and public attacks over hiring "slave" laborers. All of these challenges were of the caliber that only someone with the limitless drive and bottomless energy of a Founder/Performer could both endure and conquer.

Ray Kroc, as chronicled so wonderfully in the 2016 movie *The Founder*, was a former traveling salesmen of milkshake mixers who often listened to motivational recordings to get going before sales calls. Kroc had an epiphany concerning the power of an innovative fast-food model demonstrated in a single California store owned by the McDonald brothers. He saw in it exponential possibilities, and driven by his "burning bush" vision, skirted any number of ethical boundaries and found ways to borrow from Peter to pay Paul to get his dream of a nationwide franchise launched. For all his sharp dealings, including with the McDonald brothers themselves (who in effect lost the right to use their very name), Kroc built a machine that made working-class franchisee owners millionaires across the country in creating the legendary fast-food company that is today McDonald's.

Martha Stewart, Phil Knight, Ray Kroc—all are what we call Founder/Performers. They act like entrepreneurs more than CEOs or employees. They all have an original Founder vision and narrative that consumers increasingly and instinctively search for today. All have a story about why they developed the products and services that made their companies famous, for whom these products and services were invented, and what pain in the marketplace they were designed to relieve. And in pursuit of fulfillment of their vision, they stop at nothing. *The Founder* alludes to Kroc's most famous pronouncement concerning the morality of competition: "If any of my competitors were drowning, I'd stick a hose in their mouth and turn on the water. It is ridiculous to call this an industry. This is not. This is rat eat rat, dog eat dog. I'll kill 'em, and I'm going to kill 'em before they kill me. You're talking about the American way—of survival of the fittest."[71]

The story of the Founder/Performer has spawned a subgenre narrative, the tale of the Founder/Performer CEO who returns to the company he or she created to fix it after it has passed into the hands of others. If the primary Founder/Performer story is a classic American creation narrative, the secondary revival story is a classic American turnaround story. Steve Jobs at Apple, Howard Schultz at Starbucks, Phil Knight at Nike, Jack Dorsey at Twitter, and Tim Westergren at Pandora—each are Founder/Performer CEOs who returned as Founder/Performer turnaround CEOs. In some ways, this secondary story is even more powerful than the primary story, because it underscores how important the Founder/Performer's bold, insurgent, and unique way of thinking is to a truly disruptive insurgent enterprise.

Today, most successful upstart and insurgent brands are run by Founder/Performer entrepreneurs. They are vision-driven; their brands have become established because of the Founder/Performer feeling of frustration or of opportunity. And these Founder/Performers will journey through the seven levels of hell trying to get the new idea moving forward, let alone keep it going. Invariably, this frustration—or sense of fragile opportunity, depending on how you look at it—drives every aspect of a successful insurgent company's creation, development, and communication.

Contemporary Founder/Performer CEOs are their company's brand. They represent the brand in all they do and say. These CEOs sync their personal brand and narrative with that of their company—a trait that CEOs of every firm would do well to emulate. Think of the most iconic brands, and you will almost certainly think of the iconic CEO associated with each of them—Steve Jobs at Apple, Bill Gates at Microsoft, Dave Thomas at Wendy's, Frank Perdue at Perdue Farms, Jim Koch at Boston Beer/ Sam Adams, Michael Milken at Drexel Burnham, Fred Smith at Federal Express, Dietrich Mateschitz at Red Bull, Manoj Bhargava at 5-Hour Energy, Rupert Murdoch at News Corp, Marc Benioff at Salesforce, Reid Hoffman at LinkedIn, Brian Chesky at Airbnb, Sergey Brin at Google, Jack Ma at Alibaba, Jeff Bezos at Amazon, Larry Ellison at Oracle, Mark Pincus at Zynga, Elon Musk at SpaceX, and Mark Zuckerberg at Facebook.

Founder/Performer CEOs fight hard for their company's brand because it is *their* brand. David Morey's company worked with Microsoft for more than a decade. His business partner Scott Miller loves to tell the story of how often they came away from a meeting with Bill Gates certain they'd just been fired. At Microsoft, Gates created a culture of argument. Miller half-seriously believes he developed it in math camp: "I've got the answer!" "No, you don't, you jerk! I've got the answer!" Argument was part of Gate's personality and part of his brand. It was also a big part of the Microsoft process. Gates believed that the competitive arguments of strategy and product design ultimately allowed the true believers to triumph. Think *American Idol* for nerds.

Hell, when Microsoft was within ten years of starting up, everybody, but everybody, was super smart. The difference between the super smart mass and the super smart true believers was that the true believers fought for their ideas the way Gates fought for Microsoft itself. Almost any young product manager could get an audience with Gates and other leaders to present his or her ideas. As the product manager presented, for example, Gates always found a detail or two with which to take issue. "Taking issue" invariably involved a cascade of vulgarities, culminating in the accusation that the presenter was intentionally trying to destroy the company he had worked so hard to build. If this fusillade of jabs buckled the product manager's knees, Gates dismissed her, together with her idea. If, however, she fought for what she believed, Bill sat back and listened. What he cared about most was the intensity of a person's belief in his or her own idea.

As true believers, Founder/Performers don't put a lot of faith in advertising and sales promotion. As true believers, they believe their product does not need hype. Inherently, all Founder/Performers are entrepreneurs driven to create relevant differentiation, that is, to become famous "one magical effect at a time." They therefore find ways to be hyper-relevant in proving consumer benefits, ensuring their consumers feel they simply can't live without their product. When Gates said, "A computer on every desk and in every home," he was proclaiming his intention of making every Microsoft product a can't-live-without-it product. As their products are thus differentiated from the crowd—must-have versus strictly optional— the Founder/Performers themselves are clearly differentiated from their competitive set. They are—and believe themselves to be—different, special, and better. As Steve Jobs used to say, "Everybody else sucks."

We suggest that you adopt this as your personal brand motto: "Everybody else sucks." If you were brought up to be polite, make it your secret brand motto. The thing is, in our hyper-competitive, Internet-cluttered environment, "me-too marketing"—the traditional go-to of second-tier brands—is becoming dramatically less effective. Sameness is sunk. Following the leader with narrow differences in price or promotion just does not cut it. In today's marketplace, there is room on any consumer's menu for one sure-thing ubiquitous incumbent brand. They'll occasionally go for the market leader based on convenience, but the market followers are in trouble. They are being crushed from above by the incumbent leader and fractured from below by the insurgent brands.

BOLDNESS OVERCOMES AND PREVAILS

Beautiful, bold, audacious, and possessed of a devastating wit, the American actress and film star Tallulah Bankhead once proclaimed, "If I had to live my life again, I'd make the same mistakes, only sooner."

It is a proclamation that would suit any of the world's greatest magicians. They build their careers, one effect at a time, by accelerating the pace at which they fail—the pace at which they make the kind of mistakes that create tremendous, if not exponential, growth in the art of magic. To be sure, fear of failure has held many a performer back and caused them to fall well short of success, but momentum and velocity are the secret ingredients in the sauce of magic. This holds for business, too, especially today. Take software development. Digital technology moves so fast that the mantra of so-called agile software developers is *Fail fast, fail often, fail forward.* Put another way, the more offense you play and the faster you play offense, the safer you are and the more successful you will be. The iconic American general of World War II, George S. Patton, Jr., was nicknamed "Old Blood and Guts" because of his reputation for driving his soldiers directly into the teeth of battle. He did just that, and his celebrated Third Army moved faster and farther and killed or captured more of the enemy than any other force in the European theater—Allied or Axis. Patton's real achievement, though, was to do this while suffering fewer casualties than most of his fellow commanders. He believed that bold action saves lives. He believed that an army advancing toward an enemy was hard to kill, whereas an army hunkered down was a target waiting to be hit. The results he produced proved the virtues of playing offense. To paraphrase James Carville's winning 1992 campaign mantra: "It's the boldness, stupid!"

This is not to say that today's business leaders, like great magicians, should neglect to prepare soft landings wherever possible. For example, Jeff McBride, one of magic's greatest Founder/Performers, teaches his magical acolytes the concept of "hammocking" new material you are breaking in. This means putting untested magical effects between well-proven miracles, thereby ensuring that you will not be left without real magic for very long should a new effect fall flat.

We magicians often break in new magical effects, but the place to do so is not on live TV or during a high-paying and hyper-prestigious corporate engagement. To quote an old showbiz saying, "Starting out, every performer needs a place to be bad." So, we begin testing new material with friends and family whom we coax over to witness a quick performance. (Some people will do anything for a cocktail.) And we video the performance, looking for what is working and what needs further development. David Morey likes to move on from the friends-and-family stage to a local "independent living" facility, where he offers a charity show that includes the new material hammocked between proven effects.

John McLaughlin performs less frequently than David, but places the same emphasis on breaking in new material carefully. His technique is to immediately sit down and write an assessment of how a new piece has played. If something went wrong, why did it happen? Was it because of "dead space" in the script? An awkward moment in the handling of a prop? Doing something in the wrong sequence can afflict the details of handling or even what the magician says. Equally noted are things that went well with the new piece, such as something said by the magician or audience member that surprisingly got a laugh...or an unplanned element of choreography that heightened the effect. Such notes serve as a tool to continue refining the new piece the next time it is done.

Before professional magicians take any new piece of magical material "live," they test it over a dozen times before lower-stakes audiences. Author-entrepreneur Tim Ferriss, in his *Tools of Titans*, suggests that business leaders put their "A List" pitches in place only after they have completed ten lower-stakes presentations. As Ferriss puts it, "Pick the right audience to suck in front of."[72] But while hedging against failure is important, the key for business leaders who want to overcome and prevail is to play offense.

Consider the saga of Red Bull, which presents one of the best examples of business boldness of the past two decades. The energy drink company confronted barrier after barrier to entry into the marketplace. It treated each as just another opportunity.

When Red Bull couldn't convince The Coca-Cola Company or PepsiCo to purchase its energy drink, the company decided to go it alone—earning billions more than they might have made in any sale. Their road to profit was a sharp detour that avoided the tried-and-true marketing strategies of the market leaders.

When Red Bull couldn't get distribution through Coke or Pepsi bottlers, it went with beer distributors. Unprecedented? Well, with most beer sales in decline, this meant the distributors had a lot of energy for the energy category. And when Red Bull couldn't get placement in supermarkets because the soft drink incumbents had the muscle to block it, the company established an outsized presence in liquor stores, which undoubtedly eventually led to the brilliance of positioning the energy drink as a mixer. This gave the brand a sly "R-rated" image, which—naturally—became particularly popular with young consumers. And when Red Bull couldn't get its drink into restaurants because fountain and drink service in fast-food eateries and bars is a huge and hugely protected source of revenue for the soft drink incumbents, the company hit upon the idea of providing the product free to bouncers and bartenders in dance clubs. These "gatekeepers" initially used Red Bull only as a true solution for the problem they all shared: staying awake at all hours. Yet in this way, bouncers and bartenders became living testimonials that quickly established Red Bull as a source of energy. The gap from bartender to patron was thus quickly crossed by all those who wanted to boogie all night.

Finally, when Red Bull couldn't get a major sports sponsorship—the traditional "open sesame" that had ushered Gatorade out of obscurity in the 1970s—the company virtually created the sports category of extreme street sports. This morphed into the X-Games, which carried Red Bull further into the limelight.

Understand this: overcoming and prevailing does not necessarily require *new*. Want to invent a completely new and breakthrough magical effect? Follow the examples of great magicians like David Copperfield, Lance Burton, David Ben, Johnny Thompson, and Penn & Teller, and begin by studying the 1927 edition of Harlan Tarbell's *The Tarbell Course in Magic*, or C. Lang Neil's *The Modern Conjurer* from 1937, or Professor Hoffman's 1876 edition of *Modern Magic*, or for that matter, dip into Reginald Scot's 1584 classic *The Discoverie of Witchcraft*, and uncover long-forgotten material waiting to be reborn as "new."[73]

Want to read fresh examples of boldness? Dig into Edward Gibbon's 1789 bestseller *The Decline and Fall of the Roman Empire*, or any good history of the American Revolution. Consider. Back in 1836, Ralph Waldo Emerson wrote the "Concord Hymn" to commemorate the second of two skirmishes—one at Lexington, the second at Concord, Massachusetts—that kicked off the colonies' war for independence on April 19, 1775. On this day, it was two handfuls of militiamen against the greatest military power since the fallen Roman Empire. Great Britain had a population of about seven million within the British Isles, while the population of the American colonies was about two-and-a-half million, including half a million slaves. Measured in modern U.S. dollars, Britain's Gross Domestic Product was about $10.8 billion, whereas that of the colonies was a little over $500 million. The British crown permanently deployed some 120,000 men in the army and maintained a navy of 131 ships of the line—each mounting sixty-four guns or more—along with 139 ships of lesser classes. By the end of the day, following Lexington and Concord, the American colonies fielded about 3,800 militia troops and had no navy at all. And by the end of eight years, drawing heavily on boldness, the colonial insurgents had overcome and prevailed against their incumbent masters.

For centuries, boldness has been used successfully by our planet's revolutionaries in politics, war, and business. Boldness is what drives the strategy and tactics of the world's best Special Ops Forces today. And if he weren't dead, you could ask Osama bin Laden what it was like to be comfortably hunkered down in a walled fortress, surrounded by armed guards, in the middle of a city friendly to you, in the shadow of the academy of a military all too friendly to you, in a country mostly sympathetic to you and what you stood for, when SEAL Team 6 kicked in the door. Franklin, Washington, Adams, Jefferson, SEAL Team 6—all bold insurgents.

Bringing this all together, think about your company in very personal terms, namely, your own life. What do you regret more—the things you did or the things *you failed to do*? Are your greater regrets for the path taken or the one *not* taken? "Be bold," Goethe said, "for there is genius, power, and magic in it."

A CHECKLIST FOR THE BOLD

◆ *Make It happen.* This isn't Zen. You can't just "let it happen." It's time to fish or cut bait in the zero-sum competition of today's markets. First and foremost, in business as much as in magic, an insurgent boldness works. It focuses every resource on the solution, which is winning (which is fun).

◆ *Frame the Project.* Focus your people, company, or organization on how to think about any challenge facing them. They must win. In other words, they must deliver on all objectives—and they must do so by a definite date (such as "Election Day") which you set. To win, your organization must be smart and resourceful. It must use all actions, interactions, and communications needed to move the key consumers (who vote with their pocketbooks) to provide the margin for victory. Defining each term will force you, the leader, to create a clear definition of winning. Enliven the objectives by picturing success in terms of how your key targets will feel, think, and behave differently because of your win.

◆ *Set realistic intermediate objectives.* In framing the win, enumerate the intermediate objectives approaching it. They must be realistically achievable, and achieving each will pay a dividend in the magic of momentum, which will energize your people and sharpen their strategic vision. With each intermediate victory, your team will learn something they will never forget: how to win.

◆ *Aim Toward "Election Days."* Establish certain dates for achieving each objective and your goal. Your group will operate more effectively and efficiently if it is driven by a now-or-never "Election Day" focus. This enables your team members to understand what it means to win—and to lose. It shows them what they must do to win the votes that will turn the "election." Instill an "Election Day" discipline in your organization, and each member of the team will wake up every morning knowing whose votes they must win that day. Recall the magical lessons of Bob Iger at Disney: First, employees must feel they are a part of something great. Second, they must feel, every one of them, that they can make a difference. And third, they must know that someone will recognize the difference they themselves make.

♦ *Energize People's Work.* Don't settle for mere survival or for delivering marginal results. Today, more than ever, you must play a vigorous offense to overcome and prevail. The energy this both requires and generates is highly motivating. Why even compete, if you don't make it count by keeping score? Playing for keeps adrenalizes your organization's energy.

♦ *Play Offense.* Focus relentlessly on better and greater: better quality, better net profit, better intensity. Focus your *inner* Gladiator and "get action." Never play defense.

♦ *Take Chances.* Boldness calls for adopting the mindset of the Founder/ Performer and always swinging for the fences. This is what successful start-up companies do right now. They are bold—if only because there is not that much to lose.

♦ *Go Bigger.* Get your team working toward exponential change. Do this, and you can hold them all together with the cultural glue of being part of something great—believing they can make a difference, and that this difference will be recognized.

♦ *Exploit Speed.* Don't play safe. Keep moving. Never worry about errors of commission, but don't tolerate errors of omission, which can put your business out of the game. Always err on the side of doing more. Fail forward fast.

♦ *Drive Vision.* Focus on the future, because this is where your business' change will take your organization's employees. It's a question of space vs. time. The future is not a time. It is the place where success lives.

♦ *Love Change.* To a Founder/Performer, change means opportunity. When the market's molecules are in motion—in a fluid state of change—everything's up for grabs. And the rewards can be truly magical.

If you successfully tick off each checklist item, you will find you have the makings of a boldly insurgent culture. This is the culture that pervades the companies that succeed today. Consider the following two pairs:

First, a lot of people think Michael Dukakis gave up the White House to George H. W. Bush in 1988 when he let himself get photographed with his uncomfortably helmeted head sticking out of the hatch of an Abrams tank. Some people (George S. Patton Jr. or George C. Scott, for instance) look great in a helmet. Most don't. Dukakis looked downright goofy. Yet the very same professionals who did this to their candidate also ran the legendary "Comeback Kid" war room for Bill Clinton four years later.

What was the difference between 1988 and 1992? The insurgent orientation of the unquestioned campaign leader, Bill Clinton.

This was the candidate who once explained: "In any form of combat, whoever goes on the offense first wins.... The price of doing the same old thing is far higher than the price of change."[74]

Second, recall how Louis Gerstner used Operation Bear Hug to lead IBM's remarkable corporate turnaround in the 1990s. It enabled IBM to become a completely different company from IBM as it was under Gerstner's predecessor CEO, John Akers.

Given that Gerstner did not fire everybody and start with an all-new team, what happened? Gerstner's relentless commitment to the customer and his focus on listening to the customer and on driving culture change happened.

As a fellow Southeastern Conference football coach said of Alabama's legendary Bear Bryant, "He can beat your'n with his'n, then turn around and beat his'n with your'n." Insurgent leadership is portable. You don't leave it behind along with your desk at your last position. You bring it with you wherever you go. Use it.

Overcoming and prevailing means preparing *internally*, acting like a Founder/Performer, and fueling and filling your tanks with boldness, the boldness that marks a great magician or a great business leader. It is the boldness of a leader who is driving toward the kind of change that succeeds and wins today.

THE NINTH STRATEGY

EMPOWER BELIEF

"Magic is not tricks; it is a way."

—Tenkai Ishida

Scene: *This really happened to David Morey, who was doing his one-man play, A Magical Way of Thinking, at the D.C. Capitol Fringe Festival a few years ago. Onstage with him was a charming five-year-old from the audience. Laura was her name, and magically, she was creating a beautiful paper hat even though she had never made one before. She was finding her "inner magician"...becoming a magician in that onstage moment.*

The audience was clearly touched by her transformation, and Morey engaged with them about it, not by talking about Laura directly, but by telling another story about something that had really happened in another place and at another time.

"This effect has taught me a lot about myself," he explained. "It's reminded me that magic is good medicine. Shamans say that anything you do to relieve suffering or to bring joy into the world is magic.

"A few years ago, I was just beginning to get back into magic—I had given it up when I was just a boy, and I was doing a show in London. Some friends who saw my act volunteered me at the hospital where Princess Diana once worked.

"Well, 'volunteer' meant doing a show for the children there—about two hundred, as it turned out. Some were patients, some family members.

"One I will never forget: Sara, four years old.

"She was in the front row, in a wheelchair with tubes attached. Her mother doted and smiled, but Sara looked down, only down, sadder than any child I had ever seen.

"So the show began, and I was trying to pull two hundred pairs of eyes toward the magic. Sara, though, only looked down.

"It crossed my mind to come down from the stage to Sara—but an impulse moved me instead to invite her mother up onstage with me. In fact, I invited her to do what Laura just did: find the Magician Within.

"She looked at her daughter, left her side, and came up. Magically, as I knew it would, the hat formed in her hands. We were all under the mother's spell—magician and audience together. The girl's mother and I turned to Sara, her eyes now fixed on us, and across her face, the most beautiful smile on earth. She beamed.

"Mommy was a magician!

"On that day in London, Sara and I both grew stronger."

In this strategy, we first borrow one last time from history's greatest magicians the concepts of owning and fully believing in your intentions, whether performing magic for 5,000 people or selling your own business proposition. Second, we review the power of transparency and authenticity—prerequisites for success on the magician's stage and inside the business person's market. Finally, we gather and review all the lessons, so you can form your own "Magic List." With it, you can free yourself and your imagination to create ever more powerful magic.

At the heart of it all, at the inner core of the greatest magicians and the most successful business leaders, is the simple yet powerful concept of belief. This is to us the meaning of what the great twentieth-century Japanese magician Tenkai Ishida observed: *"Magic is not tricks; it is a way."*

What Eugene Burger taught his many students in the art of magic, including his co-authors in creating this book, was in the tradition of Tenkai. Magic, he told us, is not about tricks and not just about art. It is about life. Magic can be used as a metaphor for the philosophical framework we all bring to leadership, to business—and to the larger challenges of our lives. In this larger sense, magic is a way—a way of believing in dreams bigger than ourselves.

In business, the great innovations, the industry-disrupting, market-making, "must-have" products, always possess an element of magic. They satisfy a need or a desire by means of an apparent miracle. Untold millennia ago, someone dreamed of moving her family and all it possessed to a new home. But how could such a vast weight of things be transported? The dreamer invented the wheel, and its effect was magical. Some millennia later, people in the dark dreamed of light at the flick of a switch. Edison invented it—they called him the "Wizard of Menlo Park." Millions on the move needed to connect and communicate with someone down the block or across an ocean. Cellular communication came into being. It is all magic—or might as well be.

Think, for example, about the function of "sales" in the business world. In a real sense, all sales involve selling your own belief in something, and selling this belief is integral to any business success, whether selling a product or an idea. This means that all sales are about magic. To be sure, a product's *features* are its parts and functions—what it *does*. But a product's *benefits* are about what it promises to do for the person who buys it. Benefits are about empowerment. At their best, they are benefits born of our dreams.

In what we like to call our rational times, we may borrow from Jeff McBride's original and powerful framework and initially think of a magician as a performer and a trickster—as somebody whose job it is to entertain and distract us with "illusions" and "sleight of hand." In truth, the higher calling of the magician—as a magician's career progresses from "Trickster" to "Sorcerer" to "Oracle" and all the way to "Sage"—is rooted in vocations more profound.[75] Magicians were learned scholars and physicians of the body and the mind. Magicians were shamans. The job of the shaman is to connect people with the spiritual world, the world behind the physical realm, and to heal them—*heal* in the sense of making people whole. The Old English word *hælan*, from which the modern word heal comes, means to cure, save, and *make whole* (in Old English, *hal*.) Even today, the best magicians, the greatest magicians, don't focus on tricks and diversions. Their objective is to amaze deeply, motivate powerfully, and inspire profoundly those who watch them. Their task is to empower an audience to dream bigger dreams.

And so, this final strategy is about helping you apply the thinking of magic to create, portray, and present the benefits of whatever value you and your business offer. It is about elevating your product, your service, your company, your idea, and yourself to a level of desirability that empowers intense belief.

BENEFIT IS BELIEF

Joseph Dunninger, the greatest mentalist of his day, invariably transfixed his audiences, including the likes of Theodore Roosevelt and Thomas A. Edison, in whose homes he performed. Often, Dunninger concluded a late-career performance by approaching the footlights and addressing his audience thus, "Ladies and Gentlemen: For those who believe, no explanation is necessary. For those who do not, none will suffice."

Belief is the fuel of success in branding, politics, religion, and leadership, and it is belief that turns the promises of magical benefits into successes as real as the wheel, which over the last many thousands of years did not just allow people to relocate themselves and their belongings, but empowered them to transform their lives. Recall from the previous strategy "Shoe Dog" chairman and Nike Founder/Performer Phil Knight, who transformed sneakers—cheap shoes of rubber and fabric—into sources of perceived status and empowerment linked to the magic words *Just do it.* Inexpensive in terms of features, sneakers had traditionally commanded commensurately low prices. A pair of Nikes, however, sells well into the three figures, and consumers line up to plunk down their cash on the latest shoes. It is not the fabric and rubber they want. It is the magic. Whether it is mind reading, a card sewn into a tuxedo, a journey through one side of the Great Wall of China and out the other, a magical hat in the healing hands of a sick child's mother, or the $200 sneakers that people can't wait to buy, benefit is belief, and belief is magic. If magic brings our dreams into the living light, then belief is the fuel that empowers magic.

Eugene Burger said that all of life is about the dance between fear and courage. All—magicians and non-magicians, business leaders and leaders in other fields—all of us have fears. We fear that we are not good enough and that we will not be loved. We fear failure, which comes in many miserable forms. We fear death, and even more, we fear the manner of our death. Our fears are with us, consciously or subconsciously. The dance to which Eugene referred is a part of magic's essential framework. As we wrote in the previous strategy, overcoming and prevailing against our challenges and fighting an enemy, an enemy of our own choosing, is crucially important. The greatest enemy—in the sense of the most universal—is fear. President Franklin D. Roosevelt spoke profound truth when he told an American people hurtling deeper into the pit of a Great Depression unprecedented in its breadth and depth, "The only thing we have to fear is fear itself."

David Morey vividly remembers a corporate leadership retreat in which he participated near Los Angeles a few years ago. Five days surrounded by hyper-achievers intent on learning leadership "mastery" lessons in health, fitness, and wealth management began in a stunningly beautiful California forest, where the trees are much bigger and taller than those on the East Coast. Teams—soon to become cheering peer groups wearing different colored bandanas—were quickly formed. Each was assigned certain challenges to jostle the psyche of each team member out of the current box of whatever fear might reside inside: *"Am I good enough?" "Will I be loved?" "Will I die in fulfillment?"*

Importantly, each of that first morning's physical obstacles lurked high up in the tall trees, over one hundred feet in the air. For example: a trapeze from which participants swung to grab hold of a stationary bar; an 80-foot net they had to climb and then jump to an adjoining platform; and a narrow 50-foot balance beam on which two people, starting from opposite ends, must walk to the center, exchange places, and then walk back to their respective launch platforms.

David drew the narrow fifty-foot balance beam as his obstacle, and he began rehearsing on the ground with a French CEO, with whom he would shortly be exchanging places some one hundred feet up in the air. Teams began to cheer for members trying out this conquest of fear. Painfully, one man somehow got himself up the one hundred feet to his platform only to freeze, absolutely freeze, immune to the coaxing of several gymnastics handlers. At last, a rescuer ascended to help the still-frozen climber down.

The man's fear was not simply "irrational" or "imaginary." It was real. Nevertheless, there were nets below us intended to catch anyone who fell. They *looked* like they would hold up. Additionally, each of us wore a harness attached to a rope that we *guessed* was measured accurately enough to suspend us before we hit anything hard. So performing the challenges with which we were presented was not an act of irrationality, either. The safety measures provided a rational reason to ignore real fear.

Still, our fifty-foot narrow balance beam looked increasingly narrow and awfully high—exponentially higher than the one we had seen in the last Olympic Games. Was this a good idea? How much, after all, does fear really impact leadership "mastery?"

Our turn came.

Climbing up to the platform, David found himself thinking negative thoughts exclusively. *It's very hot out here. What if sweaty hands mean I slip? Has anyone fallen before they even get to the beginning platform?*

He began to feel weak and defeated before the real challenge even started. On the climb up, flashes of fear-fueled failure were passing through his mind, much as we hear about a person's life passing before them just before they die.

The negativity was unbidden. It assailed him. Then, equally unbidden, it all changed.

David Morey got pissed—at himself. A former athlete, hell, a former decathlete, he steeled himself with a new resolve, and without conscious will, somehow empowered new belief and new confidence.

This was the antidote to fear, and it coursed through his veins like an injection of antivenin. The poison of the venomous fear that had bitten him was neutralized, and the strength re-entered his body. The feeling was what you feel when, having had the flu, you arise one morning well. David was channeling some inner athlete or inner magician or inner something, and he found himself on the platform, walking out at that moment and seeing his partner, who immediately fell, half pulling David down with him. Braced by the rescue ropes and David's now-empowered hand on the fifty-foot narrow balance beam, the French CEO was quickly pulled back onto the beam.

And then...and then, something very interesting happened. The worst was out of the way. It was in the past, having already occurred. We had already fallen. And we were neither killed nor wounded. We were free. The worst freed us both from fear. We were then, the two of us, immune to fear.

We met one hundred feet up, at the center of the fifty-foot narrow balance beam, and said hello just as casually as two acquaintances who have met one another on a familiar street. We laughed, shook hands, and then made the exchange as we had rehearsed. That completed, we headed back to the other platform and thence the safety of home base. New confidence had bred courage that had won over this small but memorable dance with fear. Belief had displaced fear. It occurred to us both that the more we can believe, the less we will fear—from that day on, as long as we have the ability to remember the act, the feelings, and the outcome.

FIRST, OWN YOUR INTENTION

What we believe truly matters. This is how the Karate 9th Dan Black Belt chops through 584 cinderblocks: He believes he can chop through 584 cinderblocks, and he makes his intention his belief. As Napoleon Hill, bestselling author of the classic study of success, *Think and Grow Rich*, wrote: "You *can* be anything you want to be, if only you *believe* with sufficient conviction and act in accordance with your faith; for whatever the mind can conceive and *believe*, the mind can achieve."[77] At the height of World War II, the Royal Air Force (RAF) had a saying: "The difficult we do immediately, the impossible takes a little longer." And former Secretary of State Henry Kissinger once observed: "The strong grow weak through inhibition. The weak grow strong through effrontery."[78] In fact, playing offense is always about tackling the impossible and channeling effrontery. It is grabbing and holding onto an empowering belief in what you are doing.

When you are leading, and communicating as a leader—and especially when you are performing magic—playing this kind of offense requires you to reveal the internal emotion behind your belief; in the case of the magician, it is your belief in magic. In magic, playing offense requires owning your intention and conquering any fear you have about revealing this intention to your audience. This is what it means to lay it all on the line, and it is what leadership and the communication of leadership are all about.

For a magician to lay it on the line means a great deal, because magic is merciless. You conquer a finger-curling sleight-of-hand routine, only to discover the next layer of the art of performance—presentation. Perhaps the best place to begin discovering the art of presentation, or to begin to find a new way of thinking about presentation, is to work with one of magic's legends, Bob Fitch.

Fitch is a magician, dancer, choreographer, singer, director, and an actor's actor. He has appeared in twenty-seven Broadway plays and has received Broadway's Burns Mantle Tony as well as a Carbonell Award as the Best Featured Actor in a Musical. He's done it all, including theater, television, and movie roles with the likes of Katherine Hepburn, Liza Minnelli, Whoopi Goldberg, Jerry Lewis, and Steve Martin. He has also directed—both live and on TV—some of the world's greatest magicians, including Jeff McBride, David Blaine, and David Copperfield.

One of the ineluctable truths of magic is that magicians at every level rise or fall not on individual moves, sleights, or props, but on the theatrical power of their presentation. Thematically, Fitch calls this a "through-line": the belief or the *intention* behind everything you do in magic. The Fitch approach means preparing and scripting, while of course leaving some room for "jazz," but creating cues and character references that keep you aimed along your "through-line." This ensures coherence in the performance while conveying to the audience a sense of its fresh reality. It's not so much acting as it is *feeling*, really feeling what you do and say each time you do and say it.

According to Fitch, the only way you can really bring your audiences in and make what you do genuine is to be in the moment—to be feeling it as you do it. This, he teaches, means investing yourself wholly in what you do. It means *believing* it as you are doing it.

"If you are affected," Fitch counsels, "your audiences will be affected. If you can feel, then you can get others to feel!"[79]

The great acting teacher Stella Adler explained that the word *theater* comes from ancient Greek. "It means the seeing place. It is the place people come to see the truth about life and the social situation."[80] Master director Fitch works individually with students to bring them out of hiding—out from behind glitzy props and glib words, out from behind fancy sleights or canned routines, and into the hot bright spotlight, where audiences can really see them, and where audiences can see the truth. To find the truth, Fitch often asks his magician-students *Why?* Why do you do what you do, look the way you do—or say what you do? Why? Why? Why? The answers set up tremendously powerful and magical performances.

The Magic "Boot Camps" Fitch runs are attended by some of the world's greatest magicians. He brings to each camp the eye of a vulture, swooping down on each detail of his original presentational exercises. Over a number of fourteen-hour days, Fitch focuses on:

- disciplining each participant's pitch, rate, and volume across various voice exercises, and helping each learn to comfortably project what they say across a football-field distance;

- refining each participant's "body lead"—this is a mental "trick" that metaphorically and stylistically pulls performers out to meet their audience for the first time using the best possible style of walking, movement, and posture;

- teaching participants to walk to the stage, to own the stage, and through preparations and checklists ("Magic Lists"), to take total control of their surroundings, minimize stage fright, and maximize audience appeal;

- honing participants' acting ability through a range of exercises, including the dreaded "box," in which students struggle for agonizing minutes to escape from an imaginary box made of death rays and break out into a level of energy and confidence they can call on for future performances;

- aligning words and actions and making both totally genuine— for example, Fitch teaches the art of finishing each thought or sentence as you engage an audience member, directly *considering* their eyes, and then moving to the next, and then the next; and

- re-staging, re-scripting, and re-energizing even the most battle-worn effects to elevate the way audiences see the true power of magic.

Both David Morey and Eugene Burger worked with Bob Fitch, and Eugene called him "a national treasure." David believes the single most valuable insight he has gained from this work is the understanding that all performers hide behind something, but the truly great ones discover how to step forward out of hiding, into the hearts and minds of their audience. "Creativity," Fitch offers, "comes from failure, which opens up new possibilities." He continues: "So there's no failure in this work, only discovery."

"If the performer feels it, the audience will feel it," Bob Fitch says. He has taught some of the world's greatest magicians how to channel their belief and their intention so that they may open themselves up to their audience to show what they are feeling. "The greatest failure, it seems to me, is a failure of the imagination on the part of the performer to imagine that he is really doing things that are absolutely fantastic and amazing," Eugene Burger wrote some years ago. "If the performer can imagine this to be the case, he is already on his way toward communicating that energy and wonder to his audience."[81]

Magic is elevated exponentially when feeling, belief, and intention empower performance. Performance takes on more meaning and displays more magic when feeling, belief, and intention fuel what the magician is doing. Why? Because audiences remember not what you said, not what you did, but rather how you made them *feel*.

Wharton School marketing professor Jerry Wind has spent years gathering experts, assessing, and writing about the future of advertising. He notes that over time and going forward, feeling and emotion are bound to be an important part of advertising. Great advertising, great marketing, and great communications must always be anchored in belief, and they must touch or inspire consumers in truly genuine ways. This puts us in mind of an article by business author Geoffrey James titled "8 Core Beliefs of Extraordinary Bosses," which presents a great outline view of the power of belief and intention as applied to business leadership. Our own experience working with some of the best business leaders teaches us that they truly *feel* these beliefs—feel them deep in their bones. The beliefs are their core principles, which drive everything they do. Here is James's "core beliefs" list summarized:

- ◆ *"Business is an ecosystem, not a battlefield"*: Extraordinary bosses find creative ways to organize and find symbiosis by inventing new teams, creating new partnerships, and so on.

- ◆ *"A company is a community, not a machine"*: Great leaders look at their organizations as collections of people's hopes and dreams, all driving to higher purpose.

◆ *"Management is service, not control"*: Great leaders set direction and then ensure that their employees get the job done, pushing decision making downward and across teams.

◆ *"My employees are my peers, not my children"*: Extraordinary bosses value every single employee, treat each as important, and expect excellence across their organization.

◆ *"Motivation comes from vision, not from fear"*: Great leaders inspire and help employees see how they fit into a larger vision, allowing workers to feel they're part of something greater, and that they can make a difference that will be recognized.

◆ *"Change equals growth, not pain"*: Because change is inevitable, great leaders are always looking for ways to apply new ideas and approaches.

◆ *"Technology offers empowerment, not automation"*: Business success comes from leaders who adapt and ensure technologies work for their employees, rather than compelling their employees to work for technology.

◆ *"Work should be fun, not mere toil"*: Great leaders fully invest their intention and embody what they believe—creating positive organizational environments that work better, faster, and smarter. [82]

SECOND, EMBODY TRANSPARENCY

Great magicians know—by listening, watching, and learning—the emotional state of their audience. The very best do this by offering a degree of transparency into their real selves. In fact, they tell an amazing story that pulls an audience toward them, embedding their own "self" into the performance with a degree of transparency that would impress even Bob Fitch. Having created this insight into themselves, they go on to deliver a "wow" to those who experience the show.

Transparency on this level is a two-way street. The legendary Chicago close-up magician Don Alan summed it up this way: "You watch their faces, and their faces will tell you if they were fooled or not, if they are enjoying this or not. *Their faces will tell you everything."* [83] In all forms of communications, a transparently *authentic* belief in your argument is integral to arguing effectively. Conviction, transparent conviction, transparent belief that what you are saying is true—this is what makes all the difference in communications. Juries, audiences, consumers, voters, today have all been trained to spot a lack of belief or a lack of conviction. They will nail you if you are communicating something you do not fully believe. They will pick up on any failure of transparency and take it as a contradiction (small or large) or a concealment, either through deliberate trickery or an incomplete telling of the story.

Today, for all great leaders, the simple fact is that truth is the most powerful form of propaganda—a word, remember, which comes from church Latin and a body of cardinals formed in 1622 known as the *Congregatio de Propoganda Fide*—Congregation for Propagating the Faith.

Coauthor John McLaughlin, former acting head of the CIA, makes the connection between truth and propaganda by citing the "authentically truthful" Radio Free Europe and its broadcasts in the darkest days of the Cold War. During this period, Radio Free Europe relayed rigorously fact-based information behind what was then called the Iron Curtain, which separated the Soviet Union's captive satellite nations in Eastern Europe and the Baltic from the west (the "Free World"). Radio Free Europe began in 1949 as a secret CIA operation, but it was eventually exposed and is today run by the Broadcasting Board of Governors, an organization that oversees various American government-funded broadcasting. Radio Free Europe's days of combatting Soviet communism are over today, but it still disseminates authentic and truthful information to Europe, Russia, the Middle East, and elsewhere.

Whether you seek to win over a population, amaze an audience with magic, or persuade consumers to buy your product, it is crucial to be demonstrably authentic in all that you say or do. For a great magician, or for that matter *any* great actor, authenticity is manifested by transparently establishing the consistency of "character" down to the smallest details. Most effective magicians create an onstage "character." They know who they are, and they consistently align what they say with their stagecraft. The greatest magicians so clearly define their characters that they can describe them in terms varying from "pompous sophisticate" to "slightly mad professor," to "suave gentleman." Everything they do onstage—what they say, what they wear, how they move—reflects these characters. They are transparently authentic.

John McLaughlin learned the power of transparent authenticity in his intelligence career after the Cold War ended and Congress reduced his Agency's resources by 23 percent. News of this reduction created great anxiety among Agency officers who wondered whether their jobs would be eliminated. John's job was to carry out a nearly 40 percent reduction, higher than average because his office focused on the newly independent countries that in 1991 arose from the ashes of the Soviet Union, then no longer considered a threat. The reductions took the form of assignments to other lines of work, rather than outright firings—but this was equally disorienting for people who had devoted their lives to studying something that no longer existed.

The secret to getting through this period, when truly demanding work had to continue to get done, was authentic transparency. By being very transparent and honest about how the reductions would be carried out and on what timetable, John gave people the information they needed to calculate their futures. Many did not like the changes, but they now understood the rationale and personal impact and they could plan deliberately instead of dealing only from ignorance-fueled anxiety. In doing this, John learned authentic transparency and honesty build trust. And trust is probably the most precious resource for a leader, whether a government agency head or a private sector CEO—whether making organizational changes, or introducing a new product to the marketplace. If people trust you, and if the public trusts you—because you are transparently authentic— there is practically no limit to what you can accomplish.

Furthermore, in business and communications—today more than ever before—transparently believing in and selling *benefits* more than features is a common denominator among great companies and great business leaders. Great companies and their leaders focus less on how something works or on the process of its functioning than on what it *does*—on the *value* it delivers to the consumer. A product's features are its parts and functions. A product's benefits are what it promises to do for the person who buys it. Benefits are empowerment. Whatever your business, sell—and believe in—the benefits.

"Sales" is typically defined as one of several business functions, but the truth is that all business is about sales, whether it is selling a product, an idea, or a necessary change. And all sales, in turn, are about magic. In addition to selling the benefits of a business, transparency of belief is central to building and maintaining the kind of corporate marketing and branding presence necessary for success today. For example, consider again one of our favorite examples—Red Bull. For the energy drink company that created its own marketplace, the product has in many ways become secondary to the activities and context of life that Red Bull's consumers experience and enjoy. Want to see what we mean? Search "Red Bull" on YouTube. The company uses transparency in repurposing actual footage that highlights how amazingly talented extreme athletes prepare for their hardcore contests. Red Bull displays this footage both by itself and in its Web commercials. For one event, this highlighting approach earned over 40 million views—because Red Bull's target market of young consumers love to see the kind of activities to which they can relate.

Along with sponsoring extreme sports, Red Bull tells an empowering story by transparently displaying its belief that sometimes life is meant to be lived in the extreme, out toward and even beyond the edge of adventure. In Red Bull's telling of a tale, the company's customers are always the hero. Red Bull has redefined marketing in this lifestyle benefit space by telling a story about personal achievement, pushing the edge, and going farther than you thought you might be able to go. The story of extreme athletes pushing themselves harder inspires Red Bull users to do the same in their own lives. Consider this final line of a Red Bull broadcast ad: "If you believe in it, then anything is possible."

Or this "The only limit is the one you set yourself."

And this: "You can dream about it, or you can go out and make it happen."

Or heed one Red Bull fan, loyalist, and expert, Daniel Ngongang, whose recent blog captured the eight key lessons this kind of transparent, context-setting expression of belief teaches all companies about marketing today:

- ◆ "Be Customer-Centric"
- ◆ "Great Content Marketing is the Way to Go"
- ◆ "Never Underestimate the Power of Experiential Marketing"
- ◆ "Influencer Marketing is No Gimmick"
- ◆ "To Make a Big Splash, Go Viral"
- ◆ "Sponsor the Right Kind of Events"
- ◆ "Engage Consumers Via Social Media in a Clear, Consistent Manner"

- ◆ "Ditch Traditional Media and Focus on Word of Mouth and Mouse"[84]

Finally, consider the power of transparency of belief as you create and sustain the kind of corporate culture great businesses need to succeed. In our connected age, anyone interested in working for your company has more access to more information than ever before. This may be one reason, according to Jim Collins in his book *Good to Great*, that transparency, trust, loyalty, and belief in a company's mission have outpaced financial compensation in attracting executives in today's workplace. Further, a 2017 Edelman Trust Barometer study showed that 75 percent of respondents expect businesses to lead the charge in reestablishing trustworthiness in the world, both by increasing profits *and* improving social-economic conditions.[85] This may be well taken as a powerful commentary on today's dysfunctional *political* environment. Moreover, research shows businesses perform better when employees buy into their mission—making it even more important for great business leaders to understand both who they and their companies are, what drives them, and how they can make employees feel part of something bigger, something more important, even something magical.

The health of their company's culture has become mission-critical for today's great business leaders. Magical principles can help. A recent Korn Ferry study[86] pinpoints the top three culture change strategies:

- ◆ Communications of changing initiatives
- ◆ Leadership development
- ◆ Embedding culture change in management objectives

Note that each of these strategies requires a sustained commitment to transparency of belief, the kind of commitment that goes well beyond a single program, speech, or initiative. In the same study, 72 percent of executives say culture is extremely important for corporate performance, yet only 32 percent believe their organization's culture is "fully aligned with the business strategy." The importance of getting your culture aligned by "communicating changing initiatives," "developing leadership," and "embedding culture change inside management objectives" is underlined by the 72 percent versus 32 percent gap, the difference between most executives believing corporate culture is extremely important for performance and the relatively small number who see their own corporate culture as fully aligned with their business strategy. As leadership expert Seth Godin observes, "Culture is at the heart of whether you are going to get to where you want to go. Every choice is a culture-based choice. The culture you select will drive all of your choices going forward...leaders get the culture they deserve."[87]

To drive home the importance of authenticity of belief in business, we cannot stress enough the critical role of believing in and focusing on *benefits* in selling, setting a context and driving a *marketing* strategy that is truly embodied in your company's values and, finally, creating and sustaining a *corporate culture* that helps get your strategy implemented. Just as we previously listed examples of great magicians who defined both themselves and their uniqueness in a single phrase, consider the examples of *Fortune's* 2017 "World's Most Admired Companies." Notice how easily we all come to appreciate the belief that anchors each of these respective companies and defines their core:

- Apple: *"Think Different"*
- Amazon: *"World's Most Customer-Centric Company"*
- Starbucks: *"Nurturing the Human Spirit"*
- Berkshire Hathaway: *"Value Investing"*
- Disney: *"Where Dreams Come True"*
- Google: *"Don't Be Evil"*

- General Electric: *"Imagination At Work"*
- Southwest Airlines: *"Welcome Aboard"*
- Facebook: *"Be Connected"*
- Microsoft: *"Empowering Us All"*

THIRD, ALLOW FREEDOM

Awakening and empowering your own inner magician is both a process and, as Tenkai Ishida says, "a way." The first step in this journey is what Eugene Burger, in a lecture given in Chicago years ago, called the "first step in following your dreams." It is "waking up." A good way to wake up is to unclutter and thereby connect with what one of Eugene's favorite philosophical texts, the Tao Te Ching, calls the "Powers of Nothingness." In this spirit, let us begin to pull all the components of this book into what we call a "Magic List." It is an inventory of what you the business leader need to think about before you take any stage and perform any miracle.

CONCLUSION

PLAY OFFENSE WITH YOUR IMAGINATION

You are backstage, waiting to go on—and you know the greatest magicians invariably have their preshow routines down to a NASA-would-be-proud checklist of what they must do and when they must do it. Here is ours. As you review each point, each step along the way, consider specifically *how* you will get this done.

YOUR MAGIC LIST

- Focus on your audience's perceptions, on the way *they* see reality.

- Remember to check against the "6 Cs" that orient all consumers today: Control, Choice, Change, Customization, Convenience, and Connection.

- Stop and ask your audience the ten key questions covered in The First Strategy. Why? Because your audience is the boss.

- Define yourself, your program of change, and the future.

- Show your employees that they are part of something *bigger* than what your company does, that they are providing a service that can make a difference, and that this difference will be recognized.

- Avoid complacency by assuming you are behind, because you may be. Adopt the magical role of the underdog, the insurgent, the Change Leader.

- To help consumers discover your products: Keep stressing honesty, simplicity, and naturalness. Stand for authenticity. Drive a Founder/Performer narrative. And let the actual quality of what you do become your most powerful marketing device.

- Personal conviction is essential: Drive your entire business, your company, and your career across the trajectory of what you truly believe—your conviction.

- Ensure imagination is your number one corporate resource. Train your employees (and yourself) to challenge assumptions, to *invert* their approach, and to think out of the box—to think like magicians.

- Constantly encourage and reward your organization for asking better questions and for thinking creatively, sometimes skeptically, and even exponentially. Tactics of encouragement include, for example: Reverse mentoring, where leaders bring in a younger generation representative to teach them new trends and dynamics; driving differentiation, focusing on the things that make your company different, special, and better than the competition; brainstorming, to systematically and continually feed creativity and innovation; and destination planning, where every few years you chart in bold terms and granular detail what success looks like—what your company will look like when it "grows up."

- Innovate way out along the periphery of conventional wisdom and standard operating procedure. Avoid where everyone else is focused. Seek and find your creative sparks, solutions, and systems out along the marketplace periphery, outside and well away from your own bureaucratic center.

- Never get stuck playing defense. Embody and promote corporate mobility, agility, and even hostility. Move to the insurgent offense—always.

- Always think different. Stop thinking like an incumbent leader. Guard against the over-confidence that follows winning. Disrupt your Standard Operating Procedure. And remember, your own bureaucratic center hates disruption, so build your own peripheral innovation team.

- Get away to think and imagine: "Skunk Works" yourself. Continually find new mentors, angles, inputs, and ideas. Run a

"Red Team" to surface weaknesses. Empower your own inner magician, your own inner source of imagination.

- Prepare sooner, smarter, and more aggressively than your competitors. Win before the battle begins.

- Exploit the "7 Laws of Magic" (found in The Fifth Strategy) in the way you prepare and the way you manage, communicate, and lead.

- Like the greatest magicians, get at least *"One Ahead"* in your business in every possible way, especially in your strategic planning and your future.

- Script, Practice, and Rehearse everything you do—every single expression and communication of your leadership.

- Prepare your *"Outs"* for what can and will go wrong, because what *can* go wrong, *will* go wrong.

- Remember: *everything* communicates; so you must control the dialogue and control your audience's focus.

- Borrow the discipline of the great magician: Use excellent material; practice; create magical words; memorize these words; rehearse the whole; test it in the real world; and then revise and improve.

- Pivot from the prevailing dialogue to what *you* want to talk about.

- Focus on what you want your audience to focus on—while all the time defining yourself, defining change, defining the future, and differentiating. Become a category of one. Think uniqueness.

- Take over the stage—make your "opening" exceptionally strong and magical.

- Transfer ownership—tell the story of your own leadership values and your strategy and where they will take listeners.

- Transcend and rise above the petty, the political, the status quo, and build a unity of purpose that assumes the high moral ground and aims toward the future.

- Find and define an adversary, an enemy of sorts, that which you are against or do not believe in, to help crystalize what you are *for*.

- Prepare internally by visualizing your goal, your desired objective, and when necessary, by rebooting your State, your Story, and your Strategy.

- Think like a Founder/Performer to help access the unlimited focus and energy of the entrepreneur.

- Fail faster: Avoid paralysis and fast-forward decision making so that even if you fail, you will be learning and adjusting that much more quickly. And put to work your own "Checklist for the Bold"—listing big, strategic, and proactive initiatives that can increase your activism, aggressiveness, and competitiveness. In other words, play even more offense with your imagination.

What is the power of your own Magic Checklist? In using it, magicians are no different from surgeons, pilots, or master scuba divers. They don't depend on memory, or worse, accident, to ensure they are as ready as they can be before they venture onto the stage, into the patient, up to the sky, or under the waves. A Magic Checklist allows us all to be more than one step ahead, in control, and thinking differently—like a magician— and it allows us to unleash the greatest weapon any of us have at our disposal—our imagination. For this book is about channeling the truly great magician that is inside of us all to take your leadership, your business, and your career to higher places. Implicit in this mission is unlocking and empowering your imagination.

Imagination will provide you with the notes to sing the song of *your* aspirations. As magicians, as business leaders, how do we cultivate our imagination? Eugene Burger always argued for a three-step approach:

First, we must wake up to remember and act on our dreams.

Second, we must free ourselves from the tyranny of the urgent, from the pressures of the coming show or meeting or speech, by accessing our own "Magic List"—our own preshow checklist, which (we know) provides step-by-step guideposts to our success.

Third, we must practice the magical art of allowing visual images to form in our minds. We must practice this regularly and consciously.

For every one of us, the way of magic is the way of slow movement along a path of growing and learning to be a magician.[88] Whatever philosophical beliefs you hold, accept this book as an argument for "fideism," for empowering your own beliefs. In the case of the authors, these are the beliefs of the magician. Believing in what you do, say, and live is the ultimate calling of your inner magician. "I have something *wonderful* to show you tonight," was coauthor Eugene Burger's favorite preshow mantra. So it should be for all of us. We *all* have something *wonderful* to show you tonight.

"When people lack a sense of awe, there will be disaster," advises the Tao Te Ching.[89] Well, this book and its final strategy are a bet on the side of awe, on the potential of your leadership, and on what we know is the inexplicable power of your imagination.

We three authors join together in believing that there will always be magicians, because humanity is wired for it. The human heart and the human mind both cry out for magic. There will always be magicians. Why? Because we need them, because it would be necessary to invent magicians if they did not exist, and because using our imagination and thinking like a magician means we can all know a way that is magic.

And imagination can make magicians of us all.

ABOUT THE AUTHORS

DAVID MOREY

David Morey, founder and Chairman of DMG Global and Vice Chairman of Core Strategy Group, is one of America's leading strategic consultants and most sought-after speakers. As a magician, he performs on stages around the world, including at the official Inaugural Ball of the forty-fourth president of the United States, Barack Obama. He is the award-winning author of the *The Underdog Advantage* (McGraw-Hill) and *The Leadership Campaign* (Career Press), and for many years served as Adjunct Professor at Columbia University and the University of Pennsylvania. Over the years, Mr. Morey has worked with some of the world's top business leaders— and advised five Nobel Peace Prize winners and eighteen winning global presidential campaigns. His corporate clients include GE, Verizon, Pepsi, Mars, KPMG, Deloitte, McDonald's, Microsoft, Nike, P&G, Disney, Visa, The Coca-Cola Company, Linked-in, TPG, American Express, NBC, and many others.

JOHN E. McLAUGHLIN

John E. McLaughlin was deputy director and acting director of the Central Intelligence Agency from 2000 to 2004, capping a thirty-two-year career in intelligence. He is a highly-accomplished magician, performer, and speaker, focusing on foreign affairs and the application of magic principles to intelligence, business, and leadership. Mr. McLaughlin currently teaches at Johns Hopkins University's School of Advanced International Studies. During his government career, he worked in nearly every part of the world, briefed four U.S. presidents and Congress, represented the intelligence community in meetings of the National Security Council, and traveled widely to strengthen U.S. relations with national security counterparts globally. Mr. McLaughlin continues to testify before Congress and to participate in public policy debates through articles in major newspapers and commentary on television. He is the recipient of the Distinguished Intelligence Community Service Award and the National Security Medal.

EUGENE BURGER

One of magic's legendary performers, philosophers, and teachers, the late Eugene Burger was called by *Magic* magazine "one of the 100 most influential magicians of the 20th century." He amazed and delighted audiences from Las Vegas to Tokyo and, as *Stagebill* magazine proclaimed, Eugene Burger was "universally recognized as perhaps the finest close-up magician in the world." The author of fifteen best-selling books on magic, translated into many languages, Mr. Burger starred in eight instructional videos, lectured in over a dozen countries, appeared on television in the U.S., Great Britain, Canada, Belgium, Finland, and Japan, including on PBS and CNN, and was the featured speaker for top corporations and business schools. Mr. Burger's deep understanding of the psychology and philosophy behind and within magic won him many international accolades, cover stories in conjuring magazines, and four awards from Hollywood's legendary Magic Castle.

ENDNOTES

The First Strategy

1. See https://www.youtube.com/watch?v=xTxGC1OiWFs.
    (Link active at publication).

2. This effect was invented by our amazing friend and magician,
    Gene Anderson. See Gene Anderson's *The Book* (Gene Anderson,
    2016), and https://www.youtube.com/watch?v=xTxGC1OiWFs.

3. See http://www.livescience.com/6727-invisible-gorilla-test-
    shows-notice.html .

4. Sue Uneman, "Abracadabara; there's no fooling the robots,"
    Mediacom (March 23, 2017), https://www.mediacom.com/uk/
    article/index?id=abracadabra-theres-no-fooling-the-robots.

5. Linda Rodriguez McRobbie, "What magic can teach us
    about our brains," *The Boston Globe* (September 2, 2016),
    https://www.bostonglobe.com/ideas/2016/09/01/magic/
    IYE084jKTpuA5mUHmF1xKP/story.html .

6. Daniel Kahneman, *Thinking Fast and Slow* (New York: Farrar,
    Straus and Giroux, 2011), 26.

7. See more at http://illusionoftheyear.com/2007/05/the-leaning-
    tower-illusion/.

8. Bahar Gholipour, "Placebo Effect May Account for Half of Drug's
    Efficacy," *LiveScience* (January 8, 2014), http://www.livescience.
    com/42430-placebo-effect-half-of-drug-efficacy.html .

9. William Kremer, "Why are placebos getting more effective?" *BBC
    News Magazine* (October 20, 2015), http://www.bbc.com/news/
    magazine-34572482 .

10. Georgia, "Steve Jobs: You have to start with the customer experience and work backwards to the technology," *iMore* (October 26, 2013), http://www.imore.com/steve-jobs-you-have-start-customer-experience-and-work-backwards-technology .

11. Seth Godin, "define: Brand" (December 13, 2009), http://sethgodin.typepad.com/seths_blog/2009/12/define-brand.html .

12. You may see the poster at the website of Nielsen Magic, https://nnmagic.com/store/reproductions/devant-all-done-by-kindness/.

The Second Strategy

13. See http://www.achievement.org/.

14. John Gruber, "Microsoft, Past and Future," *Daring Fireball* (February 4, 2014), https://daringfireball.net/2014/02/microsoft_past_and_future.

15. Gruber, https://daringfireball.net/2014/02/microsoft_past_and_future.

16. W. I. Oliver, "Can Man Propel Himself Through the Air on His Own Power?" *Popular Aviation* (August 1932), 94-94; accessed at https://books.google.com.ph/books?id=wF6MmgXsYJAC&pg=PA94&lpg=PA94&dq=condor+cannot+fly+when+in+a+pen+with+no+top+story&source=bl&ots=3LTpAJtu9R&sig=lwCtk-_5d0q8F7KQOOYkZvYK8&hl=en&sa=X&ved=0ahUKEwj2oYK7lcPTAhXImJQKHQcAC4cQ6AEIMDAC#v=onepage&q=condor%20cannot%20fly%20when%20in%20a%20pen%20with%20no%20top%20story&f=false.

17. Thomas Jefferson to James Madison, January 30, 1787; accessed at *The Works of Thomas Jefferson,* vol. 5, http://oll.libertyfund.org/search/title/802?q=storms+in+the+physical.

18. Thomas Jefferson, "Extract from Thomas Jefferson to William Stephens Smith" (November 13, 1787), *Jefferson Quotes & Family Letters,* http://tjrs.monticello.org/letter/100 .

19. PYMNTS, "Aspirational Consumers Want 'Purposeful' Brands—
    But Are They Out There?" PYMNTS.com (July 28, 2016), http://
    www.pymnts.com/news/retail/2016/aspirational-consumers-
    purposeful-brands/.

20. PYMNTS, http://www.pymnts.com/news/retail/2016/
    aspirational-consumers-purposeful-brands/.

21. David Morey and Scott Miller, *The Underdog Advantage: Using the
    Power Of Insurgent Strategy to Put Your Business On Top*
    (New York: McGraw-Hill, 2004).

22. Cesare Civetta, "Critics and Audiences," in *The Real Toscani:
    Musicians Reveal the Maestro*. (Milwaukee: Amadeus Press, 2012).

23. Tom Lehrer, *Songs & More Songs by Tom Lehrer* (Rhino Records
    R2 72776).

24. Michel Guillaume Jean de Crèvecoeur, *Letters from an American
    Farmer* (1782; reprint ed., New York: Dutton, 1957), 43, 48.

The Third Strategy

25. See https://www.youtube.com/watch?v=CBLcinheVWg.
    (Link active at publication).

26. Judd Apatow, "David Copperfield," *Interview Magazine* (January
    18, 2017), http://www.interviewmagazine.com/culture/david-
    copperfield

27. Apatow, http://www.interviewmagazine.com/culture/david-
    copperfield

28. *Ibid*

29. *Ibid*

30. *Ibid*

31. David Copperfield, "Vanishing the Statue of Liberty," YouTube,
    https://www.youtube.com/watch?v=823GNH4Rczg.

32. Apatow, http://www.interviewmagazine.com/culture/david-copperfield/; "The Magic of David Copperfield 1991—Flying Live The Dream 1992," YouTube, https://www.youtube.com/watch?v=QCfCx0wi0Rw.

33. "*The Emperor's Club* (2002) Movie Script," Springfield! Springfield, https://www.springfieldspringfield.co.uk/movie_script.php?movie=the-emperors-club .

34. "Clarke's three laws," Wikipedia, https://en.wikipedia.org/wiki/Clarke%27s_three_laws .

35. Eugene Burger and Jeff McBride, *Mystery School: An Adventure into the Deeper Meaning of Magic* (edited by Todd Karr; Seattle: The Miracle Factory, 2003), 43-45.

The Fourth Strategy

36. See https://www.youtube.com/watch?v=f9PL-uhjG5U.

37. "Kelly's 14 Rules & Practices," Lockheed Martin, https://www.lockheedmartin.com/us/aeronautics/skunkworks/14rules.html.

38. Tony Robbins television interviews, Las Vegas Business Mastery seminar, and Tony Robbins, "When people succeed they tend to party but when they fail they tend to ponder," https://twitter.com/tonyrobbins/status/493534068282122240?lang=en.

39. Nick Bolton, "Disruptions: Apple's Next Unveiling Could Make or Break a Business," *The New York Times* (September 8, 2013), https://bits.blogs.nytimes.com/2013/09/08/disruptions-apples-next-unveiling-could-make-or-break-a-business/?mcubz=0.

40. Chicago Discussion with Robert Shapiro and Sandbox Industries team, March 19, 2014.

41. Verne Harnish and The Editors of *Fortune*, *The Greatest Business Decisions of All Time* (New York: Time Home Entertainment, 2012), Chapter 8; Kindle ed.

42. *Ibid.*

43. Discussion with Robert F. Armao, Assistant to the Governor of New York State, and Labor Counsel to the Vice President of the United States, the Honorable Nelson A. Rockefeller. November 18, 2016.

The Fifth Strategy

44. Conversation with Eugene Burger, and presentation at the McBride Magic & Mystery School class. October 15, 2014.

45. See Richard Stokes, "Jasper Maskelyne: The War Magician" (September 29, 2017), http://www.maskelynemagic.com/index. html ; Richard Stokes, "Archival Evidence" (2005), http://www. maskelynemagic.com/Resources/cam%20exp%20sec.pdf .

46. *The Guardian*, "Who coined the phrase, 'The first casualty of War is Truth'?" https://www.theguardian.com/notesandqueries/ query/0,5753,-21510,00.html.

47. For example, Harry Lorayne and Jerry Lucas, *The Memory Book* (New York: Ballantine Books, 1986).

48. Note that, in magic, we reverse the order that we are applying to business here: we practice, then script, and then rehearse. See the Sixth Strategy for a detailed discussion on this based on the great work and seven key steps of developing magic articulated by Larry Hass, Ph.D.

49. See Tony Clark, *Insider Secrets: Mastering the Craft, Show & Business of Magic* (N.p.: Tony Clark, 2016).

50. Albert Mehrabian, *Silent Messages* (Independence, KY: Wadsworth Publishing, 1981), 76.

The Sixth Strategy

51. See http://www.youtube.com/watch?v=x5lGwhbvANo;and http://www.youtube.com/watch?v=FW6oQZc_c80. (Link active at publication).

52. "Apple - Think Different - Full Version," https://www.youtube.com/watch?v=cFEarBzelBs.

53. Clarke, Arthur C., *Profiles of the Future: An Inquiry into the Limits of the Possible.* (New York: Popular Library, 1973).

54. Study by Weber Shandwick, 2012.

55. Larry Hass, Ph.D., *Inspirations: Performing Magic with Excellence* (Memphis: Theory and Art of Magic Press, 2015), Chapter 6.

56. Stratton Oakmont, Inc. "For Training Purposes Only," https://www.scribd.com/doc/265243987/Stratton-Oakmont-Training.

57. Senator Barack Obama, "A More Perfect Union" speech, delivered at the National Constitution Center, Philadelphia, PA, March 18, 2008.

58. See Juan Tamariz, *The Five Points in Magic* (Madrid: Editorial Frakson, 1988), 22 - "Shift the Gaze," and 23 - "Crossing the Gaze" (based on an idea of Slydini.) This is built on the principle of crossing your gaze in the opposite way from the direction your hands are moving and motivating the audience to follow the stronger motion of where you are looking rather than the motion of your hands.

59. See http://geniimagazine.com/wiki/index.php/John_Ramsay ; the original quote is: "If you want them to look at you, look at them. If you want them to look at 'it,' look at 'it.'"

60. Verne Harnish and the Editors of *Fortune, The Greatest Business Decisions of All Time* (New York: *Fortune* Books, 2013), 129.

61. Jerome Baldwin, "Lloyd Fredendall: The General Who Failed at the Kasserine Pass," http://warfarehistorynetwork.com/daily/wwii/lloyd-fredendall-the-general-who-failed-at-the-kasserine-pass/.

The Seventh Strategy

62. See https://www.youtube.com/watch?v=ksXbsFzdzFY.(Link active at publication.)

63. Andrew Pinard, interview with Eugene Burger, *Real Magic Magazine* 13 (October 2009).

64. See, for example, Section 5: "Choosing the Final False Solution" in Juan Tamariz's *The Magic Way*. (Madrid: Editorial Frakson, 1988), 35.

The Eighth Strategy

65. See http://www.youtube.com/watch?v=4S4pJzhmmMs. (Link active at publication.)

66. See https://www.youtube.com/watch?v=khQT5HP3zfU. (Link active at publication).

67. Aidan P. Moran, *The Psychology of Concentration in Sports Performances: A Cognitive Analysis* (New York: Routledge, 1996), and Dr. James E. Loehr and Peter J. McLaughlin, *Mentally Tough: The Principles of Winning at Sports Applied to Winning in Business* (New York: Rowman & Littlefield, 1988).

68. Jack Nicklaus, quoted in Anees A. Sheikh and Errol R. Korn, eds., *Imagery in Sports and Physical Performance*, (Amityville, NY: Baywood Publishing Company, 1994), 23.

69. Richard Branson, *The Virgin Way: Everything I Know about Leadership* (New York: Portfolio, 2014), Chapter 7; Ebook edition.

70. Anthony Robbins, *Awaken the Giant Within: How to Take Immediate Control of Your Mental, Emotional, Physical and Financial Destiny!* (New York: Free Press, 1991), chapter 7; http://sourcesofinsight.com/change-your-strategy-change-your-story-change-your-state/.

71. "Ray Kroc Quotes," http://www.evancarmichael.com/library/ray-kroc/Ray-Kroc-Quotes.html .

72. Tim Ferriss, *Tools of Titans: The Tactics, Routines, and Habits of Billionaires, Icons, and World-Class Performers* (Boston and New York: Houghton Mifflin, 2016), 314.

73. Harlan Tarbell, *The Tarbell Course in Magic* (Brooklyn: D. Robbins & Co., Inc., 1927), vol. 1-8; C. Lang Neil, *The Modern Conjurer* (New York: David Kemp & Company, 1937); Professor Hoffman, *Modern Magic* (New York: George Routledge & Sons Limited,1876); Reginald Scott, *The Discoverie of Witchcraft* (William Brome, 1584).

74. David Morey and Scott Miller, *The Underdog Advantage: Using the Power of Insurgent Strategy to Put Your Business on Top* (New York: McGraw Hill, 2004), chapter 4.

The Ninth Strategy

75. Eugene Burger and Jeff McBride, *Mystery School: An Adventure Into the Deeper Meaning of Magic* (Edited by Todd Karr; Seattle: The Miracle Factory, 2003), "Four Faces of the Magician," 73-74.

76. "584 Cement Bricks Broken By Hand in Only 57.5 Seconds!" YouTube (August 5, 2007), https://www.youtube.com/watch?v=YjakBg7mLJw.

77. Jack Canfield and Janet Switzer, *The Success Principles: How to Get from Where You Are to Where You Want to Be* (New York: HarperCollins, 2015), 43.

78. Tony Jeary, *Life Is a Series of Presentations* (New York: Simon and Schuster, 2005), 85.

79. Conversation with David Morey and presentation by Bob Fitch, at the "Fitch Magic Bootcamp," Gaithersburg, Maryland, 2004.

80. Howard Kissel, ed., *The Art of Acting* by Stella Adler (New York: Applause Books, 2000), 30.

81. Eugene Burger *Audience Involvement...A Lecture* (Notes edited and published by Phil Willmarth), (Asheville: Excelsior!! Productions, 1983), 25; later revised and reprinted in Eugene Burger, *Mastering the Art of Magic*, edited by Matthew Field and Richard Kaufman (Washington: Kaufman and Company, 2000) 67-82.

82. Geoffrey James, "8 Core Beliefs of Extraordinary Bosses," (April 23, 2012) https://www.youtube.com/watch?v=6-Hn4yeBOvI.

83. Eugene Burger, *Growing in the Art of Magic*, Second Edition (Pamphlet based on audiotapes produced in 1992, and later published by the author; Chicago: N.pub., 1996), 21; emphasis added; this material was developed and used also in Eugene Burger and Robert E. Neale, *Magic and Meaning* (Seattle: Hermetic Press, Inc., 1995).

84. Daniel Ngongang, AMABE, "8 Marketing Lessons We Can Learn From Red Bull," LinkedIn Blog, August 17, 2016; https://www.linkedin.com/pulse/8-marketing-lessons-we-can-learn-from-red-bull-daniel-ngongang-amabe .

85. Edelman, *2017 Edelman Trust Barometer,* https://www.edelman.com/trust2017/.

86. Korn Ferry Institute, "Real World Leadership: Part three: Create an engaging culture for greater impact" (February 3, 2016), https://www.kornferry.com/institute/real-world-leadership-part-three-create-an-engaging-culture-for-greater-impact .

87. Seth Godin quoted in Marissa Levin's "6 Reasons Culture Change, and 3 Ways Leaders Can Respond," https://www.inc.com/marissa-levin/6-reasons-cultures-change-and-3-ways-leaders-can-respond.html .

88. Eugene Burger, *Growing in the Art of Magic*, Second Edition (Pamphlet based on audiotapes produced in 1992, and later published by the author; Chicago: N.pub., 1996).

89. Lao Tzu, *Tao Te Ching*, Chapter 72; http://taotechingempower.
    tumblr.com/post/149315276773/chapter-72-when-people-lack-
    a-sense-of-awe.